OPERATION: BROKEN GROUND

Report of Proceedings

QUEEN & COUNTRY

OPERATION: BROKEN GROUND

Report of Proceedings

compiled by **GREG RUCKA**

illustrated by **STEVE ROLSTON**

short story illustrated & lettered by
STAN SAKAI

cover & chapter breaks by
TIM SALE

cover colors by
MATTHEW HOLLINGSWORTH

lettering by
SEAN KONOT

introduction by
WARREN ELLIS

book design by
KEITH WOOD

edited by
JAMIE S. RICH

additional series editing by
JAMES LUCAS JONES

Published by Oni Press, Inc.

JOE NOZEMACK, publisher
JAMIE S. RICH, editor in chief
JAMES LUCAS JONES, associate editor

Special thanks to Steven Birch at Servo for establishing
the initial design style for this series.

This collects issues 1-4 of the Oni Press comics series *Queen & Country*™
as well as a short story from the *Oni Press Color Special 2001*.

ONI PRESS, INC.
6336 SE Milwaukie Avenue, PMB30
Portland, OR 97202
USA

www.onipress.com

First edition: March 2002
ISBN 1-929998-21-X

1 3 5 7 9 10 8 6 4 2

PRINTED IN CANADA.

INTRODUCTION
by WARREN ELLIS

There was a time when British television was intelligent and aimed at adults. No, really. It wasn't all DIY shows and gardening series and hidden camera stunts and all the rest of the crap that pollutes the screen now. If British TV is, as we're still often told, the best in the world, then we may as well all jump under buses now. It all looks like Italian TV to me (which is the worst in the world, by a yard). Where British TV always excelled was in the many facets of the political thriller. The existential psychosis of *The Prisoner*, McGoohan's inspired genre-smashing retake on *Danger Man*, the straight spy series he starred in for many years. *Callan*, the study of a working-class government agent even grimmer than the Harry Palmer stories, the damaged Sergeant David Callan staying just inches ahead of a breakdown and an assassination Red File being placed on him instead of given to him. Edward Woodward in *The Equalizer* is the barest echo of Woodward in *Callan*. Imagine if the brains behind *The Equalizer* had not been injected with dogshit, and you kind of approach it. *Harry's Game*, the chilly and desperate story of a British agent in Northern Ireland. *Edge of Darkness*, the masterful, bone-shaking look at nuclear politics in the '80s. And after *Edge*... there were still bombshells like *GBH*, Alan Bleasdale's novel-for-television about the collapse of politics, communities and minds, but fewer and further between. In fact, as British television was losing its mind, British comics found theirs. Today, television's never been worse, and comics have never been better.

Which brings me to *Queen & Country*, and *The Sandbaggers*.

The Sandbaggers fell in the late Seventies, right in the middle of the period I'm discussing. Perhaps the most severe take on the British Secret Service abroad, it revolved around its small team of operatives, the Sandbaggers of the title, and their controller, a surviving Sandbagger now in the position of sending his own kind out into the cold. And it was cold. Cold war. Cold calculations. Cold bodies. There weren't many surviving Sandbaggers. This wasn't, as they were fond of reminding people, James Bond. The Special Operations section of the Secret Intelligence Service went through Sandbaggers the way I used to go through cigarettes: fast, and ruthlessly. Sometimes they even killed each other, to maintain the status quo, the political balance or the "special relationship." These were people able to lay their hands on all manner of guns in foreign countries in order to perform assassinations and tacit war crimes, but weren't allowed anything more dangerous than a penknife when in Britain. The Sandbaggers was very much of its time – the controller, Neil Burnside, has a berserk anti-Communist drive – but it was very intelligent, never took the easy option, and exposed the world of intel as a nightmare of bureaucracy, argument and horror.

So does *Queen & Country*. And it does it in a far more interesting milieu; a post-Cold War world where the enemies are no longer so clearly defined, and the job to be done is no longer so clearly described. The modern intel structure is designed to face off against one big enemy with many arms. But in a world where the Soviet Union is now a trivia question, an intelligence service has to look at two dozen little enemies all waving their arms at once. In 1979, intel could at least lay sandbags against the tide.

In 2001: well. As many events this year have shown, we're living in floodlands. This new world, the world of *Queen & Country*, is much more dangerous, and makes much less sense.

Lesser writers, the Tom Clancys and the like, deal with their new worlds of spies and technoporn by jingoistically shoving other nationalities into the shoes of Evil Empire, so that they can play the same simple games. Greg Rucka is not a lesser writer. As an author, he thrives in political, moral and emotional complexity. Down among the gravemoss and the strangleweed. Rucka, who first came to prominence as a gifted crime novelist, wrote as his first work for comics the cracklingly intelligent thriller *Whiteout*, a crime story set in the Antarctic and featuring, as a secondary player, an enigmatic and untrustworthy British agent called Lily Sharpe. Lily Sharpe is not unlike *Queen & Country's* protagonist, Tara Chace. *Whiteout* and the work in hand are very different pieces, with different sets of underlying rights. If we are not now implying that Lily Sharpe is Tara Chace, then we are certainly suggesting that in Lily Sharpe, Greg Rucka saw the foundation of a larger story. He also, bless 'im, saw *The Sandbaggers*.

Queen & Country, then, is a spy story in a complexifying world; a real world, where every single bullet has consequence, and where every single step you take in your job will come back to haunt you. Watching the horrible tumble of dominos set off by one solitary gunshot makes *Queen & Country* perhaps the most compelling comic of the last year.

Everything Rucka does here is captured perfectly by the sharp pens of artist Steve Rolston. This was his first professional work, not that you'd know it unless you were told. The slight cartooniness of Steve's well-realised figures gives them an emotional transparency: they practically shiver with hate, slump with exhaustion, get still and chill with fear. It's hard to find an artist in adventure comics who knows how to draw more than two faces, or who knows what real clothes look like. Steve Rolston makes getting it right look easy. His clear-line style is reminiscent of the European approach to thriller comics, and Rolston shares with those old masters an attention to detail and *mise en scène* that grounds the story just as much as Rucka's well-heard dialogue.

Queen & Country is one of the best illustrations I know of the cold hard fact that a lot of people try to ignore: of all the visual narrative media, comics are now the place where the most intelligent and challenging work is done. Start here, with one of my favourites.

Warren Ellis
Trafalgar Square
December 2001

Warren Ellis is the popular creator of such noteable works of modern graphic literature as Transmetropolitan, Planetary, Strange Kisses, Lazarus Churchyard, The Authority, *and* Minstry of Space. *His groundbreaking essays on the comics industry have been published in the volumes* Come In Alone *and* From the Desk Of... 1 & 2, *and he has also compiled* Available Light, *a book of prose and photographs. He is currently editing* Night Radio, *an anthology showcasing new talent, for Avatar Press, developing the Oni Press comics series* The Operation, *and is one of the curators of artbomb.net.*

CHAPTER 1

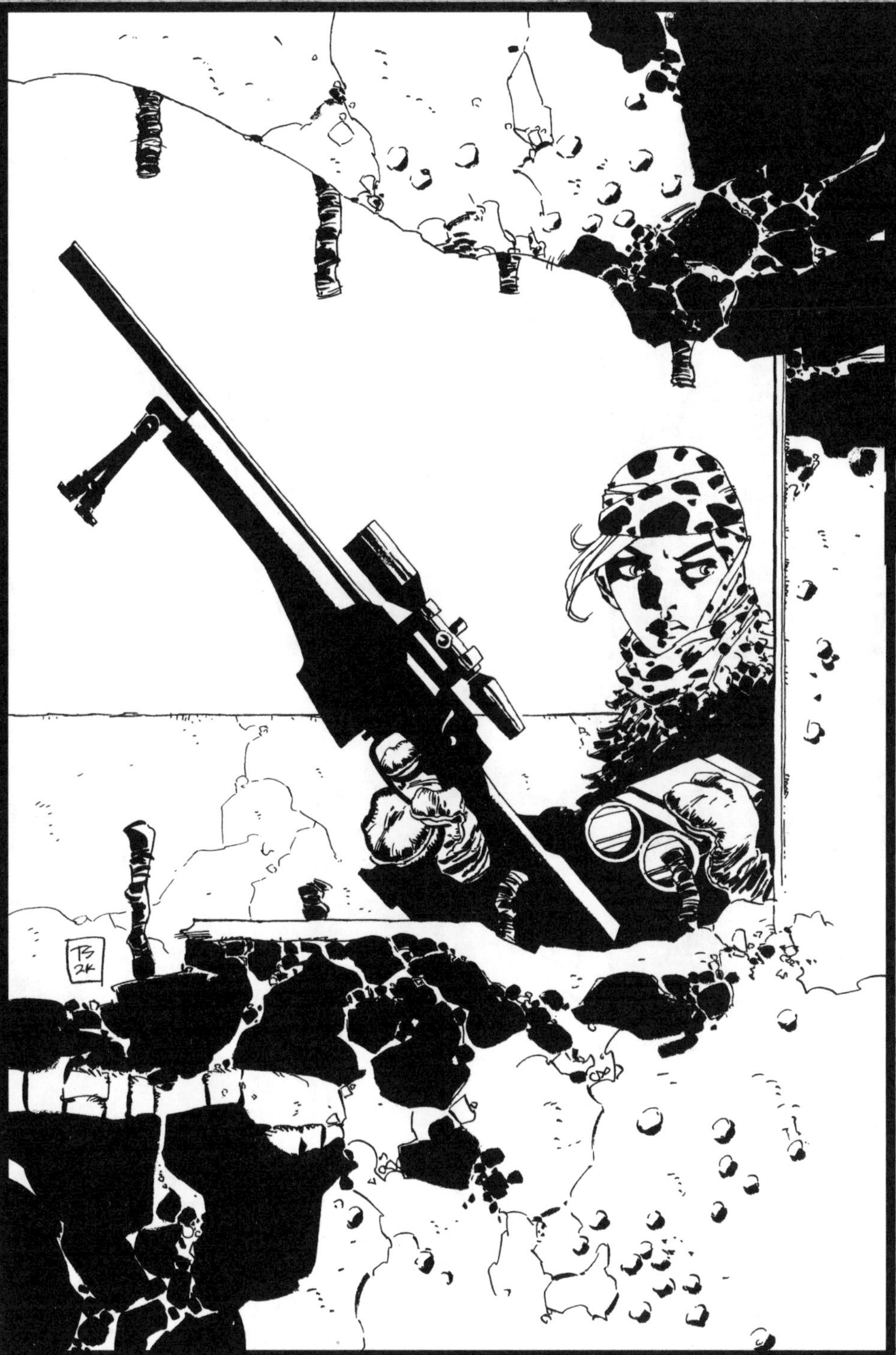

ROSTER

C

Ubiquitous code-name for the current head of S.I.S.. Real name is Sir Wilson Stanton Davies.

DONALD WELDON

Deputy Chief of Service, has oversight of all aspects of Intelligence gathering and operations. Immediate superior to Crocker.

PAUL CROCKER

Director of Operations, encompassing all field work in all theaters of operations. In addition to commanding individual stations, has direct command of the Special Section-sometimes referred to as Minders -used for special operations.

TOM WALLACE

Head of the Special Section, a Special Operations Officer with the designation Minder One. Responsible for the training and continued well-being of his unit, both at home and in the field. Six year veteran of the Minders.

TARA CHASE

Special Operations Officer, designated Minder Two. Entering her third year as Minder.

EDWARD KITTERING

Special Operations Officer, designated Minder Three. Has been with the Special Section for less than a year.

OPS ROOM STAFF:

ALEXIS

Mission Control Officer (also called Main Communications Officer)- responsible for maintaining communications between the Operations Room and the agents in the field.

RON

Duty Operations Officer, responsible for monitoring the status and importance of all incoming intelligence, both from foreign stations and other sources.

KATE

Personal Assistant to Paul Crocker, termed P.A. to D.Ops. Possibly the hardest and most important job in the Service.

OTHERS:

ANGELA CHANG

CIA Station Chief in London. Has an unofficial intelligence-sharing arrangement with Crocker.

SIMON RAYBURN

Director of Intelligence for S.I.S. (D. Int), essentially Crocker's opposite number. Responsible for the evaluation, interpretation, and dissemination of all acquired intelligence.

DAVID KINNY

Crocker's opposite number at M.I.5, also called the Security Services, with jurisdiction primarily confined to within the U.K.

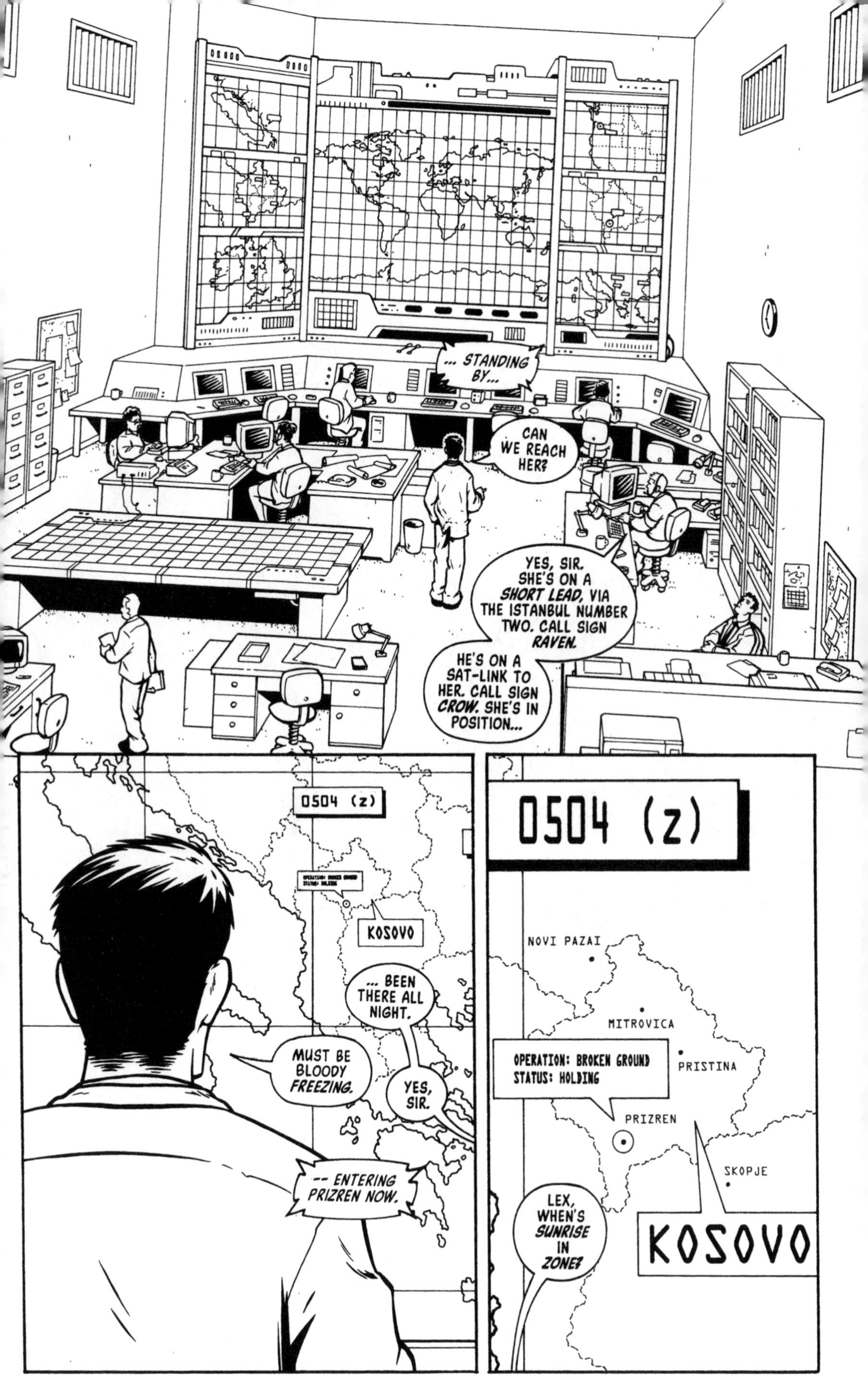
... STANDING BY...
CAN WE REACH HER?
YES, SIR. SHE'S ON A SHORT LEAD, VIA THE ISTANBUL NUMBER TWO. CALL SIGN RAVEN.
HE'S ON A SAT-LINK TO HER. CALL SIGN CROW. SHE'S IN POSITION...
0504 (z)
KOSOVO
... BEEN THERE ALL NIGHT.
MUST BE BLOODY FREEZING.
YES, SIR.
-- ENTERING PRIZREN NOW.
0504 (z)
NOVI PAZAI
MITROVICA
PRISTINA
OPERATION: BROKEN GROUND
STATUS: HOLDING
PRIZREN
SKOPJE
KOSOVO
LEX, WHEN'S SUNRISE IN ZONE?

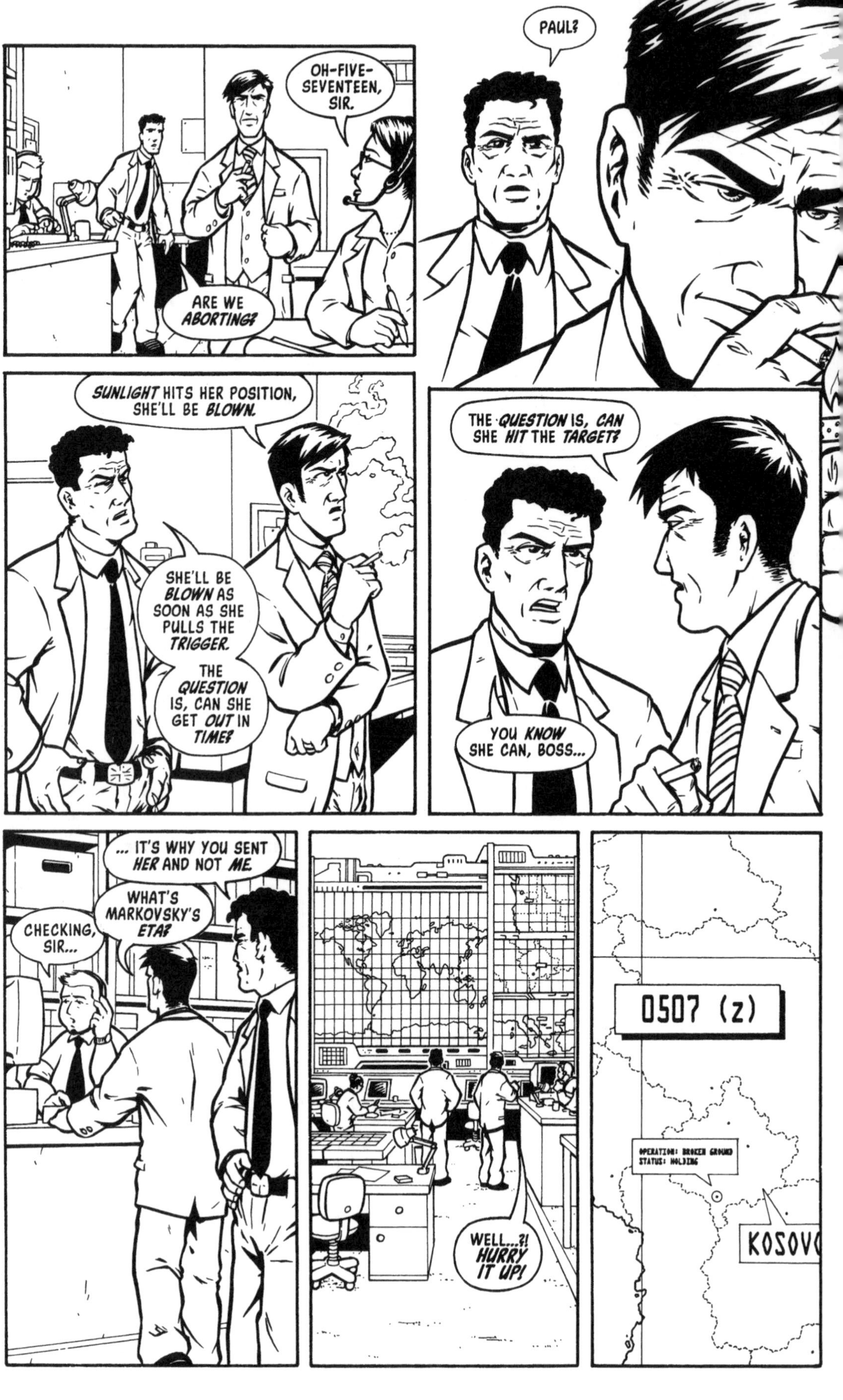
OH-FIVE-SEVENTEEN, SIR.
ARE WE ABORTING?
PAUL?
SUNLIGHT HITS HER POSITION, SHE'LL BE BLOWN.
SHE'LL BE BLOWN AS SOON AS SHE PULLS THE TRIGGER.
THE QUESTION IS, CAN SHE GET OUT IN TIME?
THE QUESTION IS, CAN SHE HIT THE TARGET?
YOU KNOW SHE CAN, BOSS...
... IT'S WHY YOU SENT HER AND NOT ME.
WHAT'S MARKOVSKY'S ETA?
CHECKING, SIR...
WELL...?! HURRY IT UP!
0507 (z)
OPERATION: BROKEN GROUND
STATUS: HOLDING
KOSOV

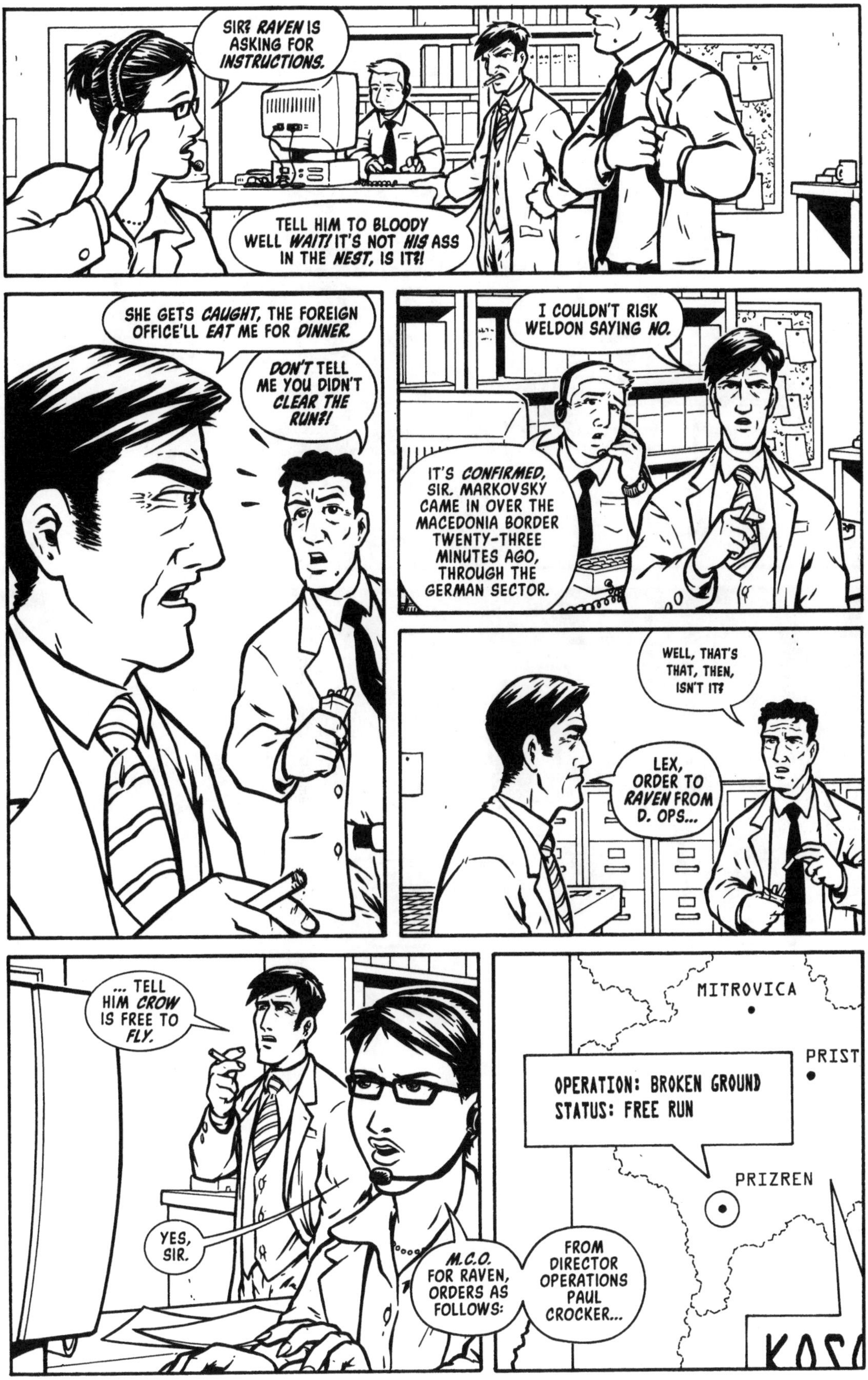

SIR? RAVEN IS ASKING FOR INSTRUCTIONS.
TELL HIM TO BLOODY WELL WAIT! IT'S NOT HIS ASS IN THE NEST, IS IT?!
SHE GETS CAUGHT, THE FOREIGN OFFICE'LL EAT ME FOR DINNER.
DON'T TELL ME YOU DIDN'T CLEAR THE RUN?!
I COULDN'T RISK WELDON SAYING NO.
IT'S CONFIRMED, SIR. MARKOVSKY CAME IN OVER THE MACEDONIA BORDER TWENTY-THREE MINUTES AGO, THROUGH THE GERMAN SECTOR.
WELL, THAT'S THAT, THEN, ISN'T IT?
LEX, ORDER TO RAVEN FROM D. OPS...
... TELL HIM CROW IS FREE TO FLY.
YES, SIR.
M.C.O. FOR RAVEN, ORDERS AS FOLLOWS:
FROM DIRECTOR OPERATIONS PAUL CROCKER...
MITROVICA
PRIST
OPERATION: BROKEN GROUND
STATUS: FREE RUN
PRIZREN
KOSO

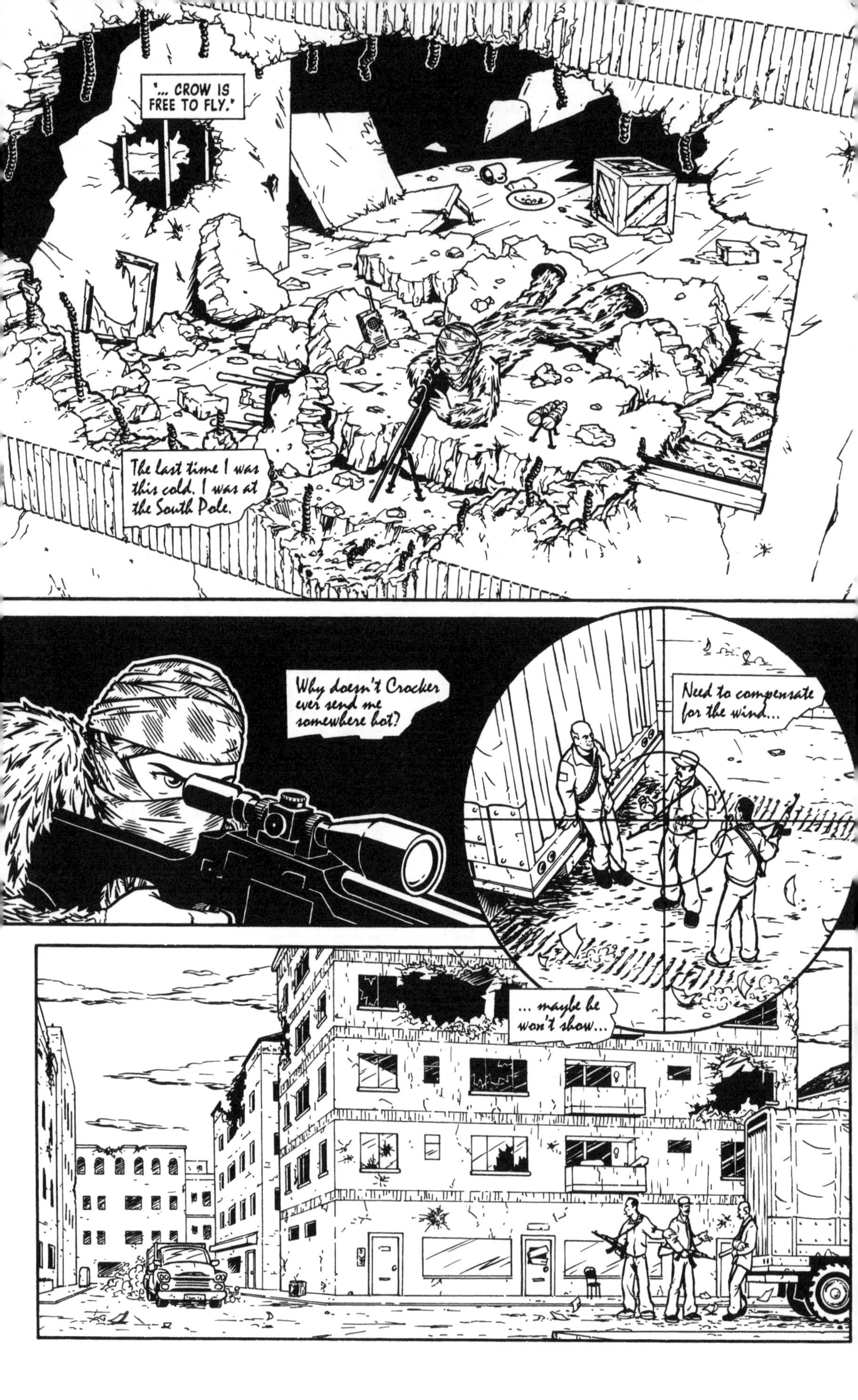
"... CROW IS FREE TO FLY."
The last time I was this cold, I was at the South Pole.
Why doesn't Crocker ever send me somewhere hot?
Need to compensate for the wind...
... maybe he won't show...

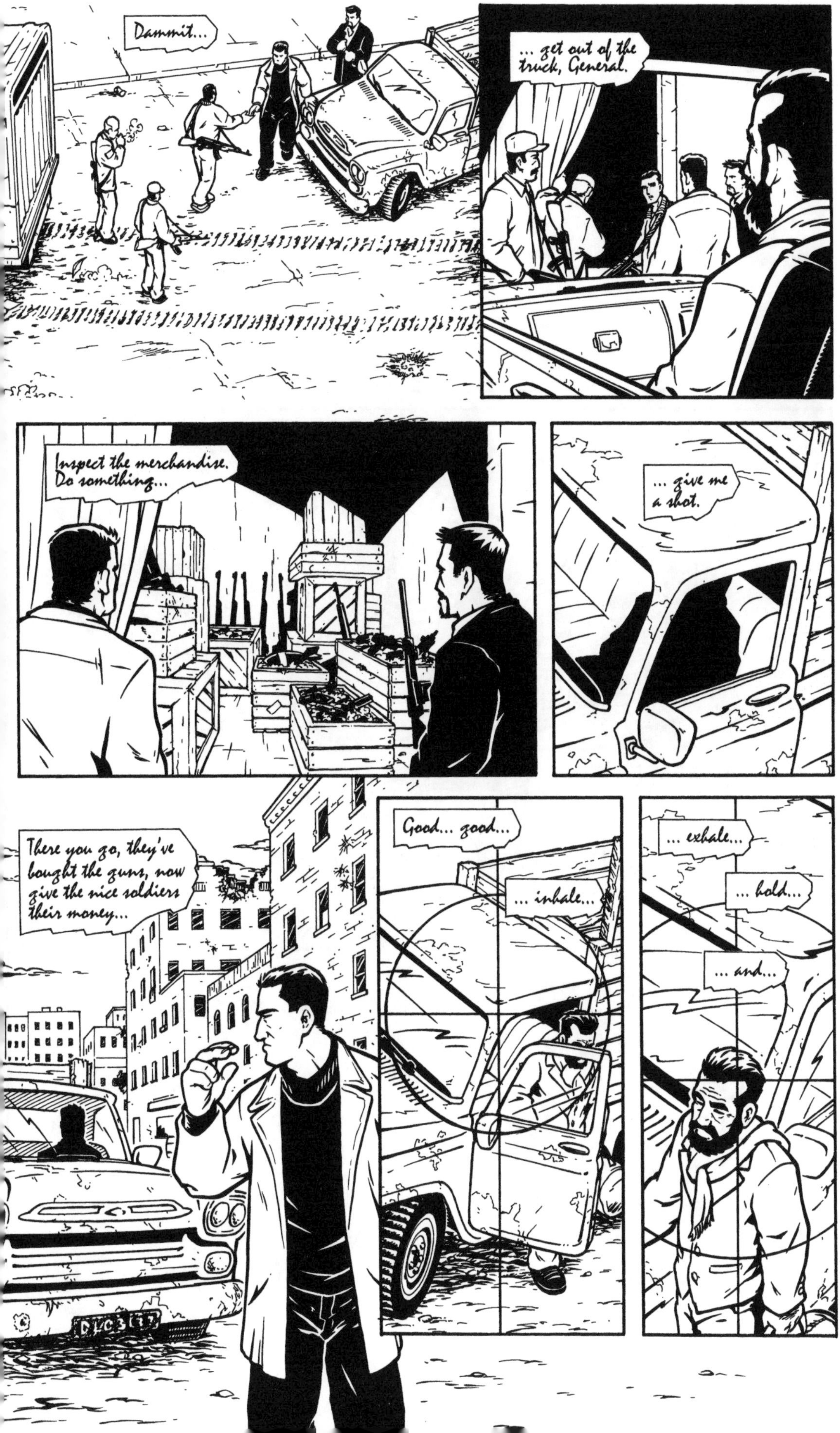
Dammit...
... get out of the truck, General.
Inspect the merchandise. Do something...
... give me a shot.
There you go, they've bought the guns, now give the nice soldiers their money...
Good... good...
... inhale...
... exhale...
... hold...
... and...

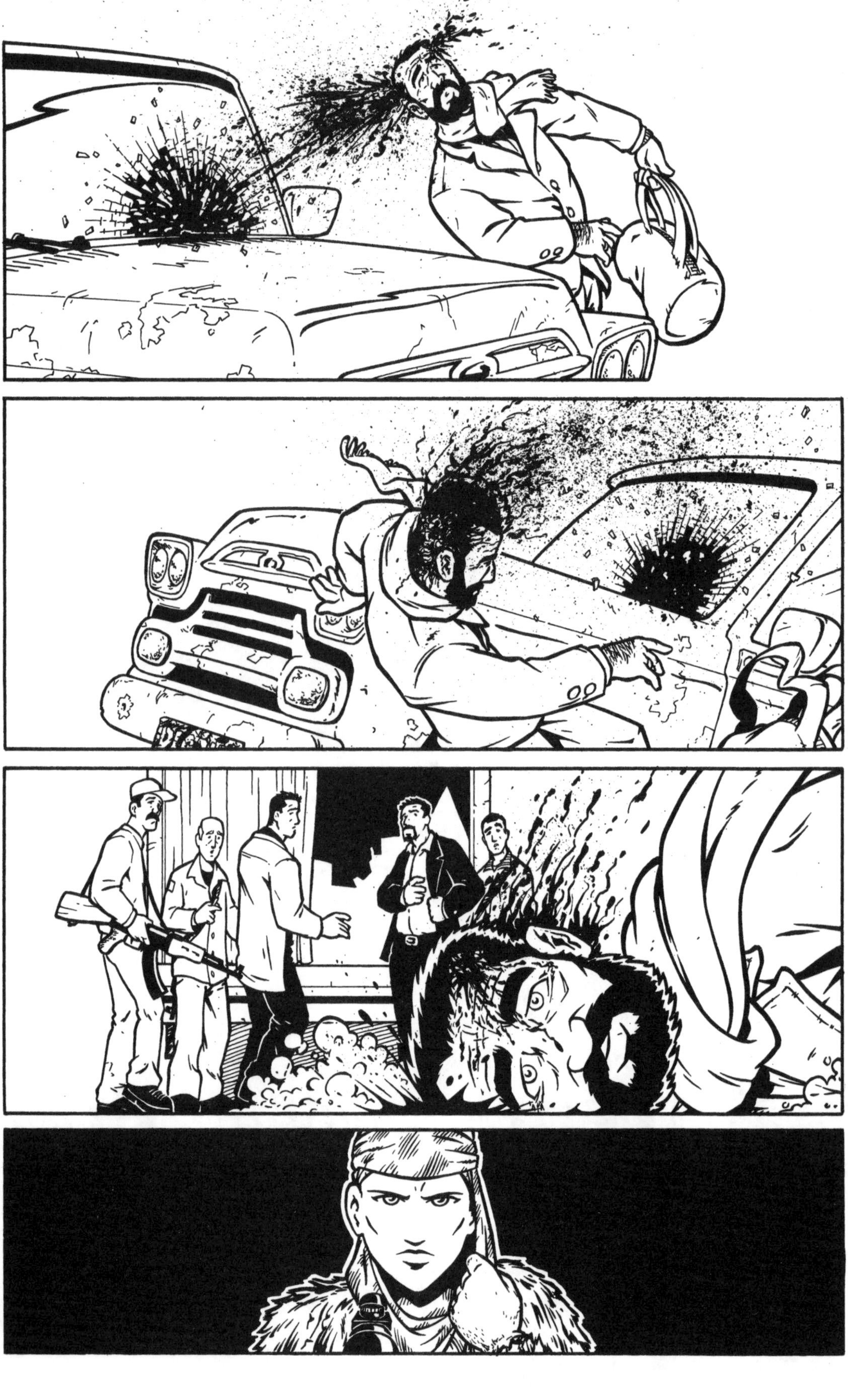

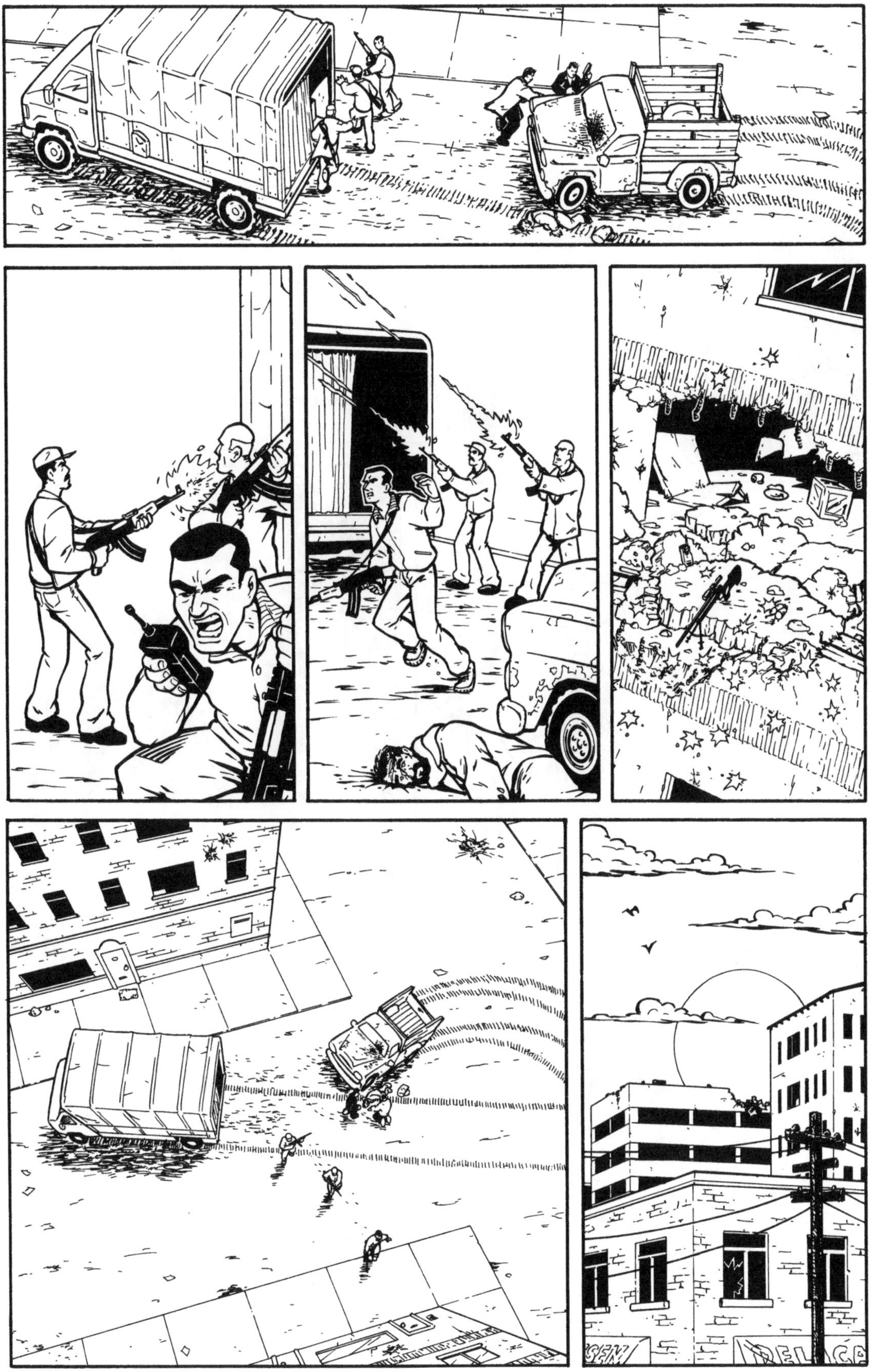

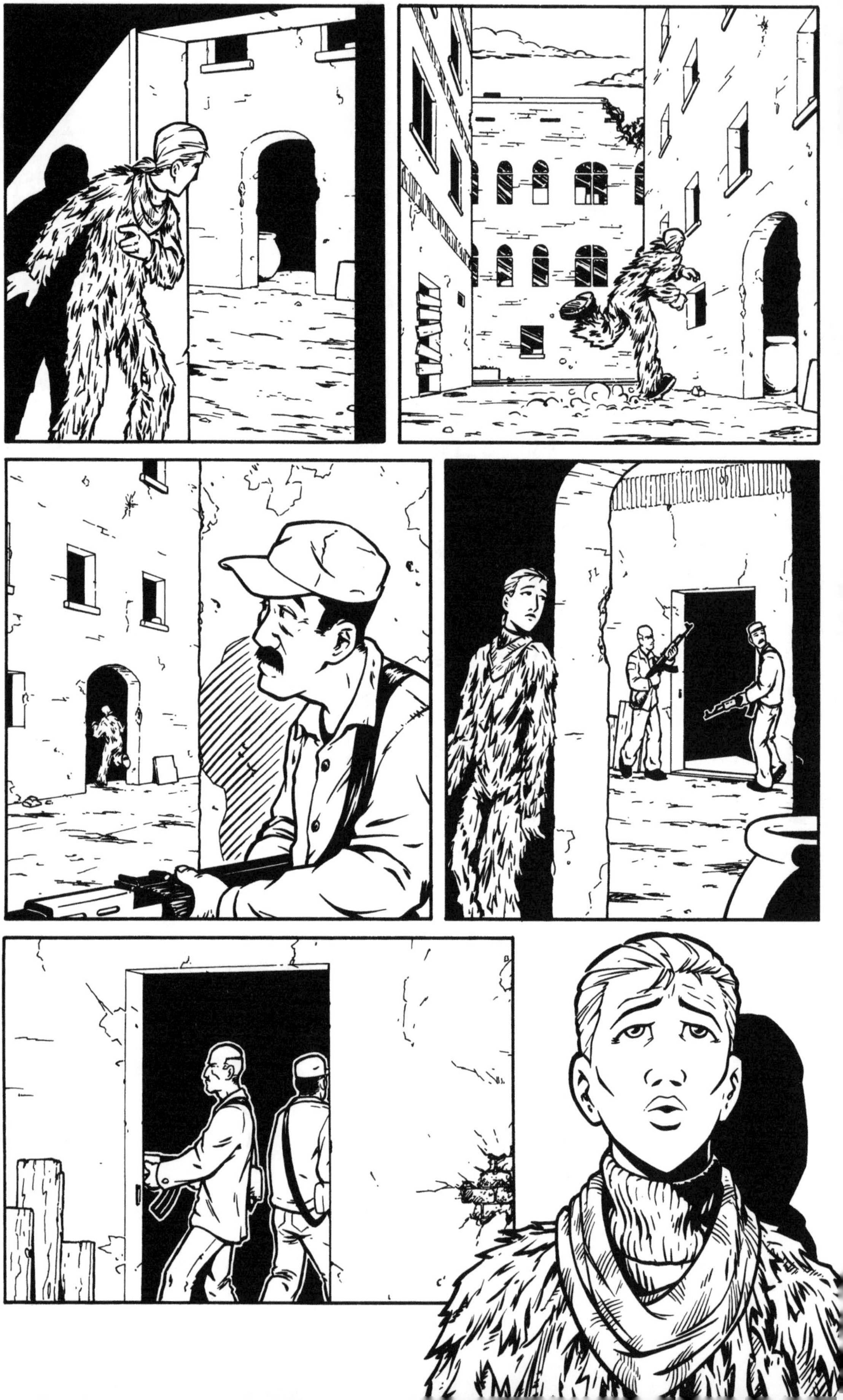

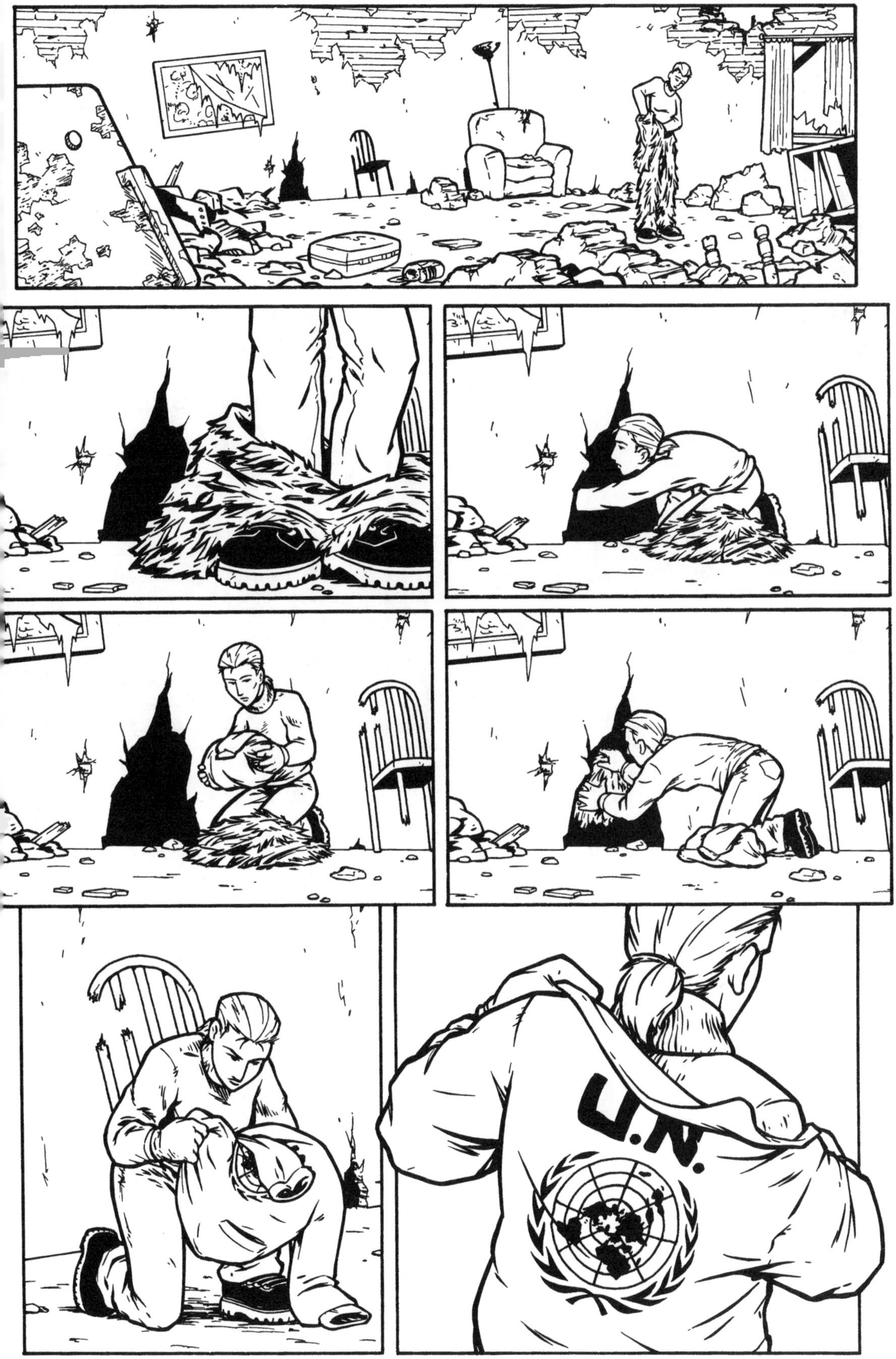
U.N.

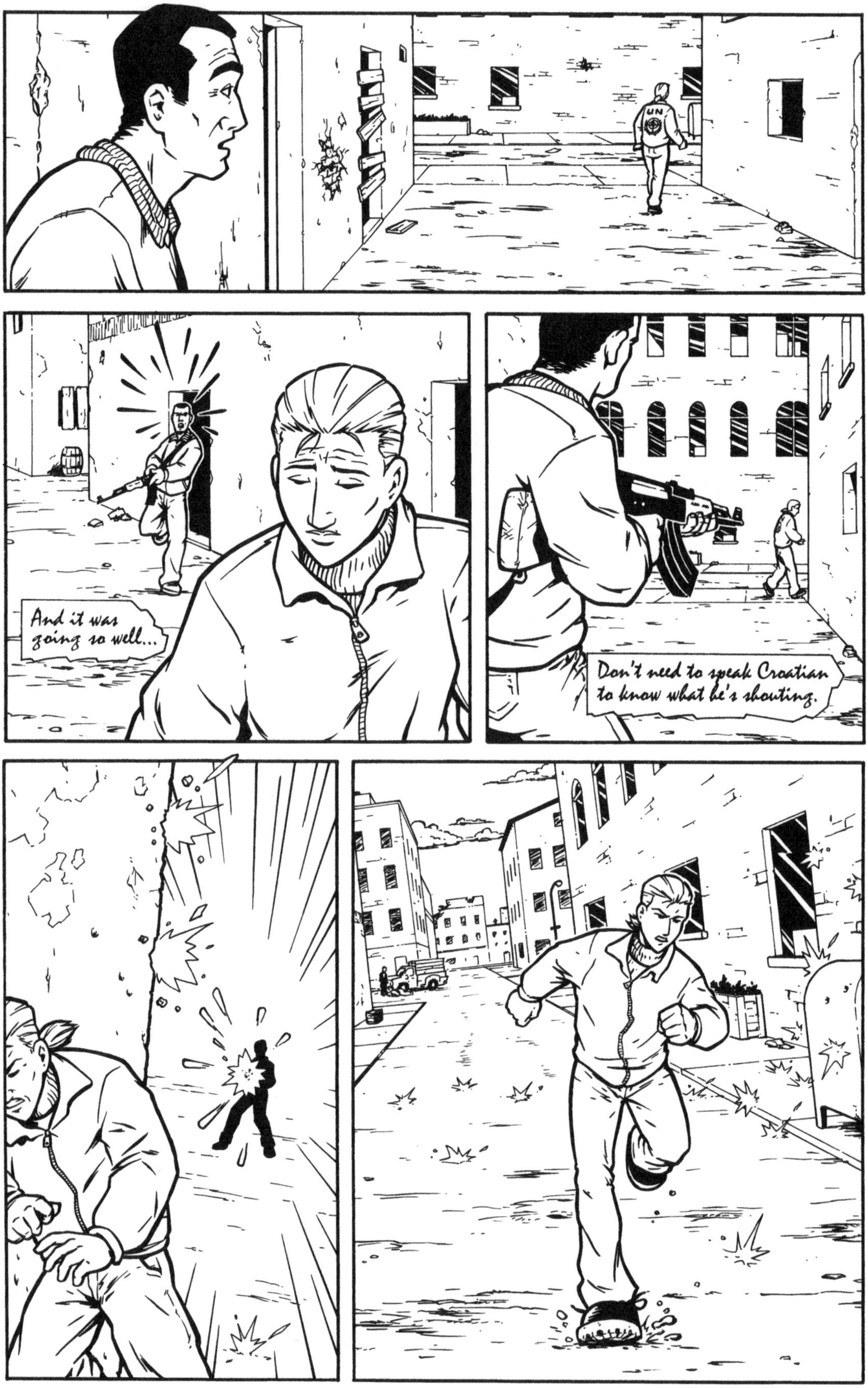

And it was going so well...
Don't need to speak Croatian to know what he's shouting.

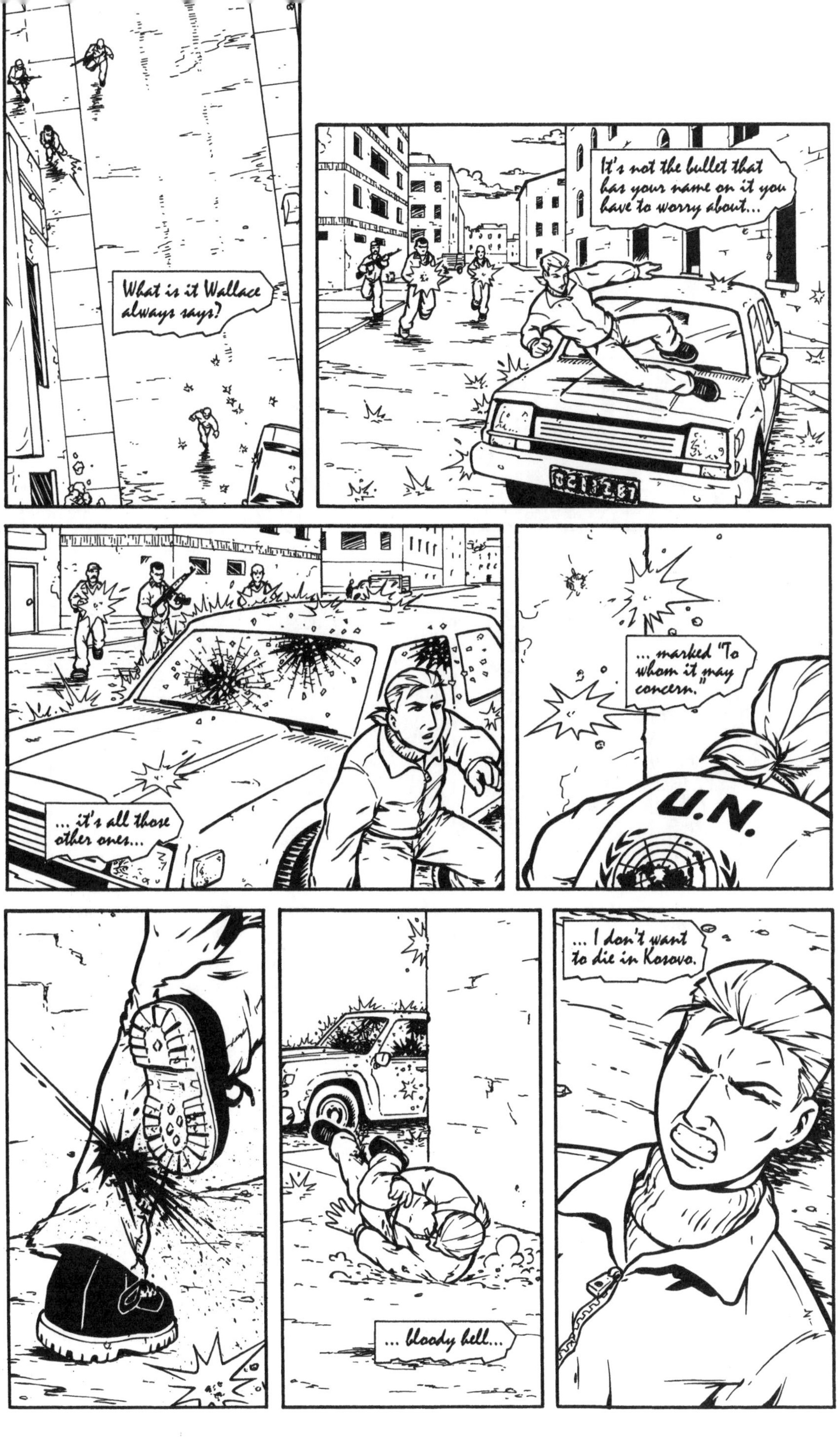
What is it Wallace always says?
It's not the bullet that has your name on it you have to worry about...
... it's all those other ones...
... marked "To whom it may concern."
U.N.
... bloody hell...
... I don't want to die in Kosovo.

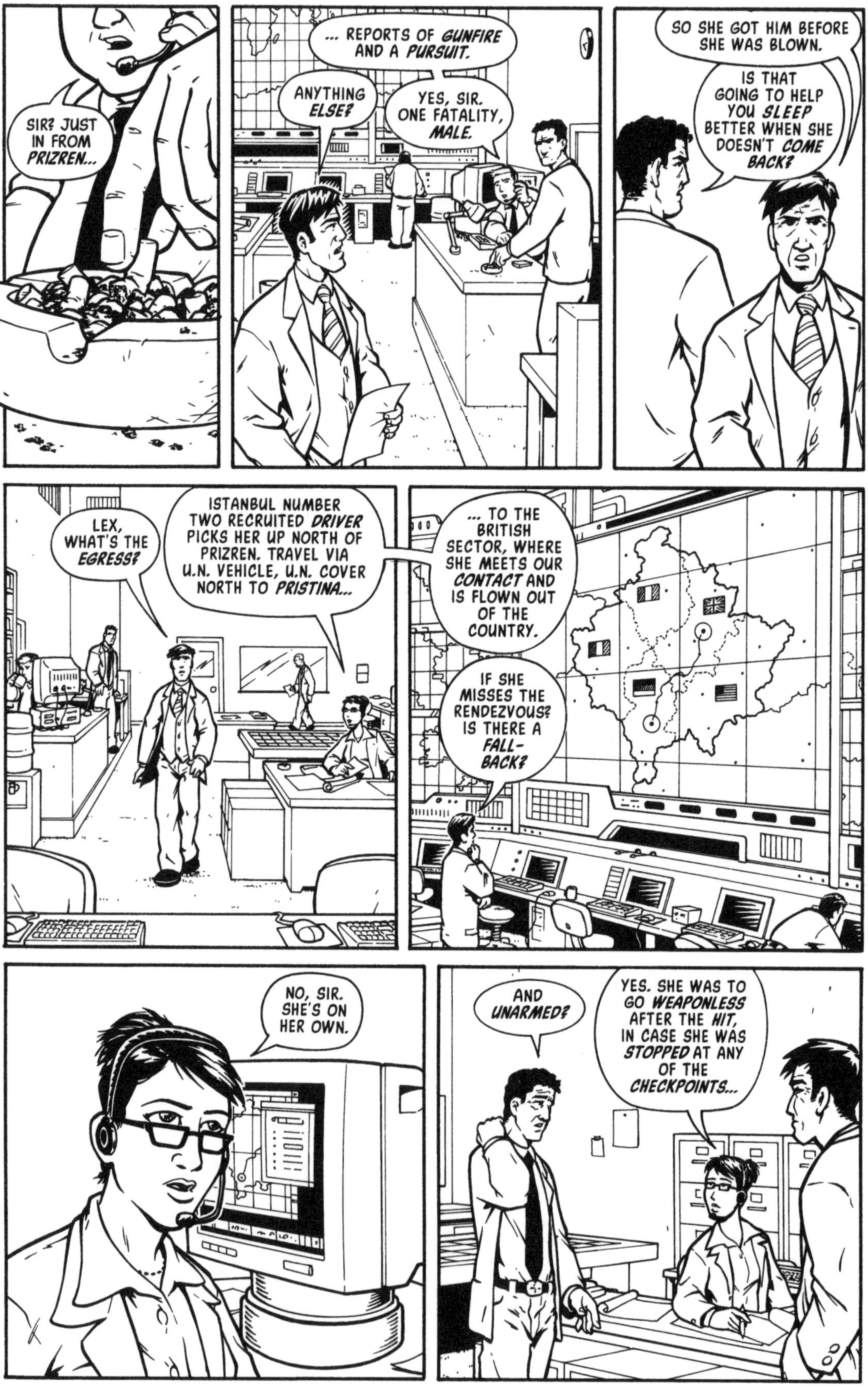
SIR? JUST IN FROM PRIZREN...
... REPORTS OF GUNFIRE AND A PURSUIT.
ANYTHING ELSE?
YES, SIR. ONE FATALITY, MALE.
SO SHE GOT HIM BEFORE SHE WAS BLOWN.
IS THAT GOING TO HELP YOU SLEEP BETTER WHEN SHE DOESN'T COME BACK?
LEX, WHAT'S THE EGRESS?
ISTANBUL NUMBER TWO RECRUITED DRIVER PICKS HER UP NORTH OF PRIZREN. TRAVEL VIA U.N. VEHICLE, U.N. COVER NORTH TO PRISTINA...
... TO THE BRITISH SECTOR, WHERE SHE MEETS OUR CONTACT AND IS FLOWN OUT OF THE COUNTRY.
IF SHE MISSES THE RENDEZVOUS? IS THERE A FALL-BACK?
NO, SIR. SHE'S ON HER OWN.
AND UNARMED?
YES. SHE WAS TO GO WEAPONLESS AFTER THE HIT, IN CASE SHE WAS STOPPED AT ANY OF THE CHECKPOINTS...

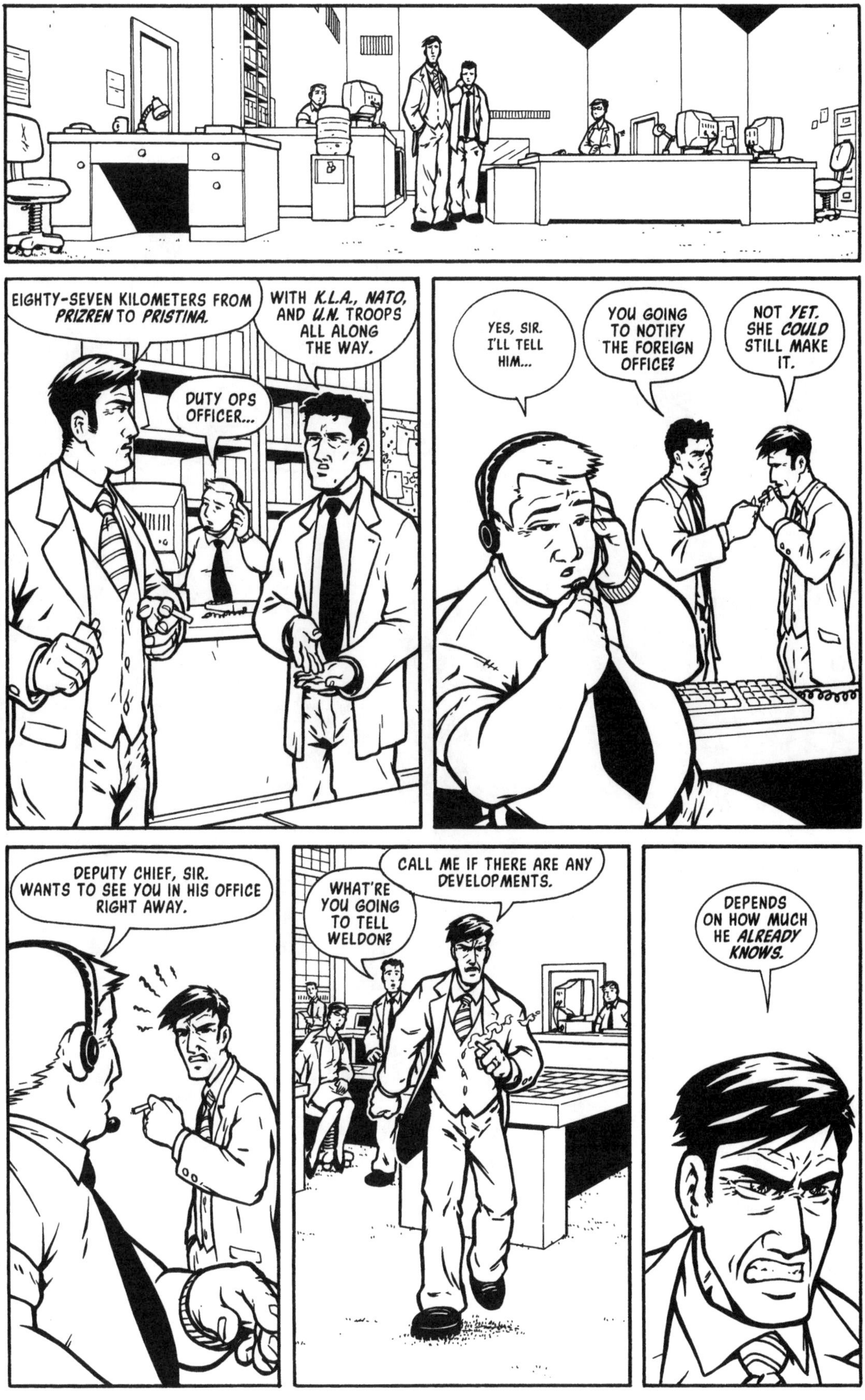
EIGHTY-SEVEN KILOMETERS FROM PRIZREN TO PRISTINA.
WITH K.L.A., NATO, AND U.N. TROOPS ALL ALONG THE WAY.
DUTY OPS OFFICER...
YES, SIR. I'LL TELL HIM...
YOU GOING TO NOTIFY THE FOREIGN OFFICE?
NOT YET. SHE COULD STILL MAKE IT.
DEPUTY CHIEF, SIR. WANTS TO SEE YOU IN HIS OFFICE RIGHT AWAY.
CALL ME IF THERE ARE ANY DEVELOPMENTS.
WHAT'RE YOU GOING TO TELL WELDON?
DEPENDS ON HOW MUCH HE ALREADY KNOWS.

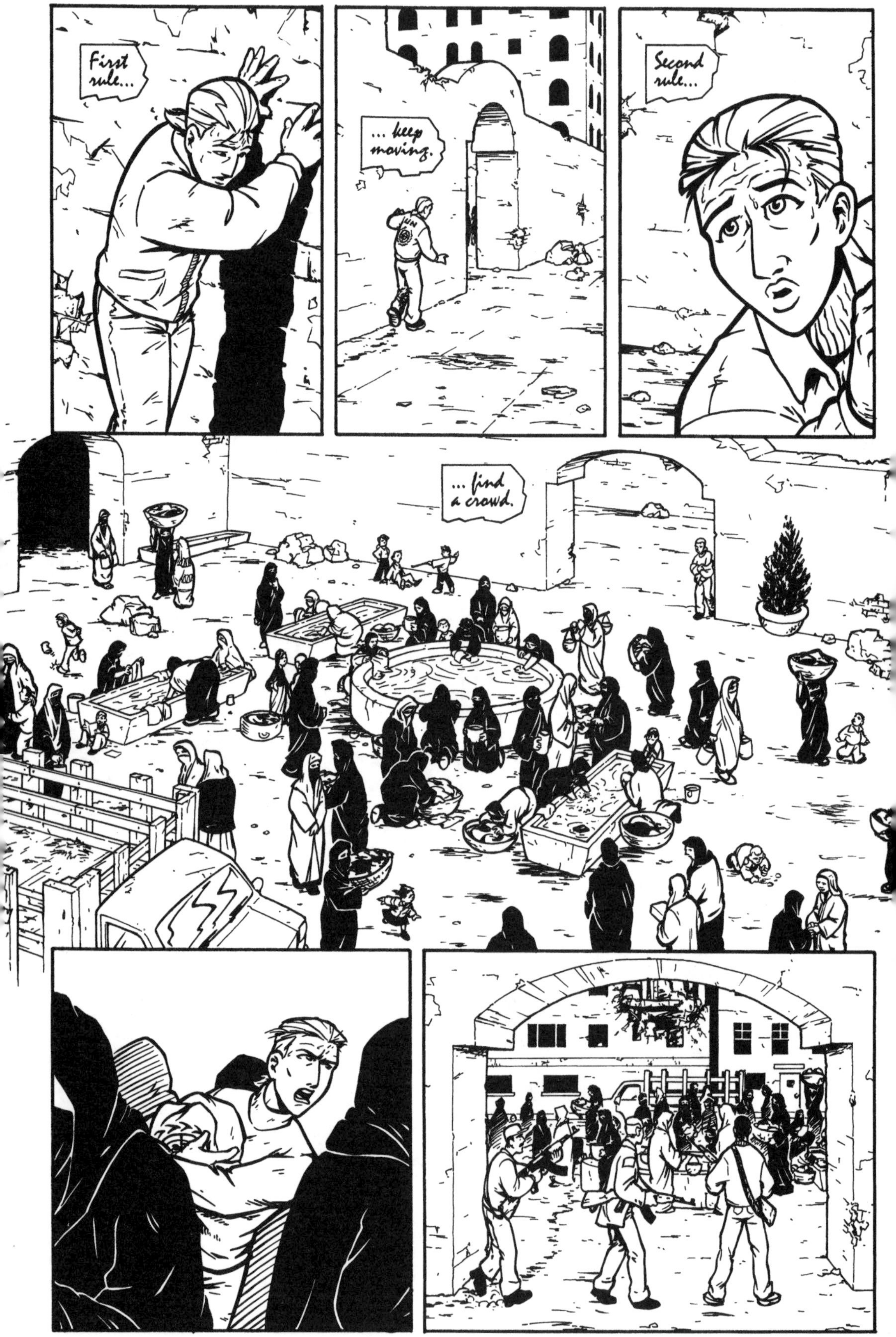

First rule...
... keep moving.
Second rule...
... find a crowd.

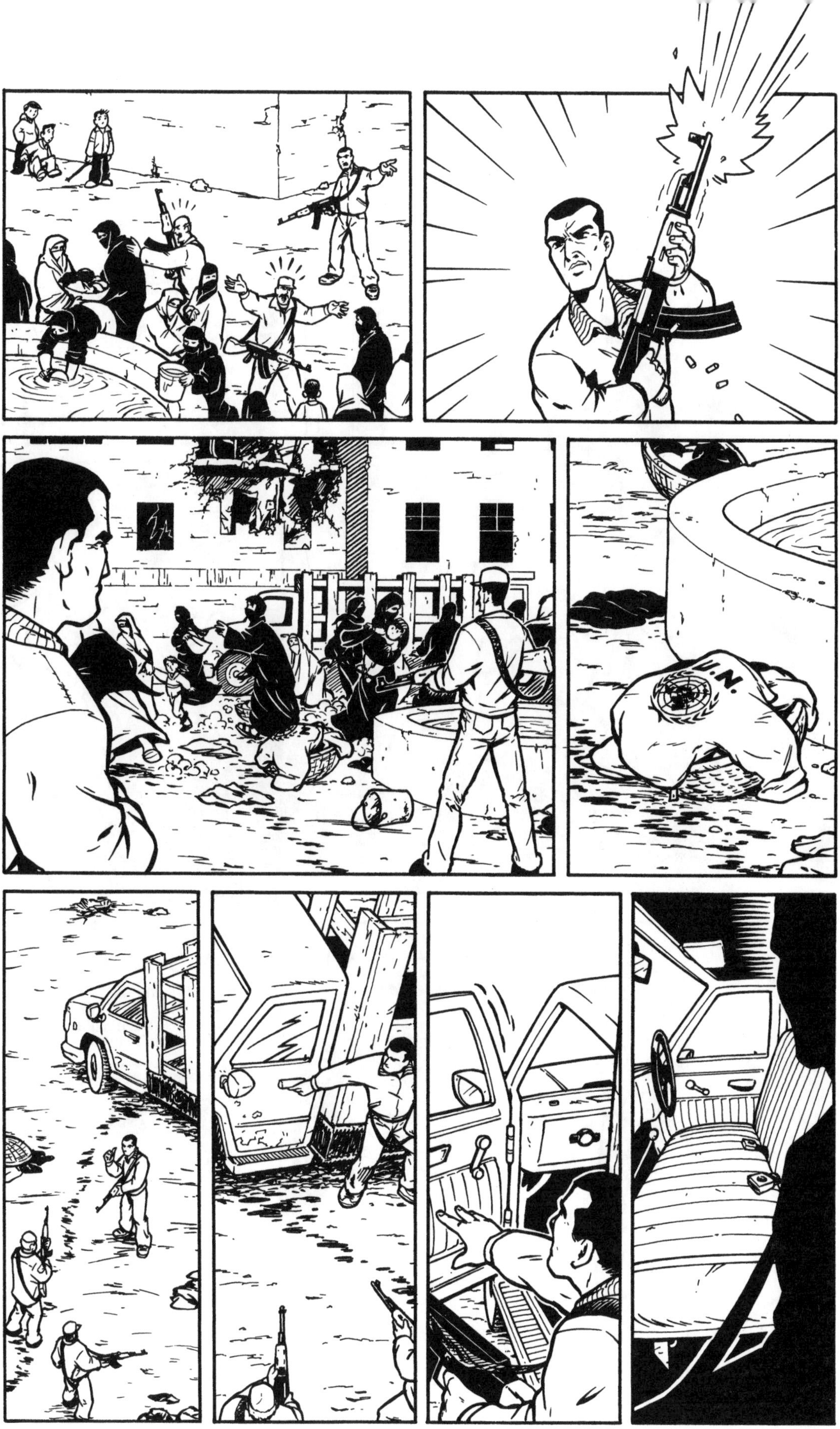
U.N.

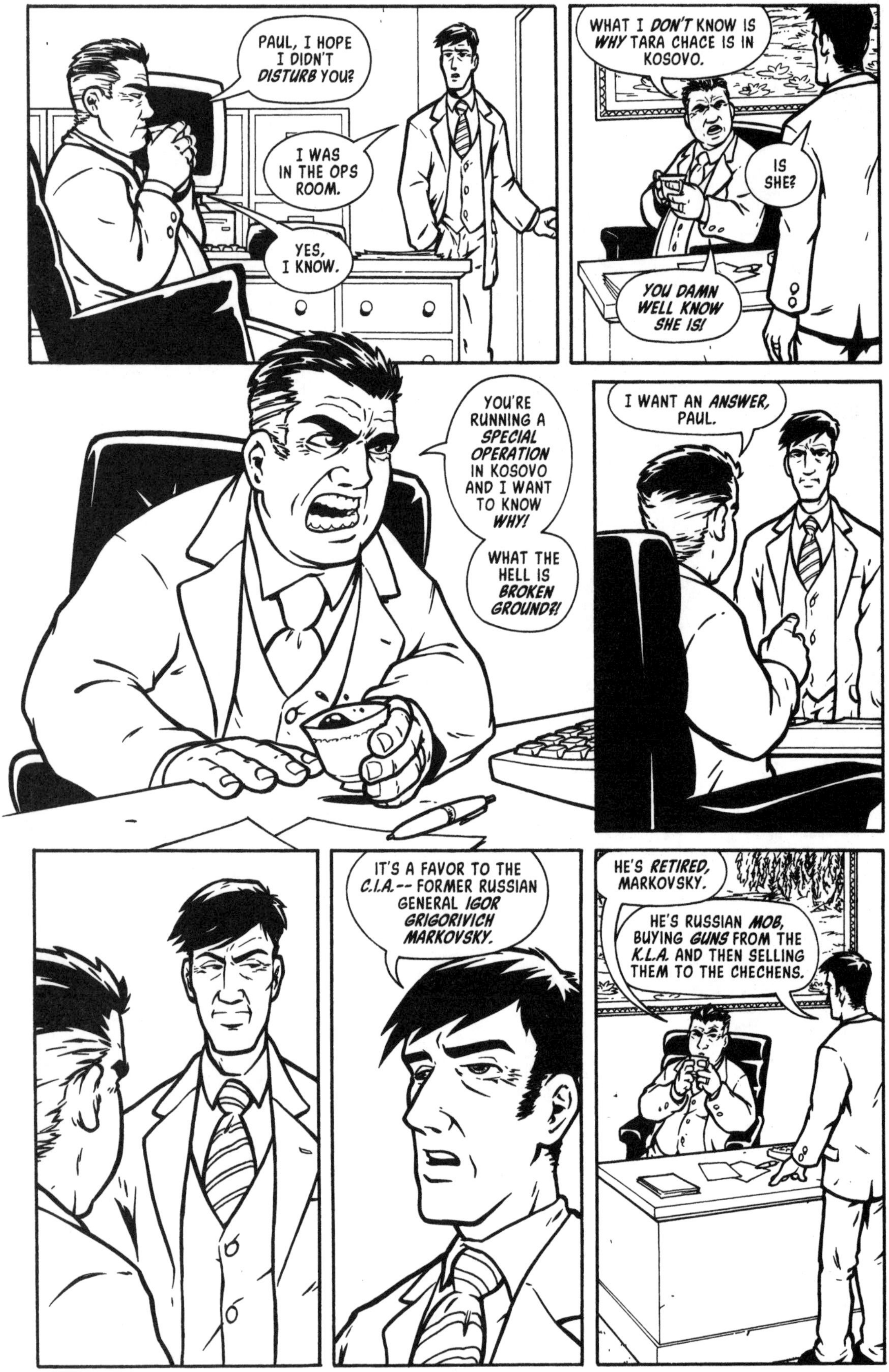
PAUL, I HOPE I DIDN'T *DISTURB* YOU?
I WAS IN THE OPS ROOM.
YES, I KNOW.
WHAT I *DON'T* KNOW IS *WHY* TARA CHACE IS IN KOSOVO.
IS SHE?
YOU DAMN WELL KNOW SHE IS!
YOU'RE RUNNING A *SPECIAL OPERATION* IN KOSOVO AND I WANT TO KNOW *WHY!*
WHAT THE HELL IS *BROKEN GROUND?!*
I WANT AN *ANSWER,* PAUL.
IT'S A FAVOR TO THE *C.I.A.*-- FORMER RUSSIAN GENERAL *IGOR GRIGORIVICH MARKOVSKY.*
HE'S *RETIRED,* MARKOVSKY.
HE'S RUSSIAN *MOB,* BUYING *GUNS* FROM THE *K.L.A.* AND THEN SELLING THEM TO THE CHECHENS.

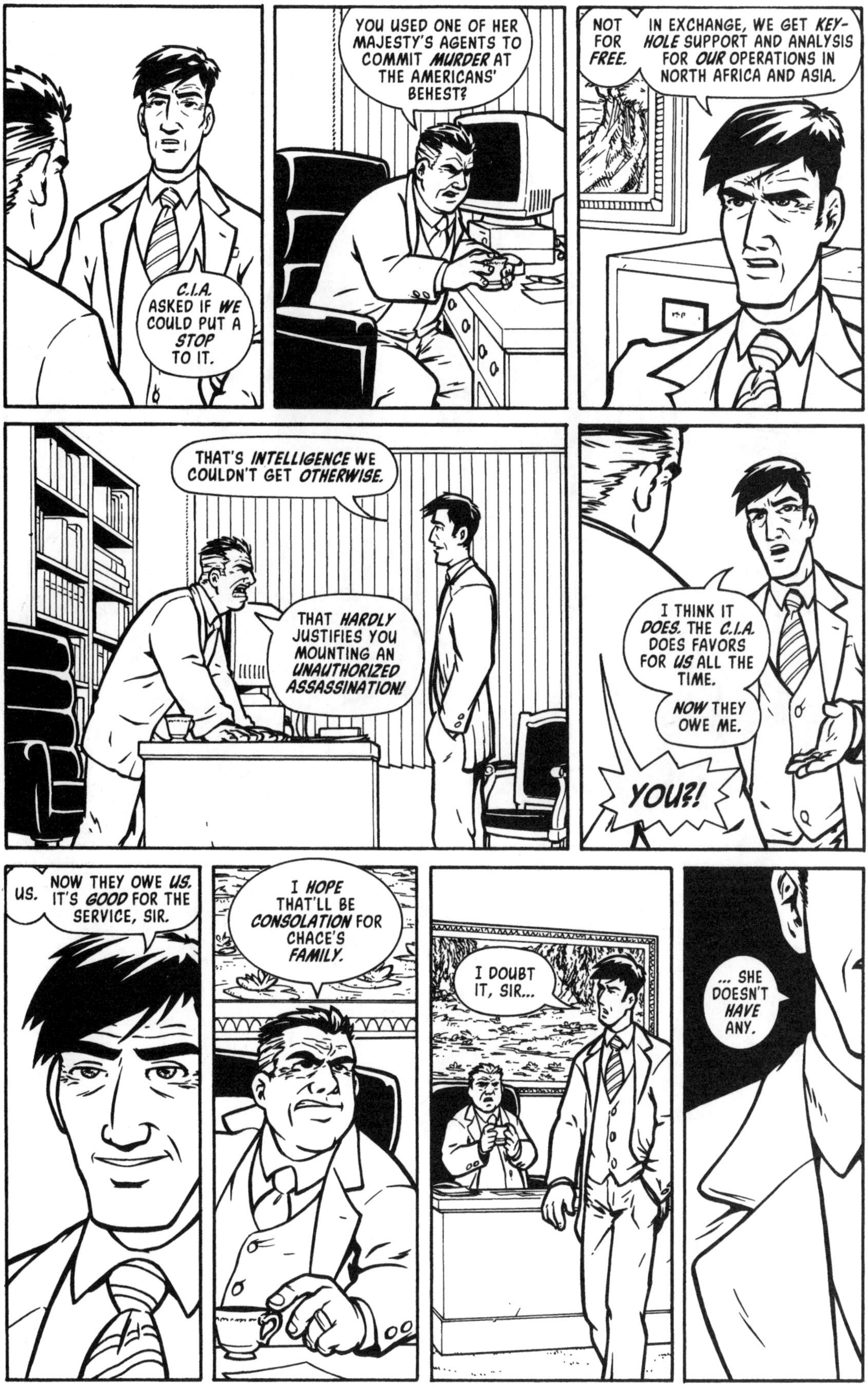
C.I.A. ASKED IF WE COULD PUT A STOP TO IT.
YOU USED ONE OF HER MAJESTY'S AGENTS TO COMMIT MURDER AT THE AMERICANS' BEHEST?
NOT FOR FREE.
IN EXCHANGE, WE GET KEY-HOLE SUPPORT AND ANALYSIS FOR OUR OPERATIONS IN NORTH AFRICA AND ASIA.
THAT'S INTELLIGENCE WE COULDN'T GET OTHERWISE.
THAT HARDLY JUSTIFIES YOU MOUNTING AN UNAUTHORIZED ASSASSINATION!
I THINK IT DOES. THE C.I.A. DOES FAVORS FOR US ALL THE TIME.
NOW THEY OWE ME.
YOU?!
US.
NOW THEY OWE US. IT'S GOOD FOR THE SERVICE, SIR.
I HOPE THAT'LL BE CONSOLATION FOR CHACE'S FAMILY.
I DOUBT IT, SIR...
... SHE DOESN'T HAVE ANY.

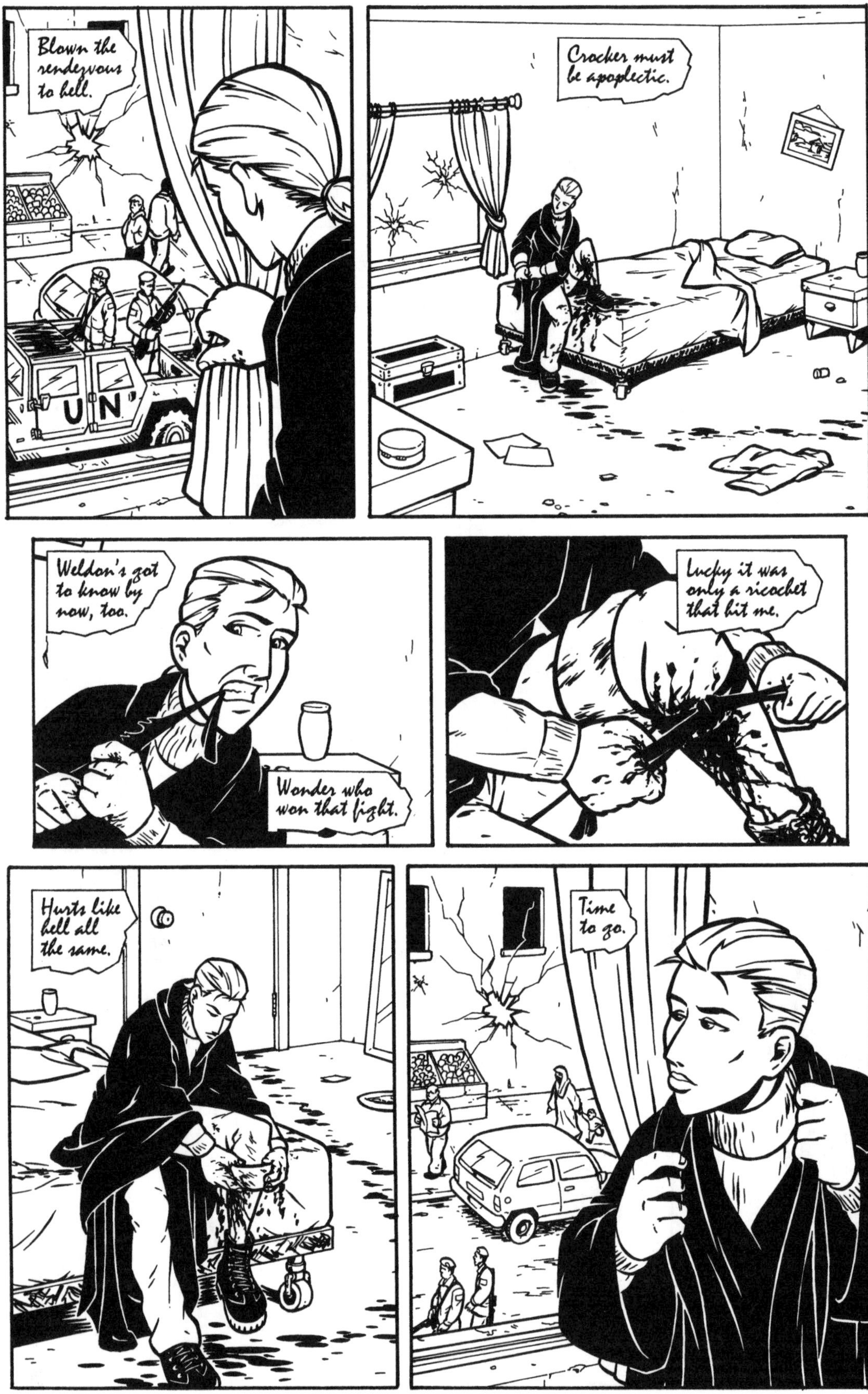
Blown the rendezvous to hell.
Crocker must be apoplectic.
Weldon's got to know by now, too.
Wonder who won that fight.
Lucky it was only a ricochet that hit me.
Hurts like hell all the same.
Time to go.

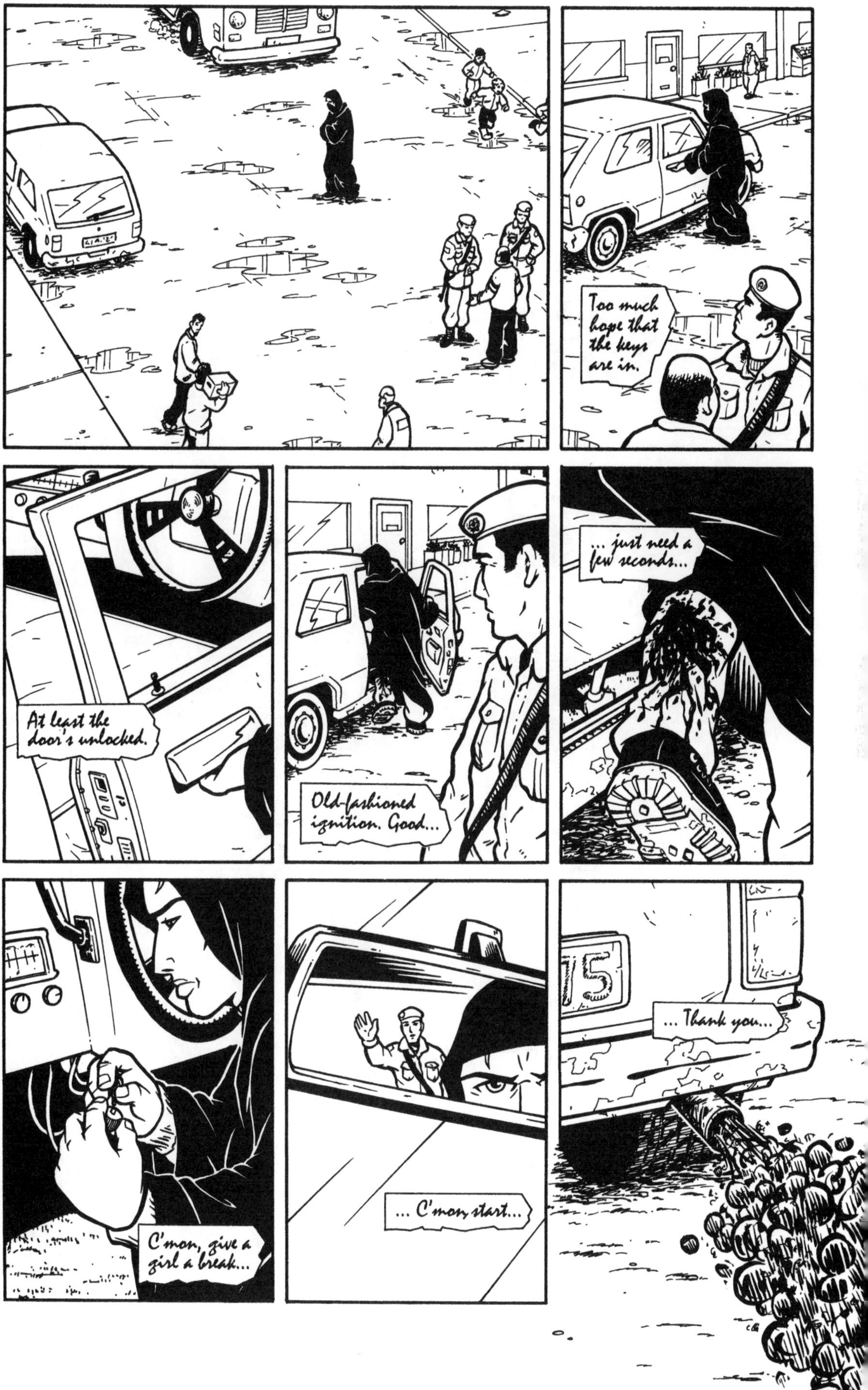
Too much hope that the keys are in.
At least the door's unlocked.
Old-fashioned ignition. Good...
... just need a few seconds...
C'mon, give a girl a break...
... C'mon start...
... Thank you...

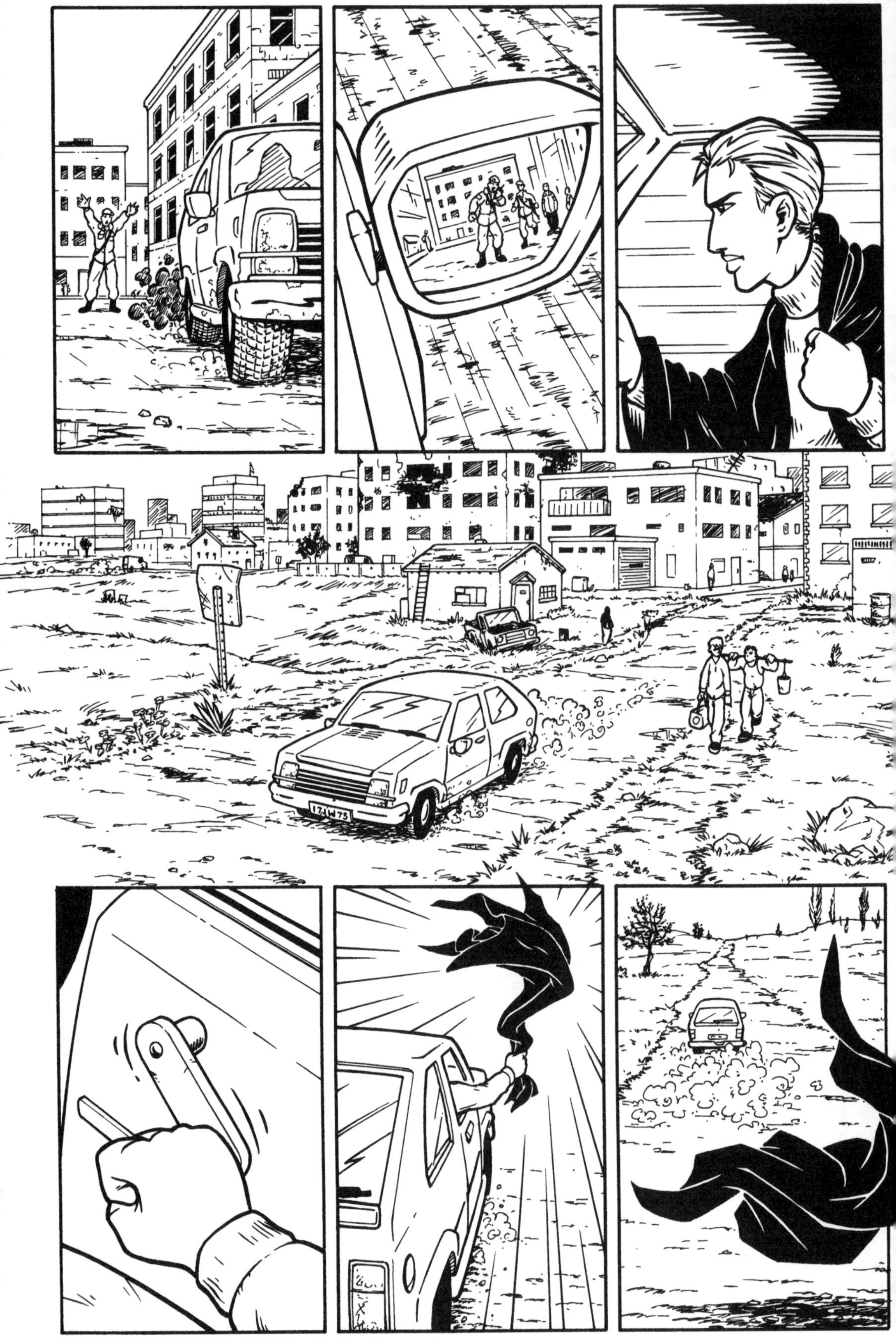

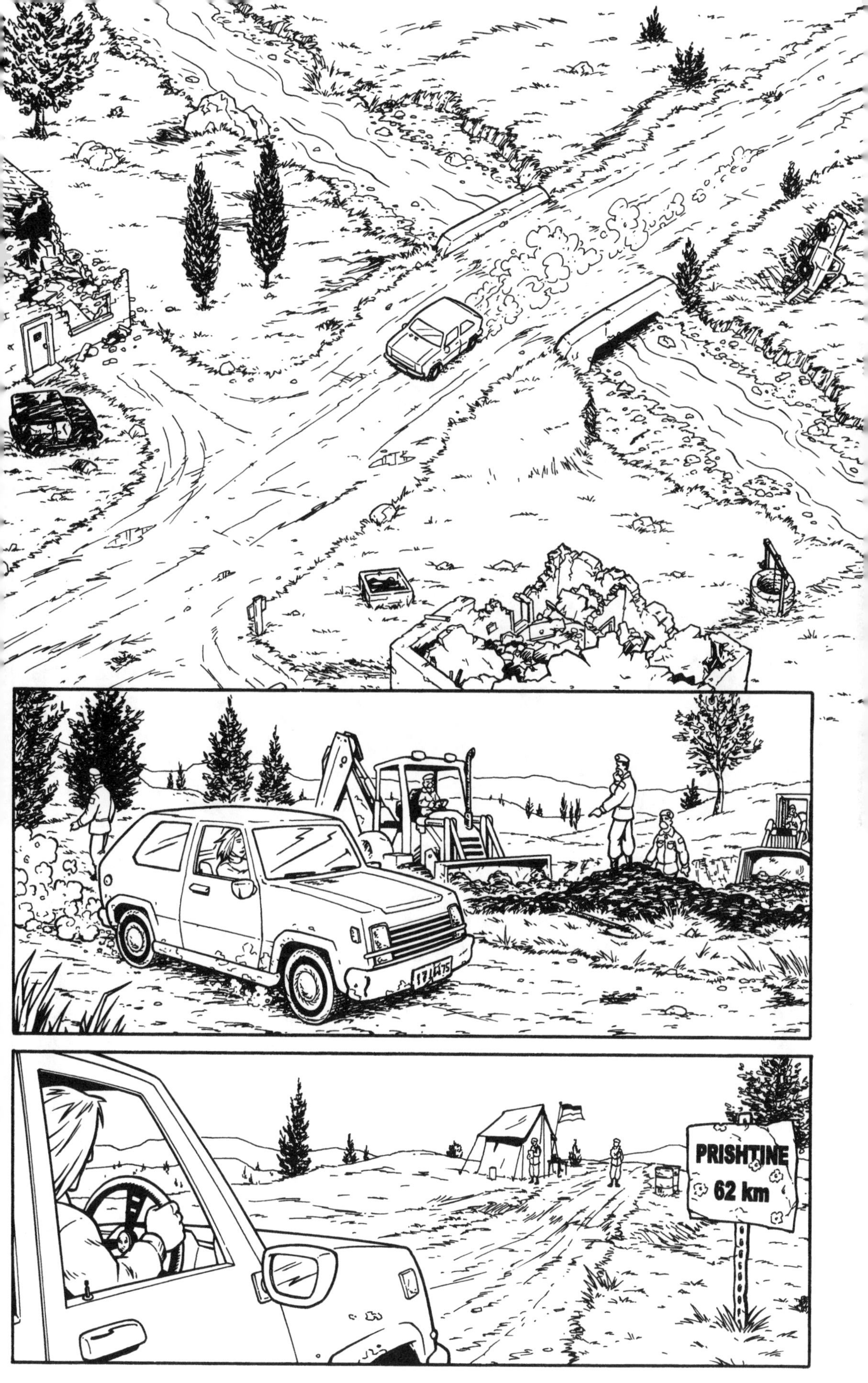
PRISHTINE
62 km

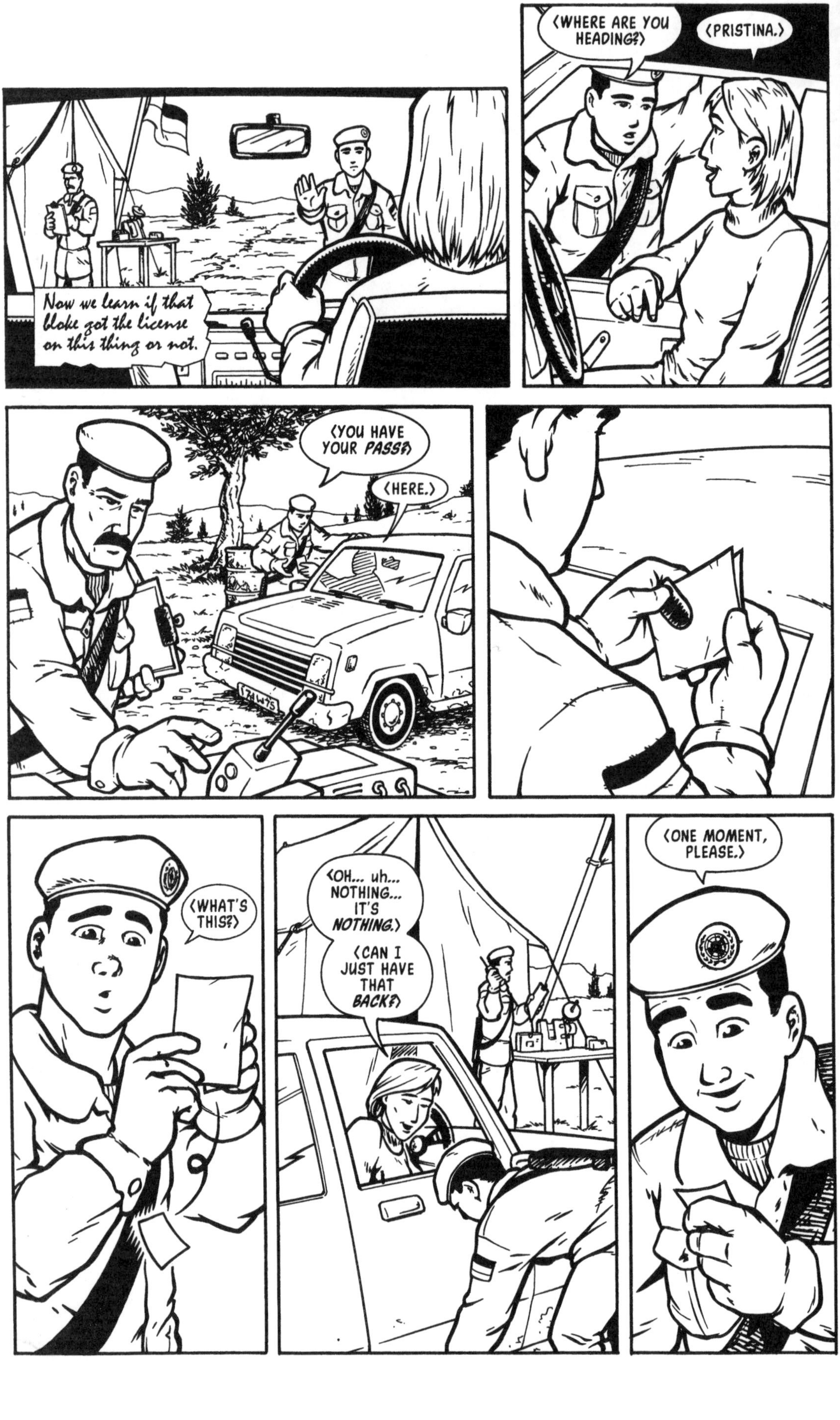
Now we learn if that bloke got the license on this thing or not.
<WHERE ARE YOU HEADING?>
<PRISTINA.>
<YOU HAVE YOUR PASS?>
<HERE.>
<WHAT'S THIS?>
<OH... uh... NOTHING... IT'S NOTHING.>
<CAN I JUST HAVE THAT BACK?>
<ONE MOMENT, PLEASE.>

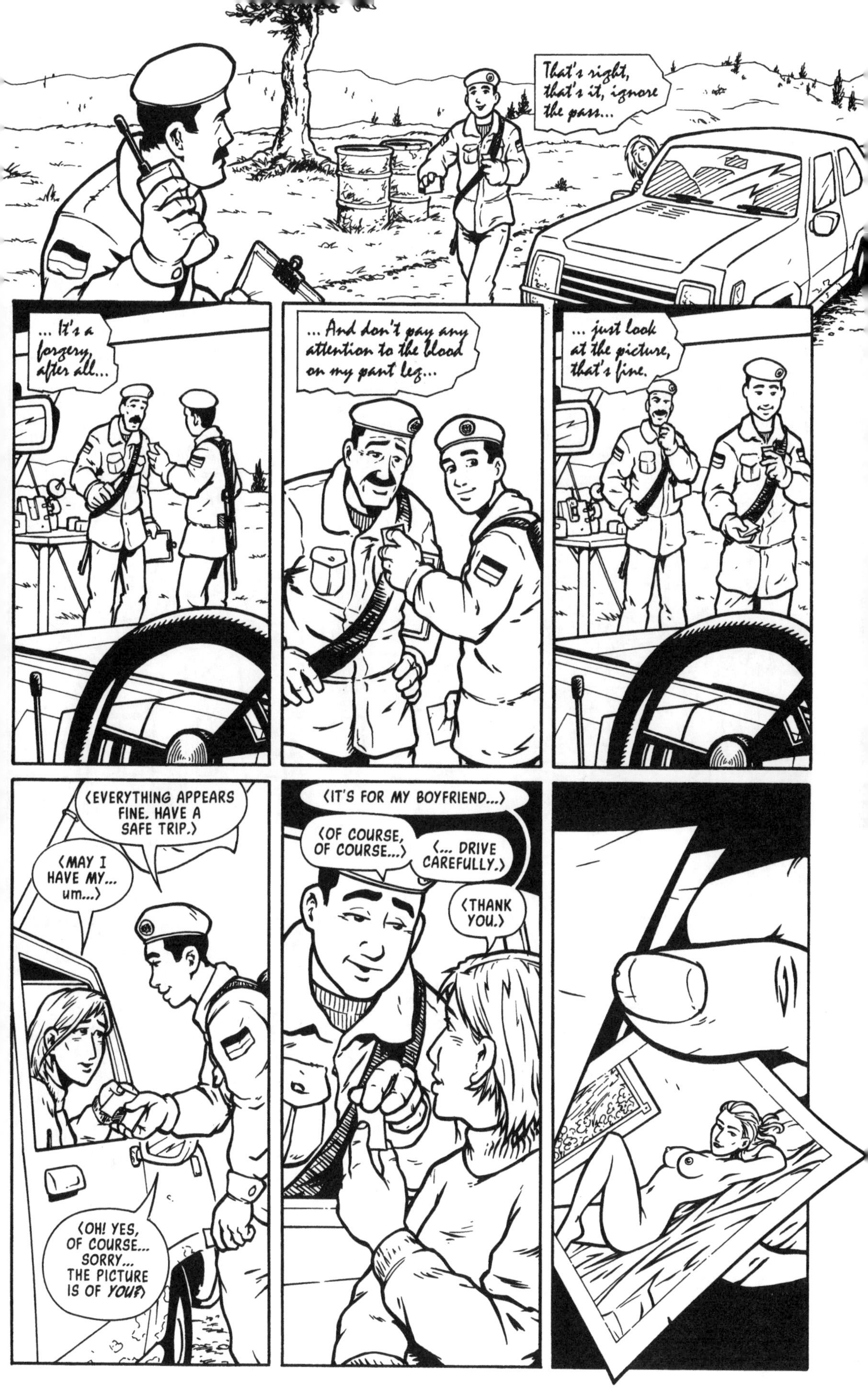
That's right, that's it, ignore the pass...
... It's a forgery, after all...
... And don't pay any attention to the blood on my pant leg...
... just look at the picture, that's fine.
‹EVERYTHING APPEARS FINE. HAVE A SAFE TRIP.›
‹MAY I HAVE MY... um...›
‹OH! YES, OF COURSE... SORRY... THE PICTURE IS OF *YOU*?›
‹IT'S FOR MY BOYFRIEND...›
‹OF COURSE, OF COURSE...›
‹... DRIVE CAREFULLY.›
‹THANK YOU.›

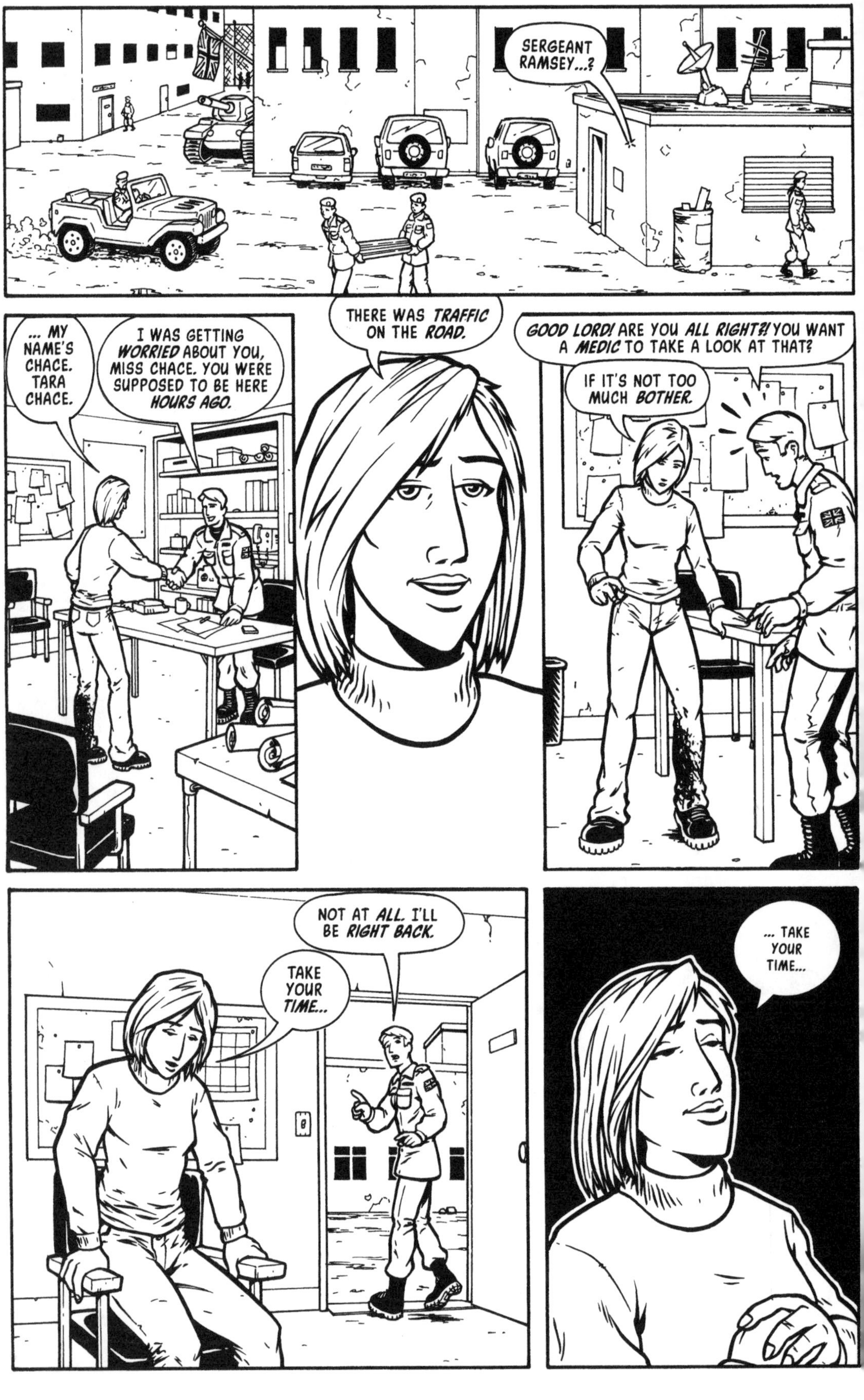
SERGEANT RAMSEY...?
... MY NAME'S CHACE. TARA CHACE.
I WAS GETTING WORRIED ABOUT YOU, MISS CHACE. YOU WERE SUPPOSED TO BE HERE HOURS AGO.
THERE WAS TRAFFIC ON THE ROAD.
GOOD LORD! ARE YOU ALL RIGHT?! YOU WANT A MEDIC TO TAKE A LOOK AT THAT?
IF IT'S NOT TOO MUCH BOTHER.
NOT AT ALL. I'LL BE RIGHT BACK.
TAKE YOUR TIME...
... TAKE YOUR TIME...

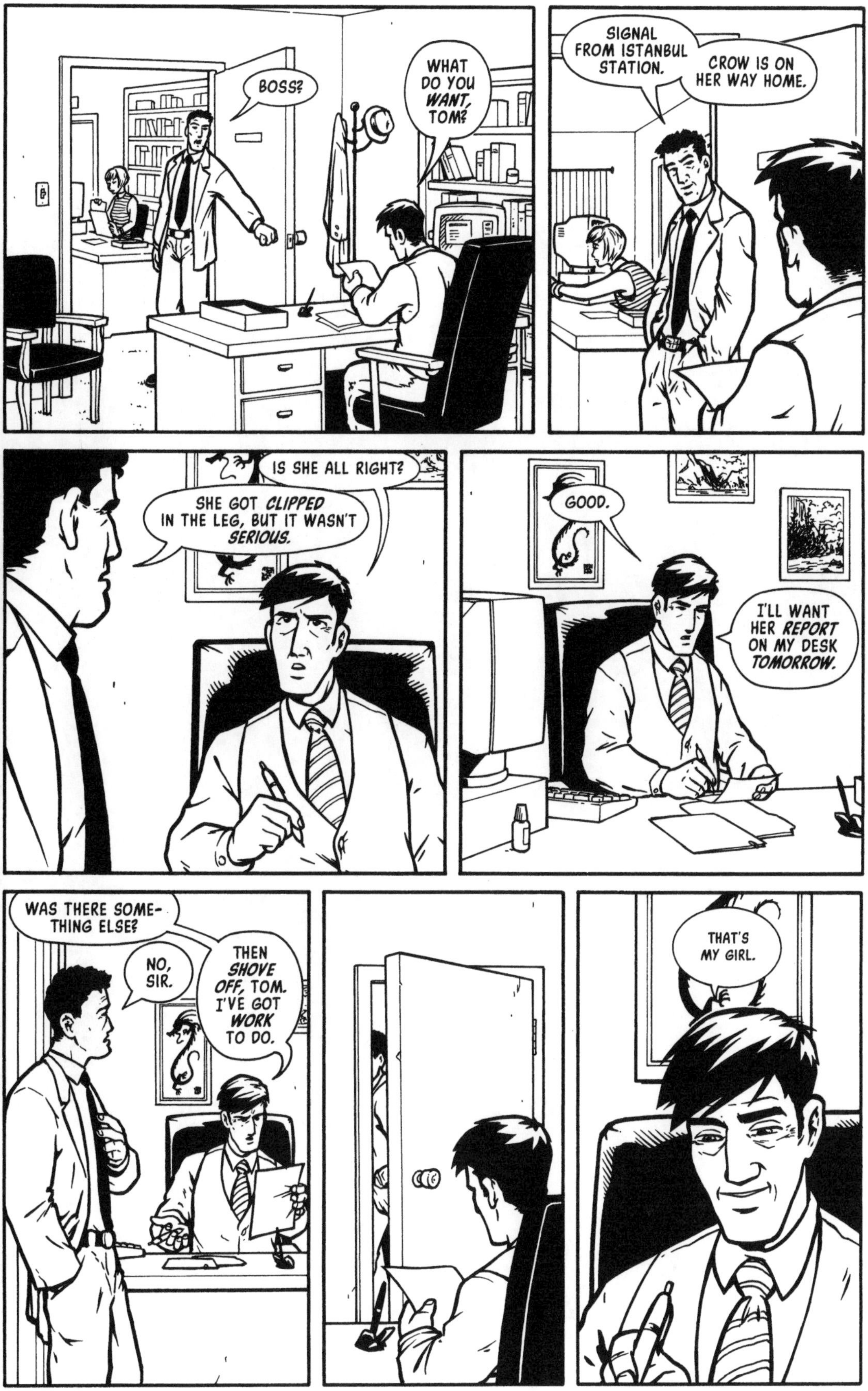
BOSS?
WHAT DO YOU WANT, TOM?
SIGNAL FROM ISTANBUL STATION.
CROW IS ON HER WAY HOME.
IS SHE ALL RIGHT?
SHE GOT CLIPPED IN THE LEG, BUT IT WASN'T SERIOUS.
GOOD.
I'LL WANT HER REPORT ON MY DESK TOMORROW.
WAS THERE SOME-THING ELSE?
NO, SIR.
THEN SHOVE OFF, TOM. I'VE GOT WORK TO DO.
THAT'S MY GIRL.

CHAPTER 2

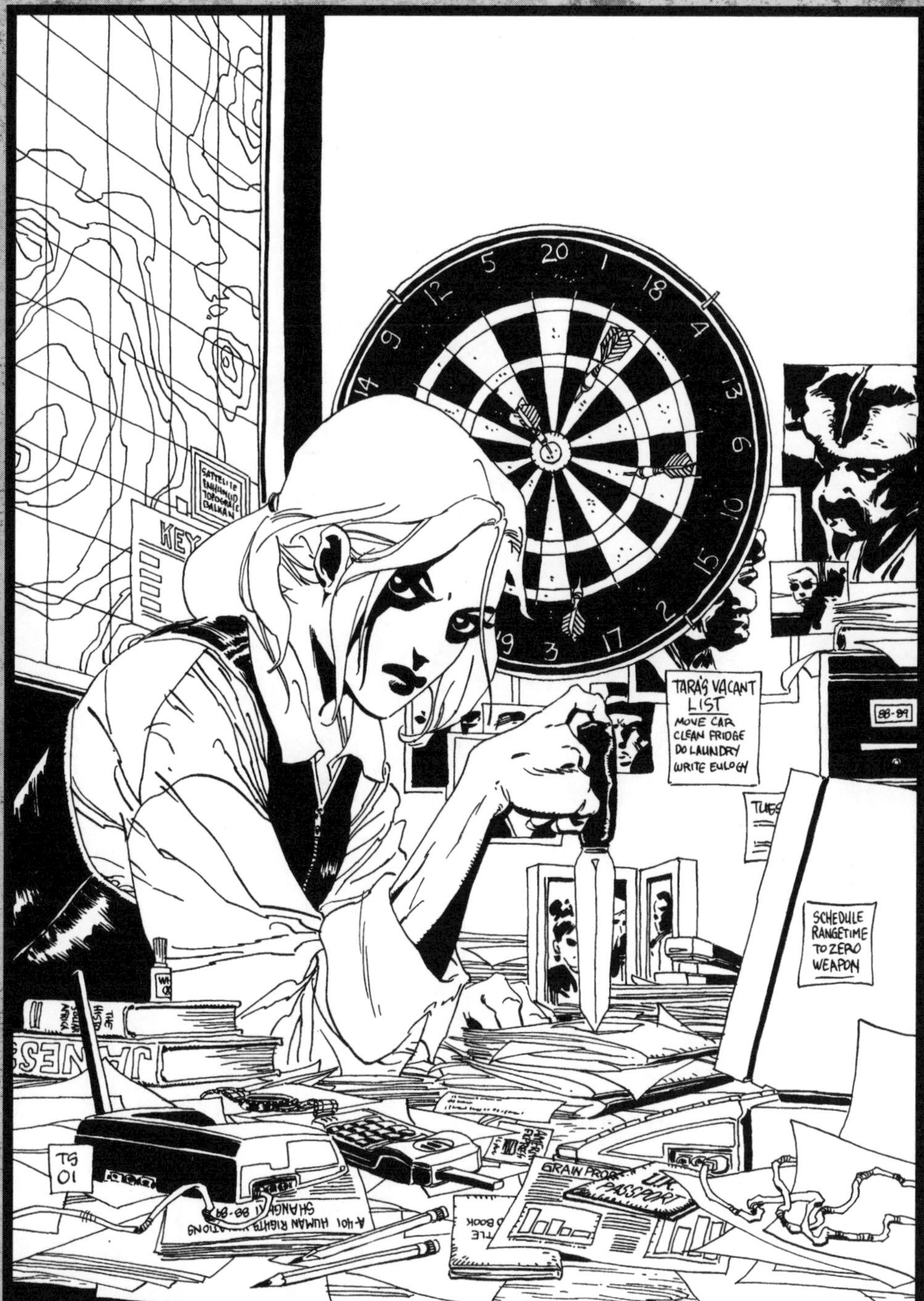

KEY
TARA'S VACANT LIST
MOVE CAR
CLEAN FRIDGE
DO LAUNDRY
WRITE EULOGY
88-89
SCHEDULE RANGETIME TO ZERO WEAPON
TG 01

★★

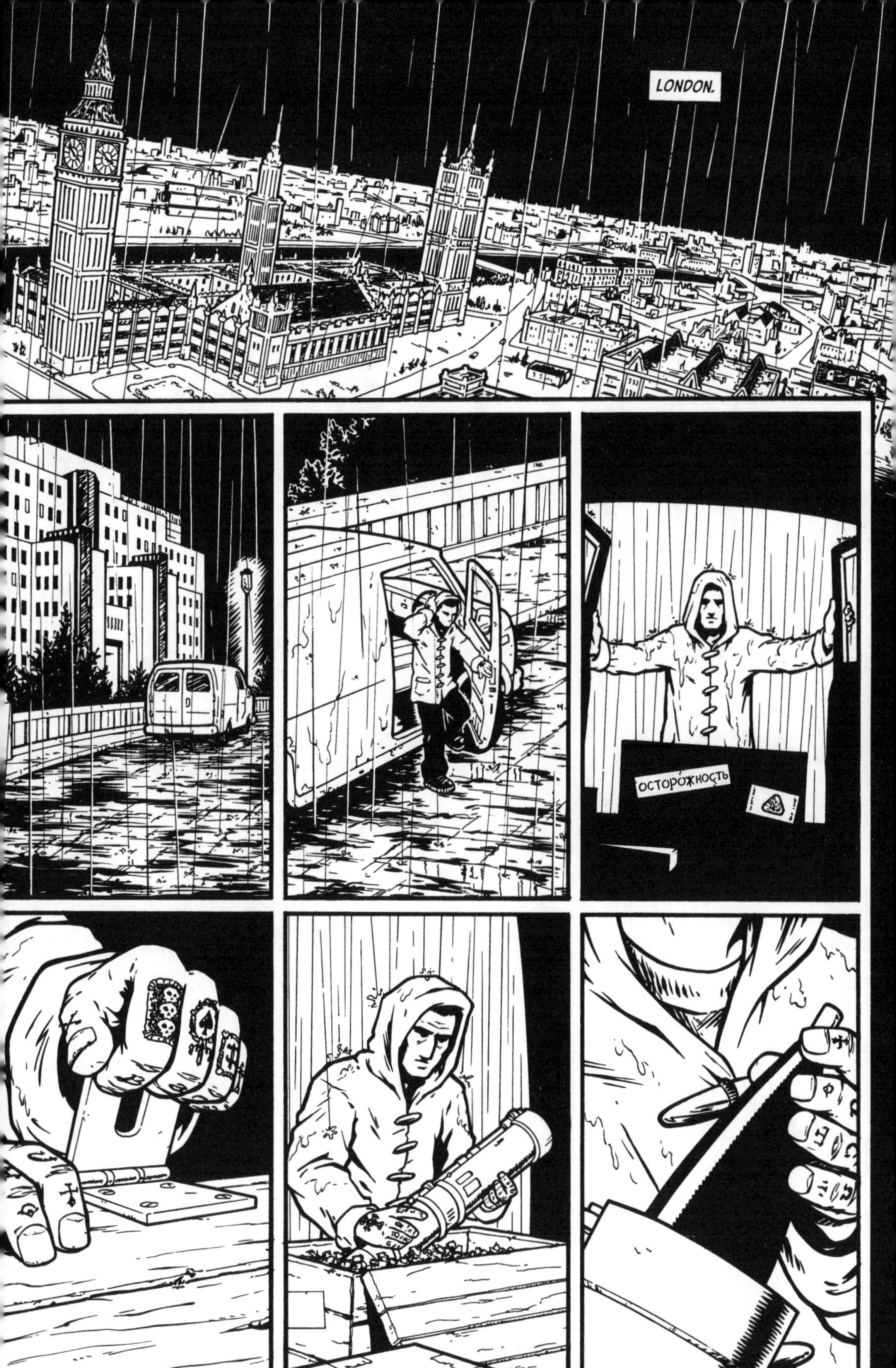
LONDON.
ОСТОРОЖНОСТЬ

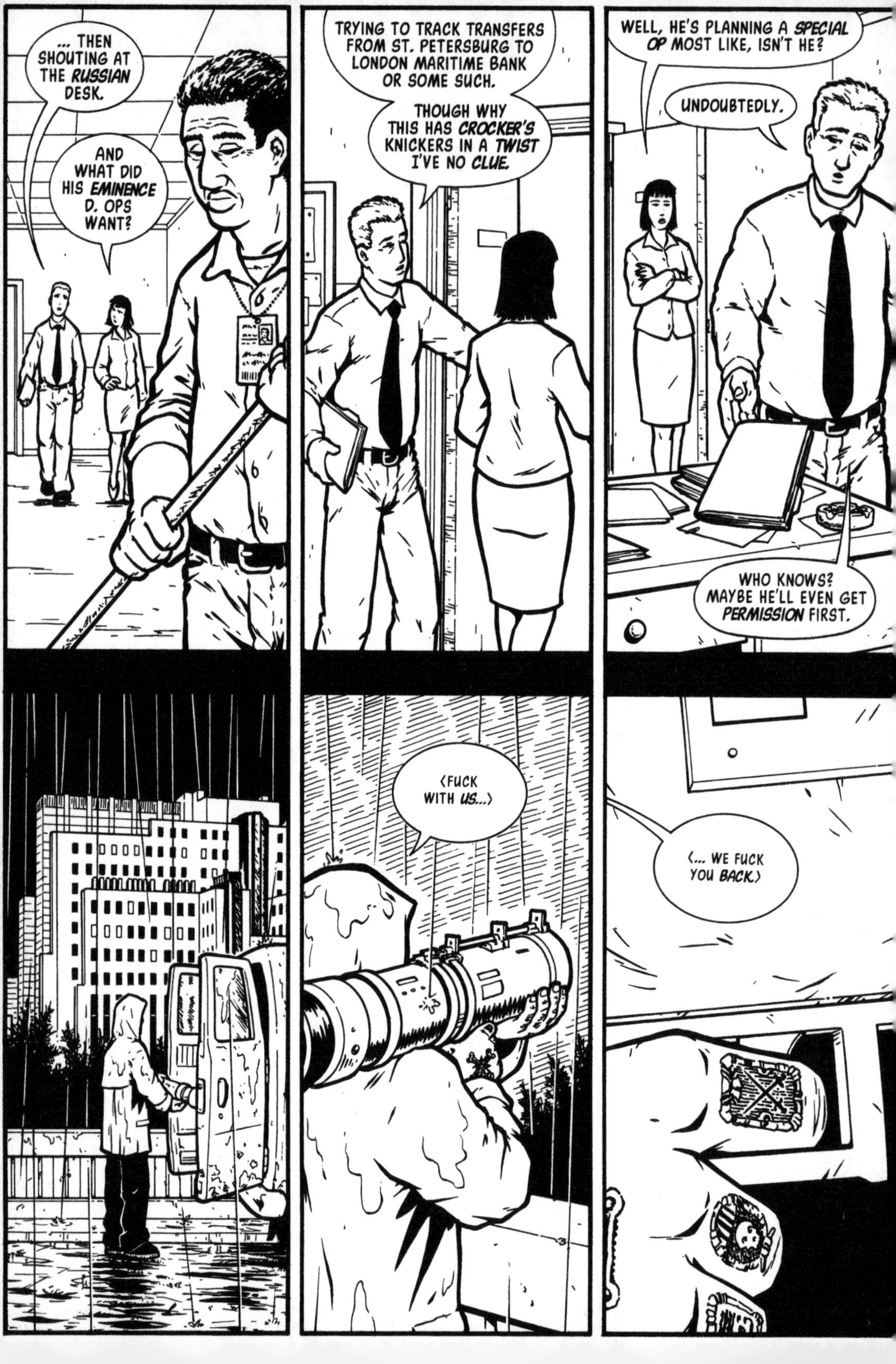
... THEN SHOUTING AT THE RUSSIAN DESK.
AND WHAT DID HIS EMINENCE D. OPS WANT?
TRYING TO TRACK TRANSFERS FROM ST. PETERSBURG TO LONDON MARITIME BANK OR SOME SUCH.
THOUGH WHY THIS HAS CROCKER'S KNICKERS IN A TWIST I'VE NO CLUE.
WELL, HE'S PLANNING A SPECIAL OP MOST LIKE, ISN'T HE?
UNDOUBTEDLY.
WHO KNOWS? MAYBE HE'LL EVEN GET PERMISSION FIRST.
<FUCK WITH US...>
<... WE FUCK YOU BACK.>

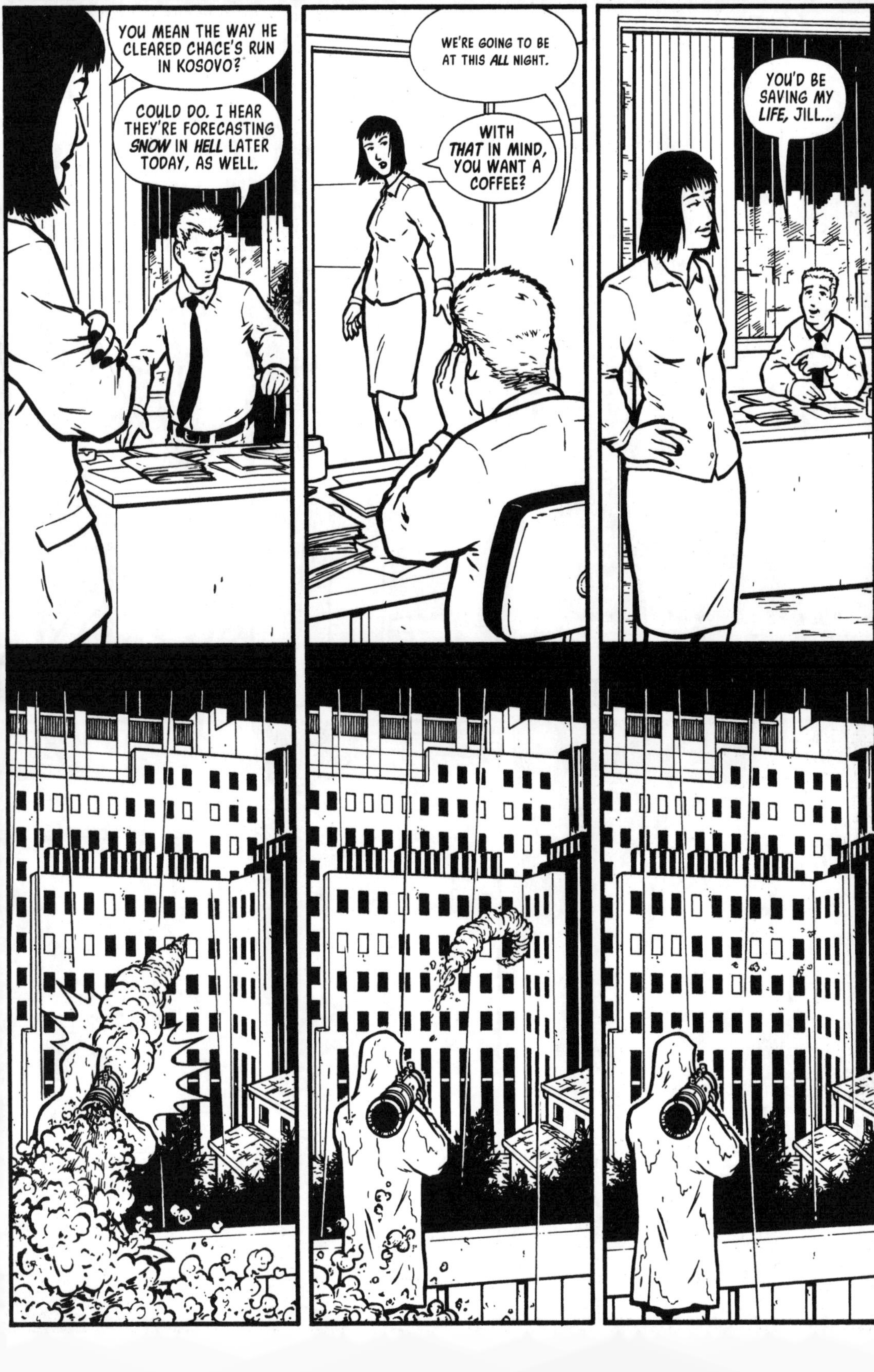
YOU MEAN THE WAY HE CLEARED CHACE'S RUN IN KOSOVO?
COULD DO. I HEAR THEY'RE FORECASTING SNOW IN HELL LATER TODAY, AS WELL.
WE'RE GOING TO BE AT THIS ALL NIGHT.
WITH THAT IN MIND, YOU WANT A COFFEE?
YOU'D BE SAVING MY LIFE, JILL...

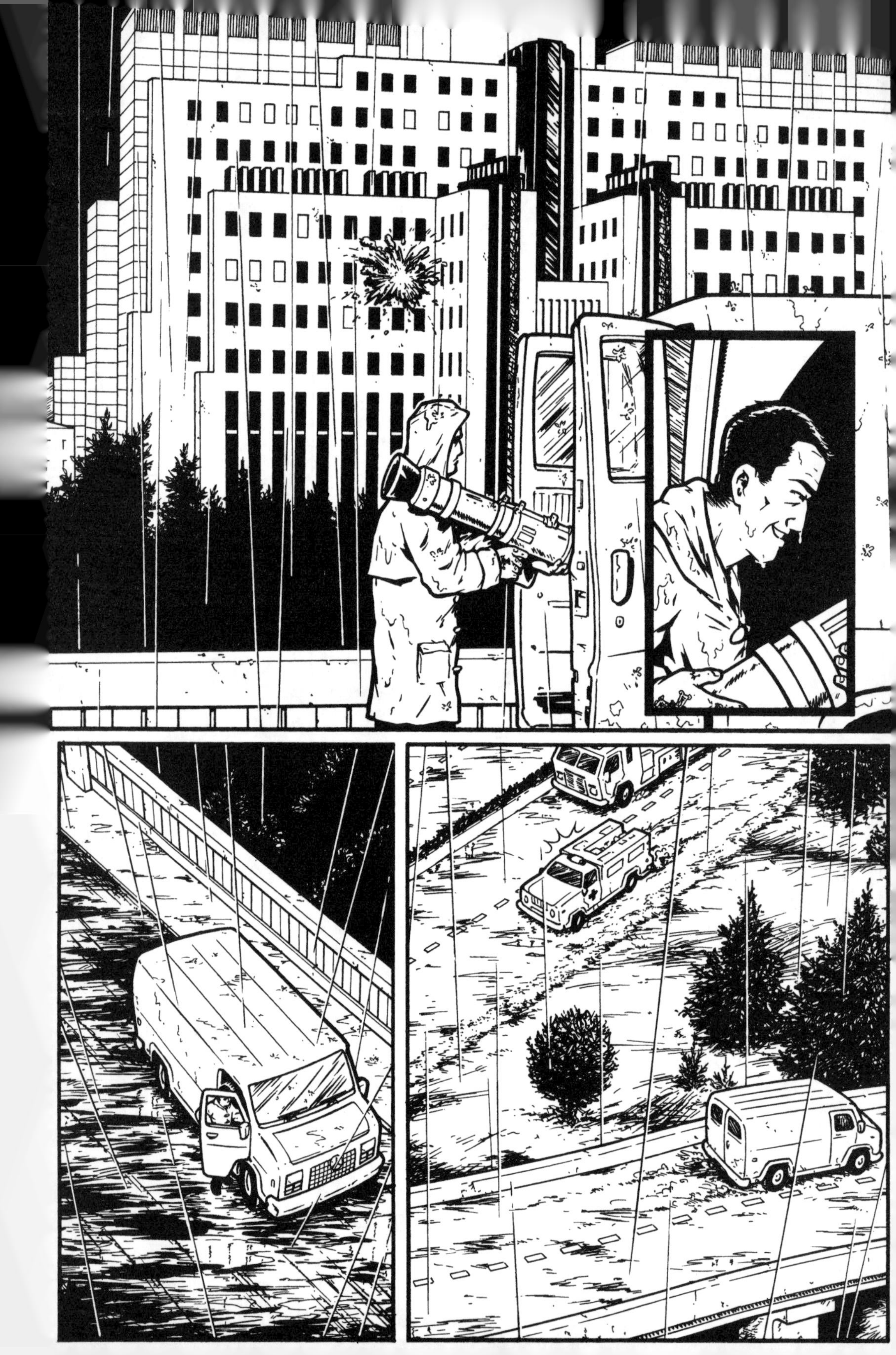

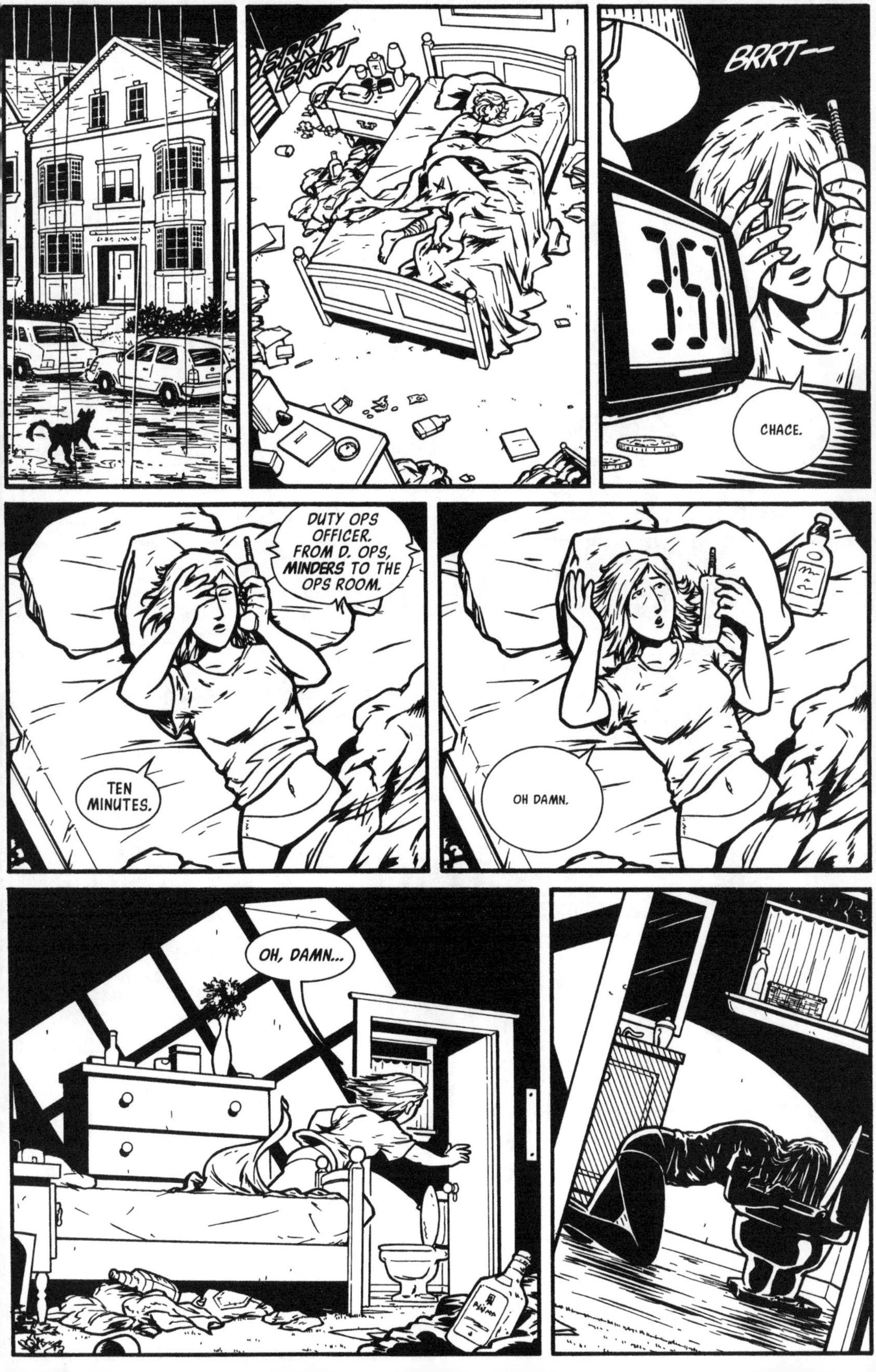
BRRT BRRT
BRRT—
CHACE.
DUTY OPS OFFICER. FROM D. OPS, MINDERS TO THE OPS ROOM.
TEN MINUTES.
OH DAMN.
OH, DAMN...

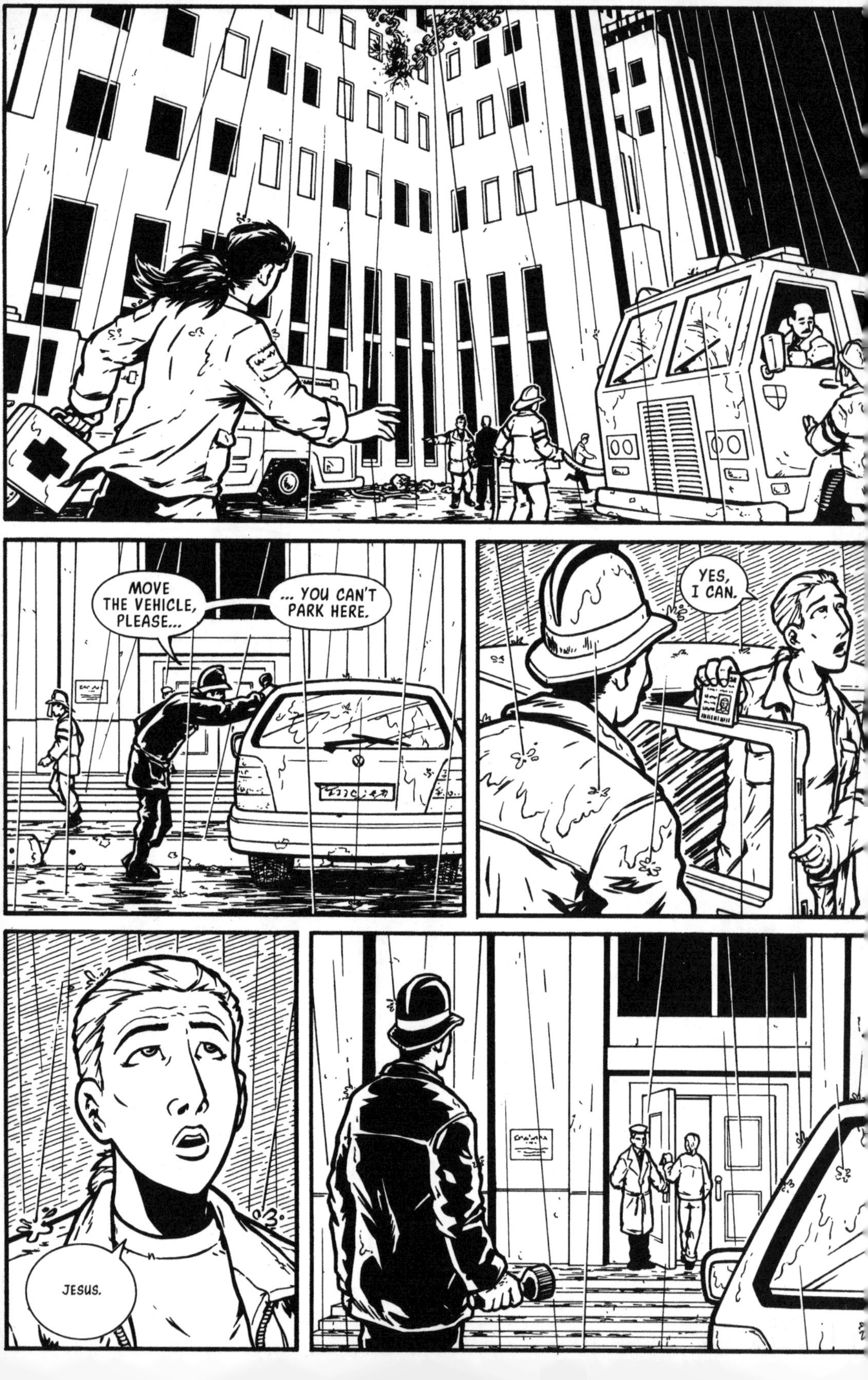
MOVE THE VEHICLE, PLEASE...
... YOU CAN'T PARK HERE.
YES, I CAN.
JESUS.

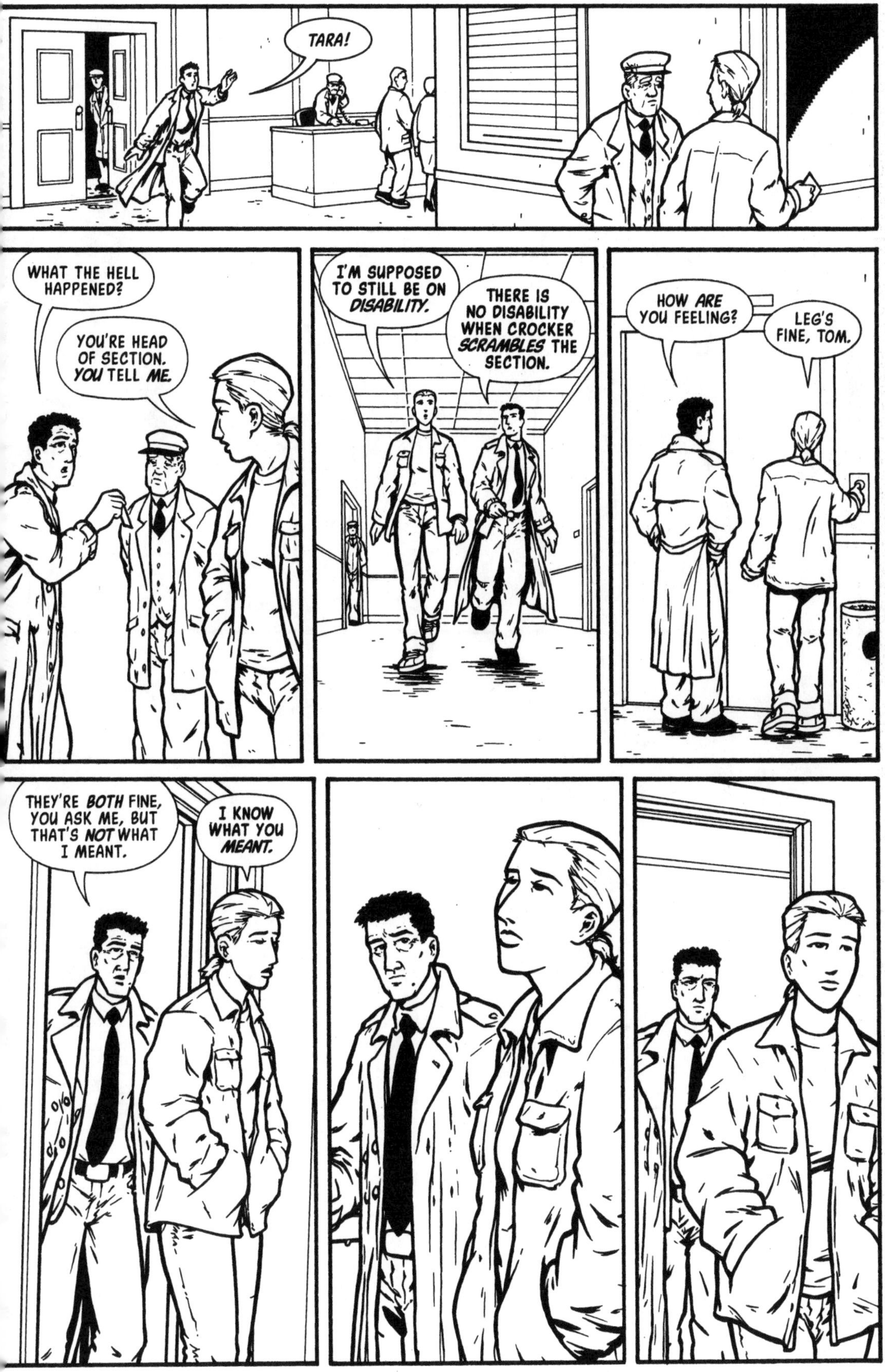
TARA!
WHAT THE HELL HAPPENED?
YOU'RE HEAD OF SECTION. YOU TELL ME.
I'M SUPPOSED TO STILL BE ON DISABILITY.
THERE IS NO DISABILITY WHEN CROCKER SCRAMBLES THE SECTION.
HOW ARE YOU FEELING?
LEG'S FINE, TOM.
THEY'RE BOTH FINE, YOU ASK ME, BUT THAT'S NOT WHAT I MEANT.
I KNOW WHAT YOU MEANT.

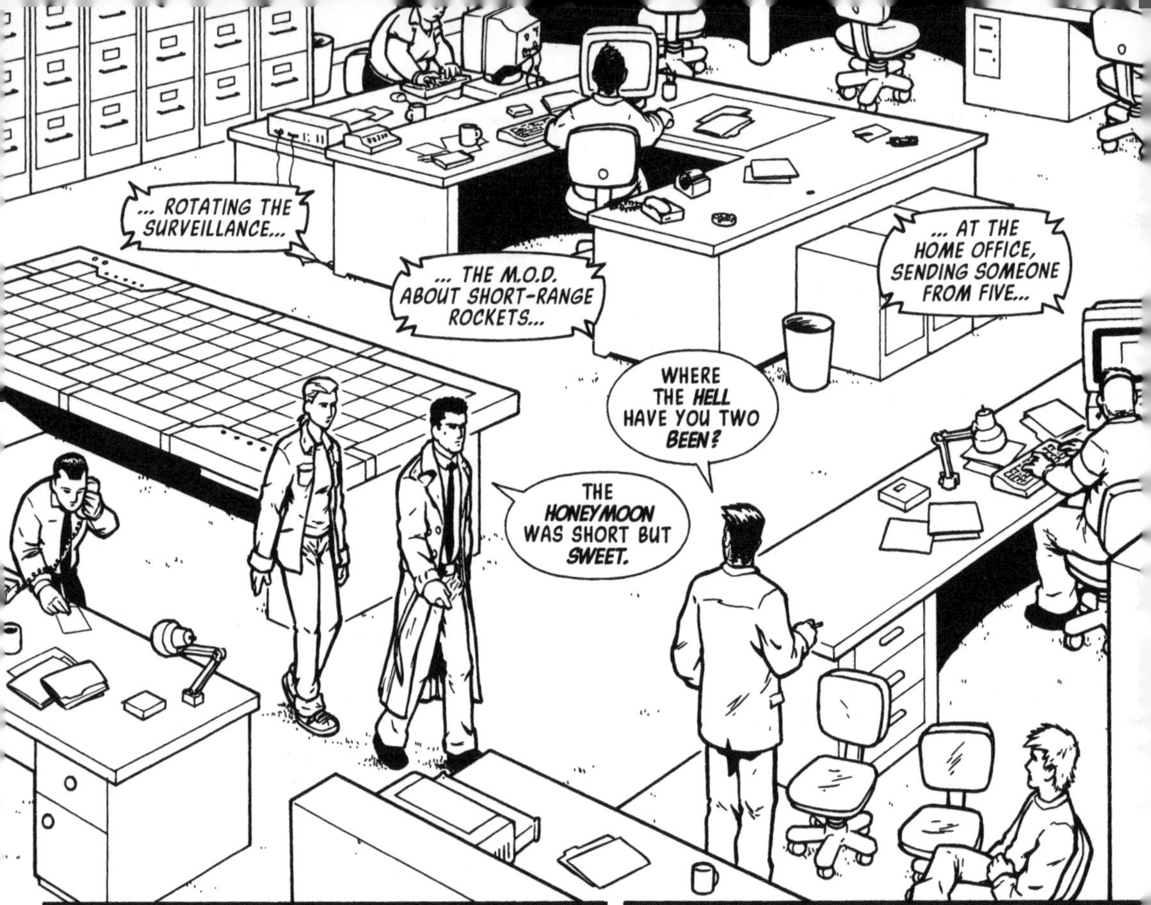
... ROTATING THE SURVEILLANCE...
... THE M.O.D. ABOUT SHORT-RANGE ROCKETS...
... AT THE HOME OFFICE, SENDING SOMEONE FROM FIVE...
WHERE THE *HELL* HAVE YOU TWO *BEEN?*
THE *HONEYMOON* WAS SHORT BUT *SWEET.*

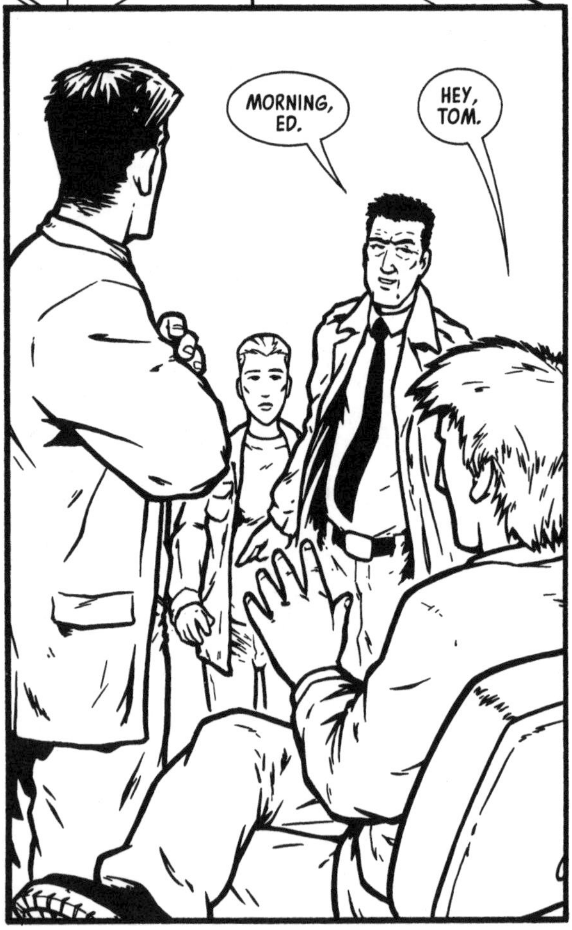
MORNING, ED.
HEY, TOM.

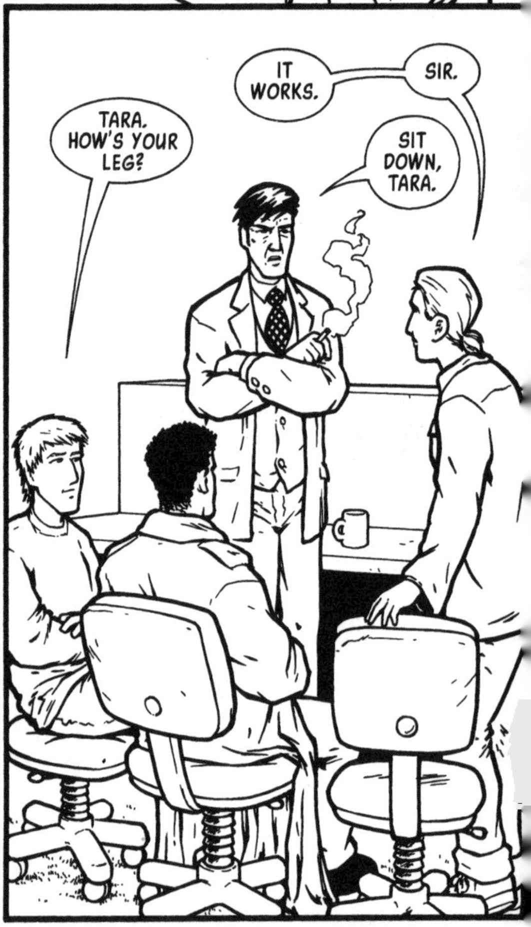
TARA. HOW'S YOUR LEG?
IT WORKS.
SIR.
SIT DOWN, TARA.

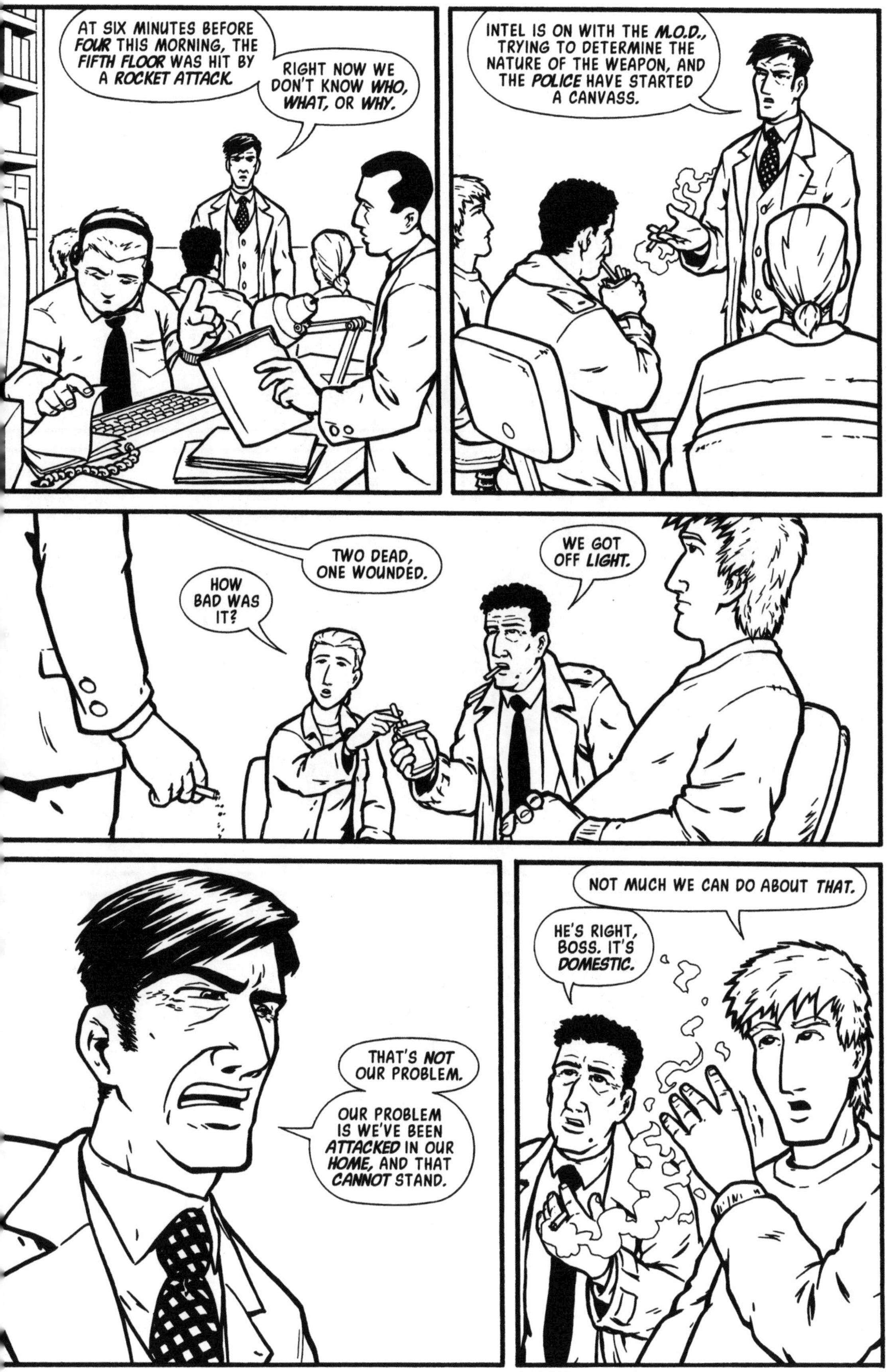
AT SIX MINUTES BEFORE FOUR THIS MORNING, THE FIFTH FLOOR WAS HIT BY A ROCKET ATTACK.
RIGHT NOW WE DON'T KNOW WHO, WHAT, OR WHY.
INTEL IS ON WITH THE M.O.D., TRYING TO DETERMINE THE NATURE OF THE WEAPON, AND THE POLICE HAVE STARTED A CANVASS.
HOW BAD WAS IT?
TWO DEAD, ONE WOUNDED.
WE GOT OFF LIGHT.
THAT'S NOT OUR PROBLEM.
OUR PROBLEM IS WE'VE BEEN ATTACKED IN OUR HOME, AND THAT CANNOT STAND.
NOT MUCH WE CAN DO ABOUT THAT.
HE'S RIGHT, BOSS. IT'S DOMESTIC.

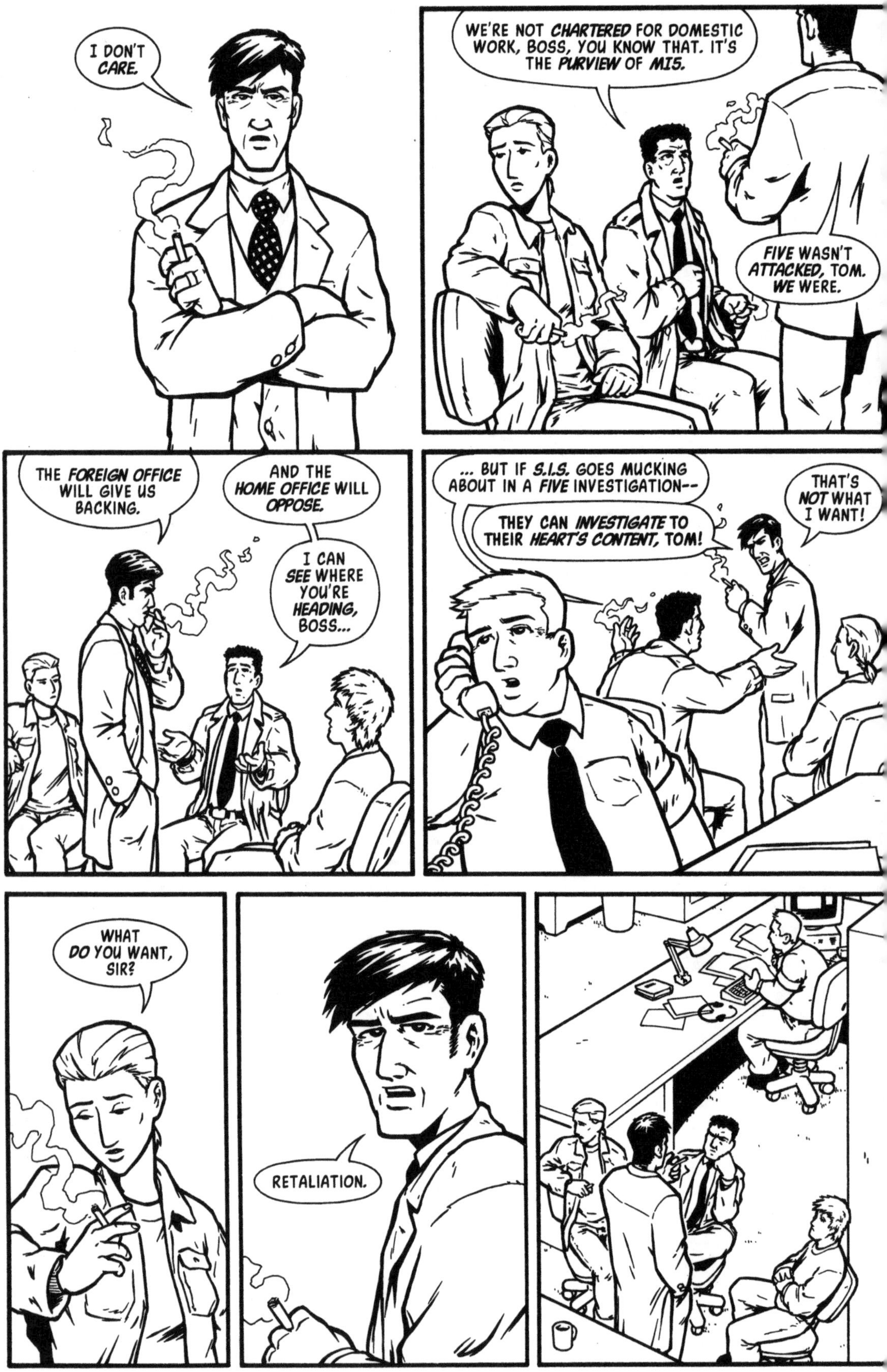
I DON'T CARE.
WE'RE NOT CHARTERED FOR DOMESTIC WORK, BOSS, YOU KNOW THAT. IT'S THE PURVIEW OF MI5.
FIVE WASN'T ATTACKED, TOM. WE WERE.
THE FOREIGN OFFICE WILL GIVE US BACKING.
AND THE HOME OFFICE WILL OPPOSE.
I CAN SEE WHERE YOU'RE HEADING, BOSS...
... BUT IF S.I.S. GOES MUCKING ABOUT IN A FIVE INVESTIGATION--
THEY CAN INVESTIGATE TO THEIR HEART'S CONTENT, TOM!
THAT'S NOT WHAT I WANT!
WHAT DO YOU WANT, SIR?
RETALIATION.

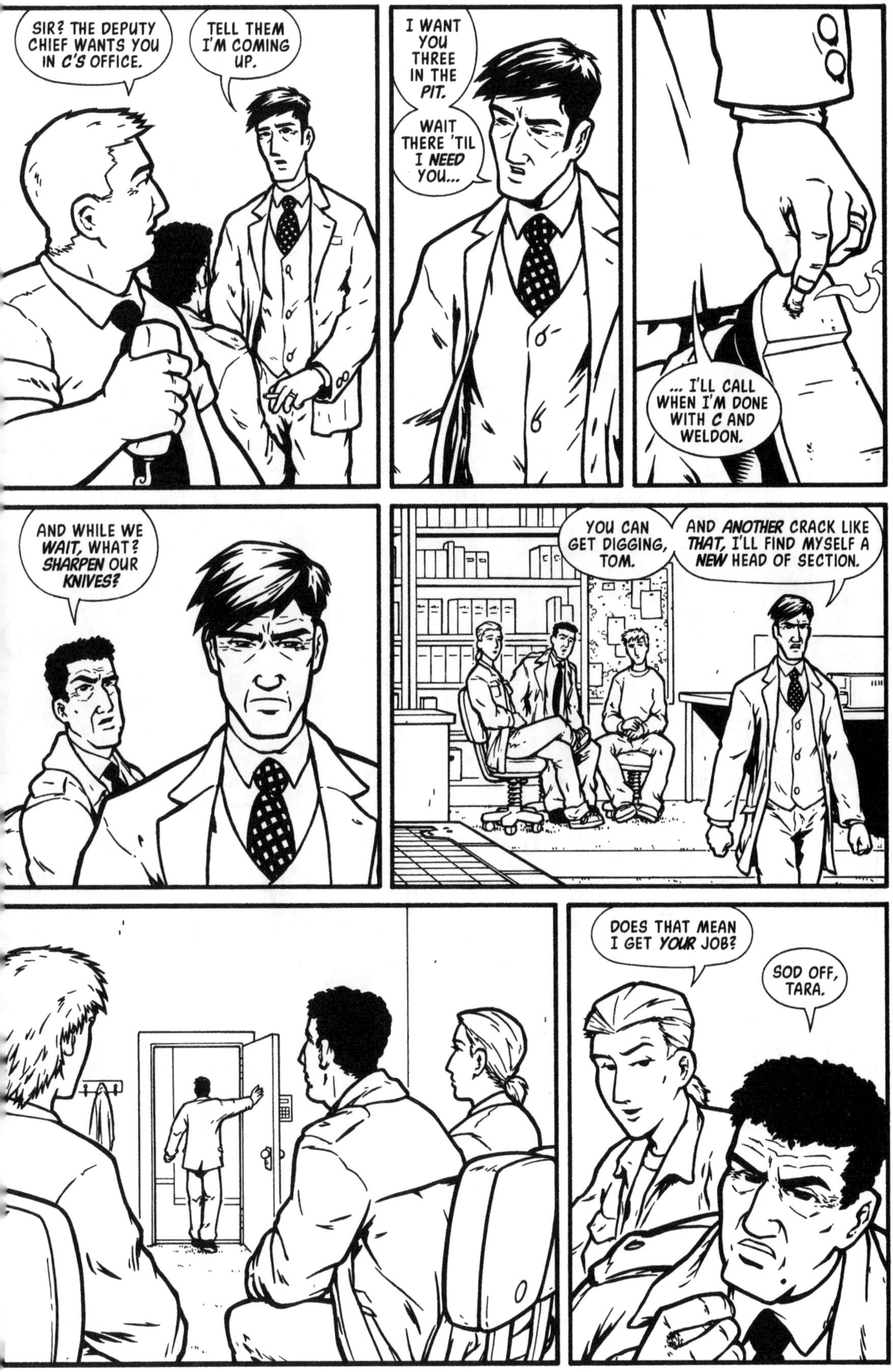
SIR? THE DEPUTY CHIEF WANTS YOU IN C'S OFFICE.
TELL THEM I'M COMING UP.
I WANT YOU THREE IN THE PIT.
WAIT THERE 'TIL I NEED YOU...
... I'LL CALL WHEN I'M DONE WITH C AND WELDON.
AND WHILE WE WAIT, WHAT? SHARPEN OUR KNIVES?
YOU CAN GET DIGGING, TOM.
AND ANOTHER CRACK LIKE THAT, I'LL FIND MYSELF A NEW HEAD OF SECTION.
DOES THAT MEAN I GET YOUR JOB?
SOD OFF, TARA.

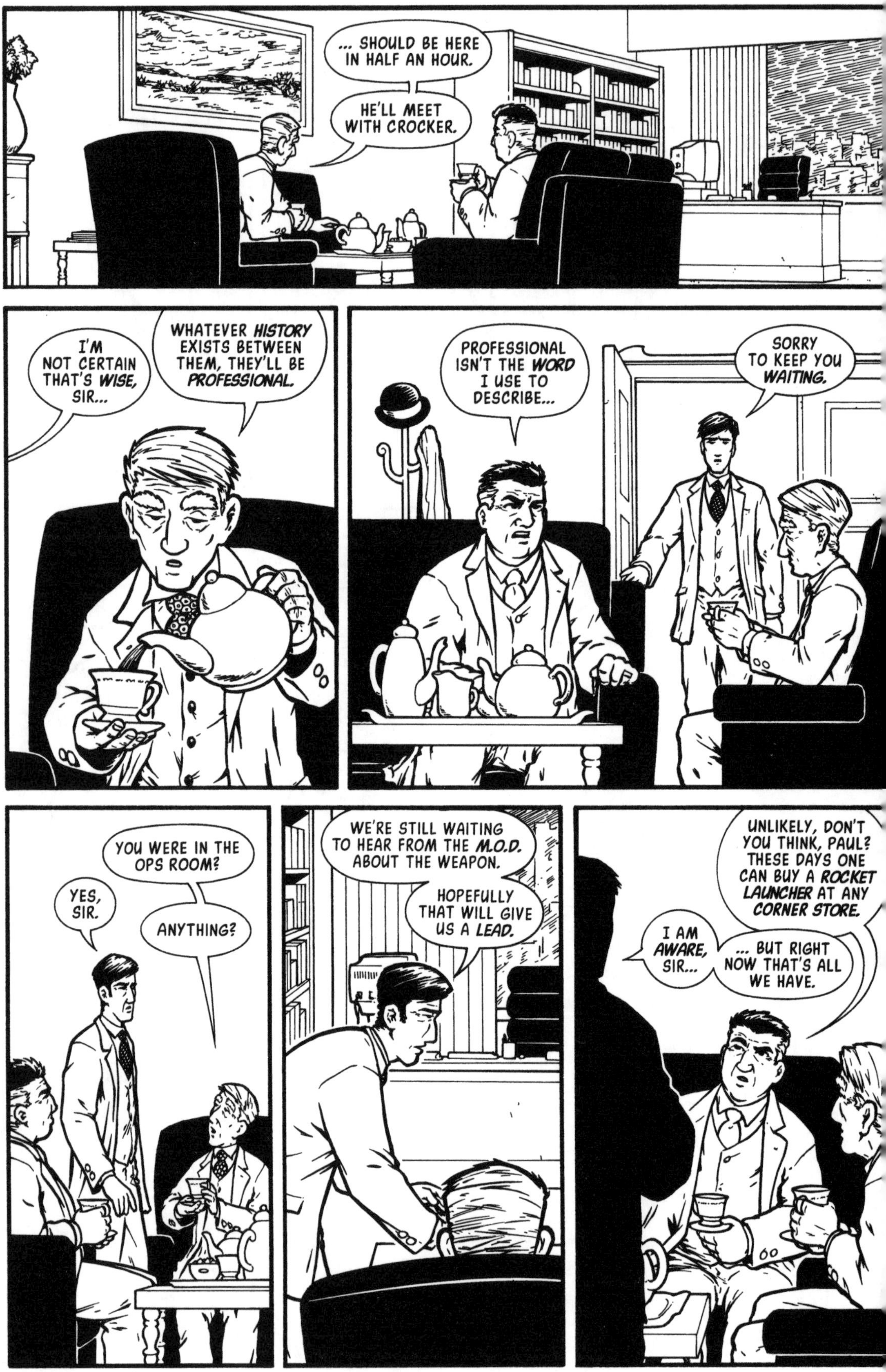
... SHOULD BE HERE IN HALF AN HOUR.
HE'LL MEET WITH CROCKER.
I'M NOT CERTAIN THAT'S WISE, SIR...
WHATEVER HISTORY EXISTS BETWEEN THEM, THEY'LL BE PROFESSIONAL.
PROFESSIONAL ISN'T THE WORD I USE TO DESCRIBE...
SORRY TO KEEP YOU WAITING.
YOU WERE IN THE OPS ROOM?
YES, SIR.
ANYTHING?
WE'RE STILL WAITING TO HEAR FROM THE M.O.D. ABOUT THE WEAPON.
HOPEFULLY THAT WILL GIVE US A LEAD.
UNLIKELY, DON'T YOU THINK, PAUL? THESE DAYS ONE CAN BUY A ROCKET LAUNCHER AT ANY CORNER STORE.
I AM AWARE, SIR...
... BUT RIGHT NOW THAT'S ALL WE HAVE.

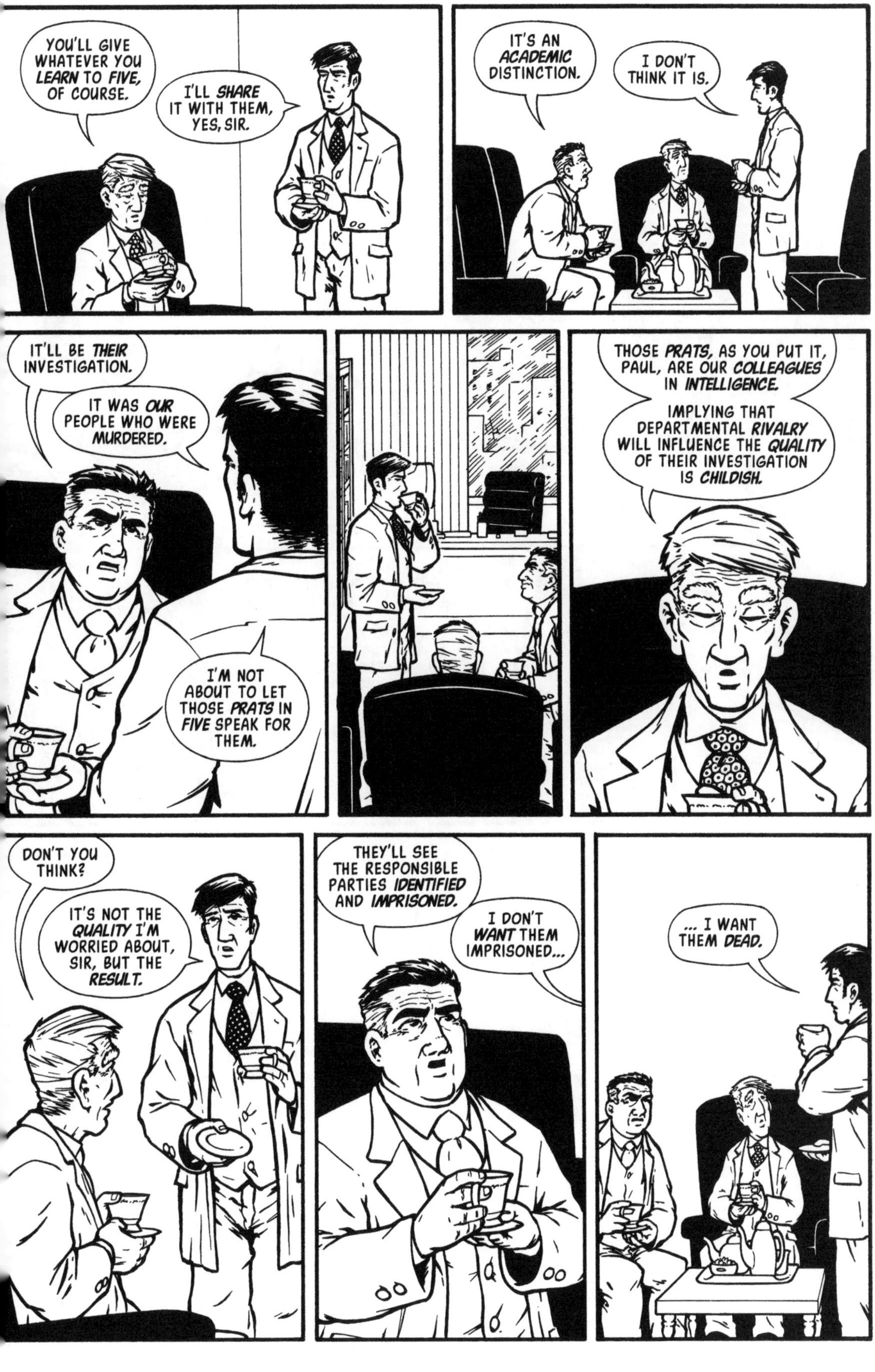
YOU'LL GIVE WHATEVER YOU LEARN TO FIVE, OF COURSE.
I'LL SHARE IT WITH THEM, YES, SIR.
IT'S AN ACADEMIC DISTINCTION.
I DON'T THINK IT IS.
IT'LL BE THEIR INVESTIGATION.
IT WAS OUR PEOPLE WHO WERE MURDERED.
I'M NOT ABOUT TO LET THOSE PRATS IN FIVE SPEAK FOR THEM.
THOSE PRATS, AS YOU PUT IT, PAUL, ARE OUR COLLEAGUES IN INTELLIGENCE.
IMPLYING THAT DEPARTMENTAL RIVALRY WILL INFLUENCE THE QUALITY OF THEIR INVESTIGATION IS CHILDISH.
DON'T YOU THINK?
IT'S NOT THE QUALITY I'M WORRIED ABOUT, SIR, BUT THE RESULT.
THEY'LL SEE THE RESPONSIBLE PARTIES IDENTIFIED AND IMPRISONED.
I DON'T WANT THEM IMPRISONED...
... I WANT THEM DEAD.

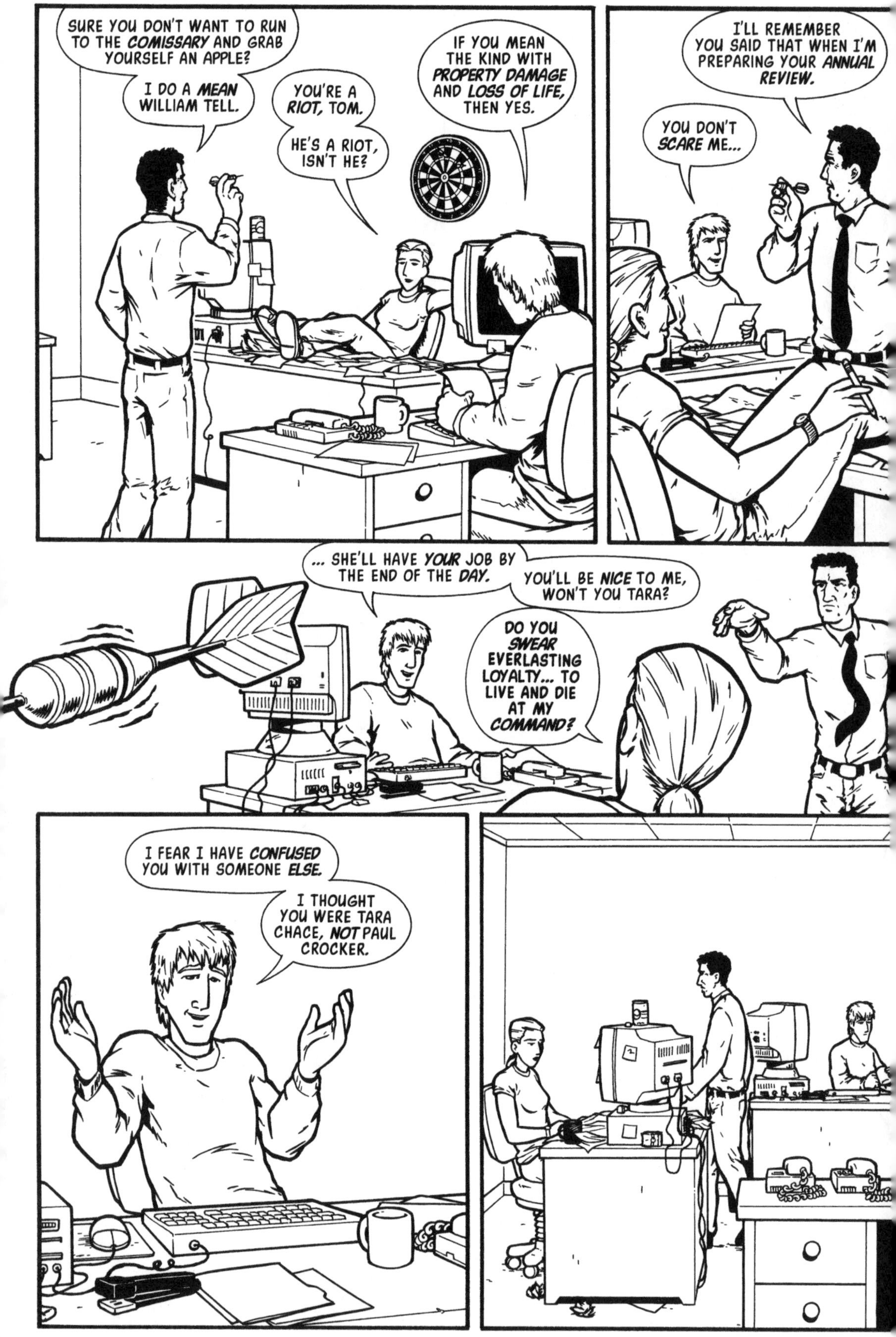
SURE YOU DON'T WANT TO RUN TO THE COMISSARY AND GRAB YOURSELF AN APPLE?
I DO A MEAN WILLIAM TELL.
YOU'RE A RIOT, TOM.
HE'S A RIOT, ISN'T HE?
IF YOU MEAN THE KIND WITH PROPERTY DAMAGE AND LOSS OF LIFE, THEN YES.
I'LL REMEMBER YOU SAID THAT WHEN I'M PREPARING YOUR ANNUAL REVIEW.
YOU DON'T SCARE ME...
... SHE'LL HAVE YOUR JOB BY THE END OF THE DAY.
YOU'LL BE NICE TO ME, WON'T YOU TARA?
DO YOU SWEAR EVERLASTING LOYALTY... TO LIVE AND DIE AT MY COMMAND?
I FEAR I HAVE CONFUSED YOU WITH SOMEONE ELSE.
I THOUGHT YOU WERE TARA CHACE, NOT PAUL CROCKER.

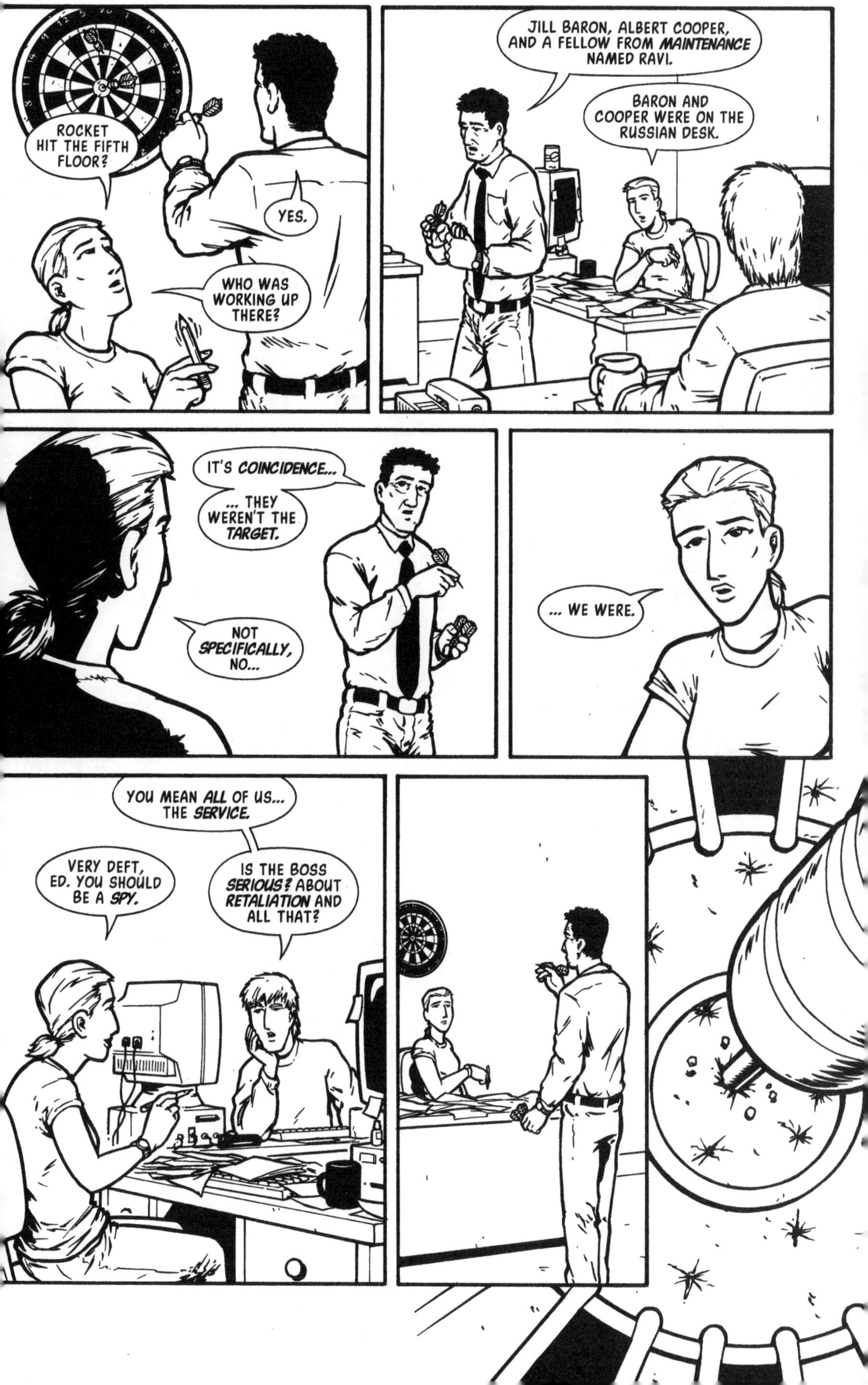
ROCKET HIT THE FIFTH FLOOR?
YES.
WHO WAS WORKING UP THERE?
JILL BARON, ALBERT COOPER, AND A FELLOW FROM *MAINTENANCE* NAMED RAVI.
BARON AND COOPER WERE ON THE RUSSIAN DESK.
IT'S *COINCIDENCE...*
... THEY WEREN'T THE *TARGET.*
NOT *SPECIFICALLY,* NO...
... WE WERE.
YOU MEAN *ALL* OF US... THE *SERVICE.*
VERY DEFT, ED. YOU SHOULD BE A *SPY.*
IS THE BOSS *SERIOUS?* ABOUT *RETALIATION* AND ALL THAT?

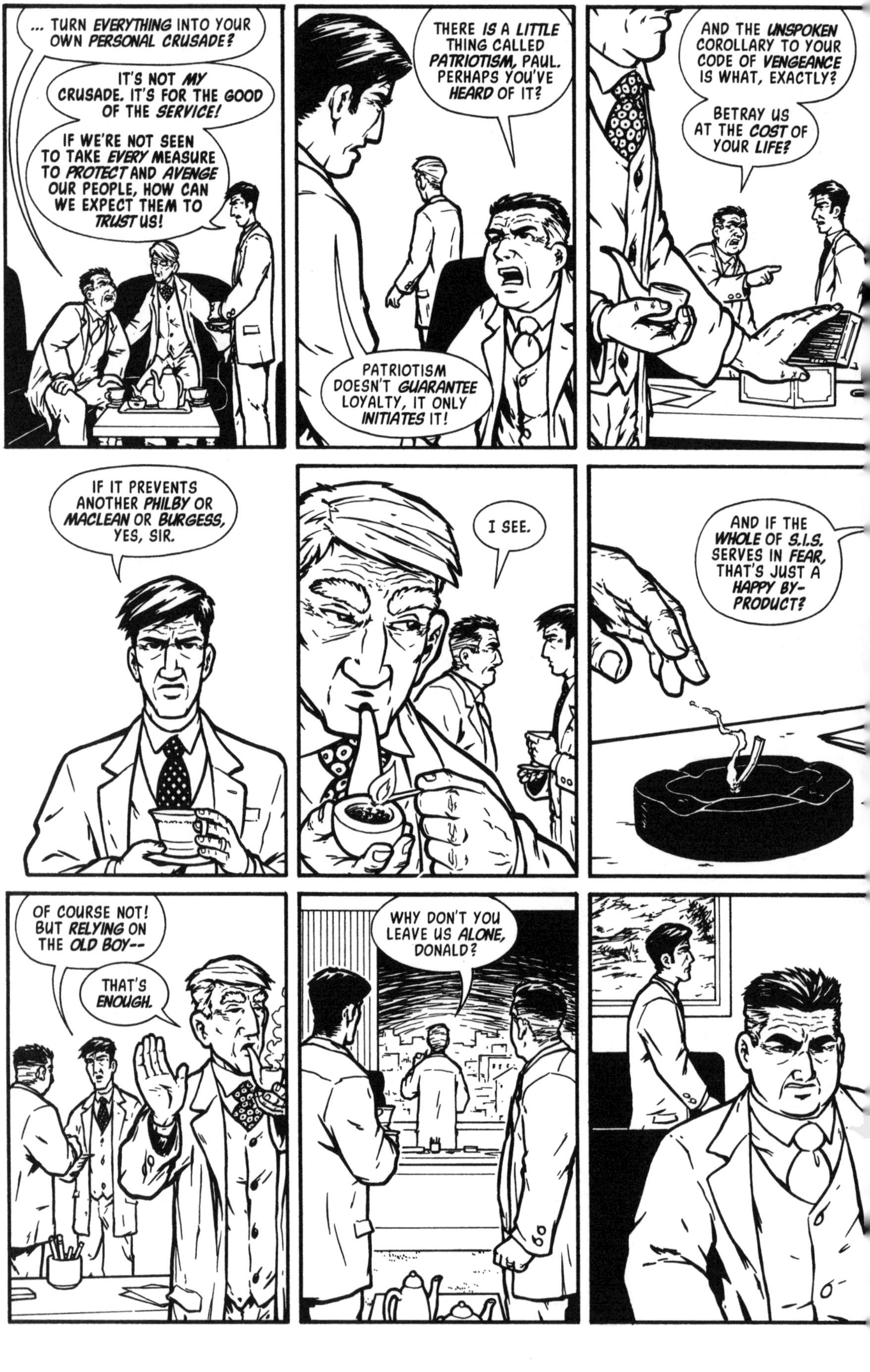
... TURN EVERYTHING INTO YOUR OWN PERSONAL CRUSADE?
IT'S NOT MY CRUSADE. IT'S FOR THE GOOD OF THE SERVICE!
IF WE'RE NOT SEEN TO TAKE EVERY MEASURE TO PROTECT AND AVENGE OUR PEOPLE, HOW CAN WE EXPECT THEM TO TRUST US!
THERE IS A LITTLE THING CALLED PATRIOTISM, PAUL. PERHAPS YOU'VE HEARD OF IT?
PATRIOTISM DOESN'T GUARANTEE LOYALTY, IT ONLY INITIATES IT!
AND THE UNSPOKEN COROLLARY TO YOUR CODE OF VENGEANCE IS WHAT, EXACTLY?
BETRAY US AT THE COST OF YOUR LIFE?
IF IT PREVENTS ANOTHER PHILBY OR MACLEAN OR BURGESS, YES, SIR.
I SEE.
AND IF THE WHOLE OF S.I.S. SERVES IN FEAR, THAT'S JUST A HAPPY BY-PRODUCT?
OF COURSE NOT! BUT RELYING ON THE OLD BOY--
THAT'S ENOUGH.
WHY DON'T YOU LEAVE US ALONE, DONALD?

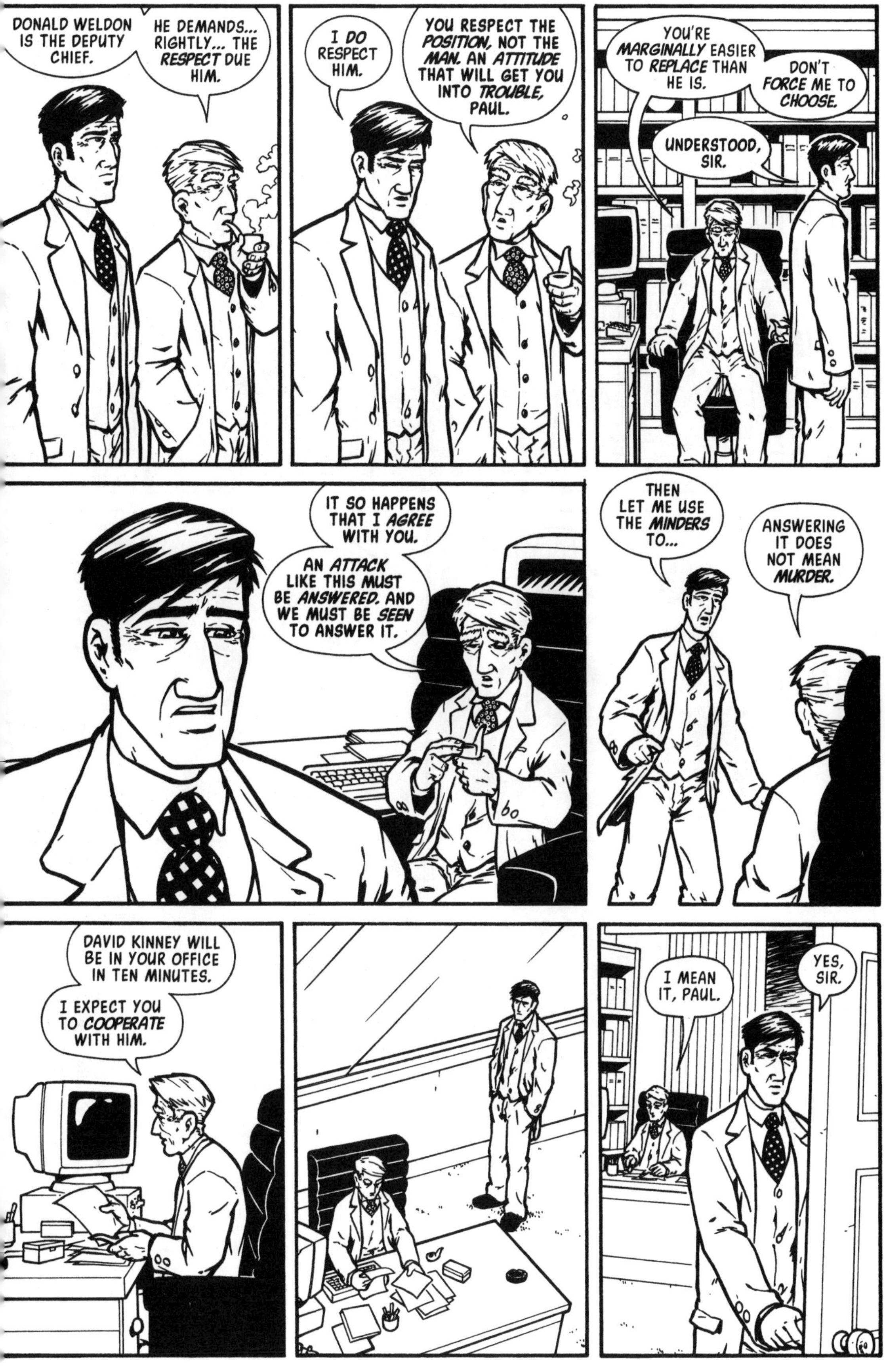
DONALD WELDON IS THE DEPUTY CHIEF.
HE DEMANDS... RIGHTLY... THE RESPECT DUE HIM.
I DO RESPECT HIM.
YOU RESPECT THE POSITION, NOT THE MAN. AN ATTITUDE THAT WILL GET YOU INTO TROUBLE, PAUL.
YOU'RE MARGINALLY EASIER TO REPLACE THAN HE IS.
DON'T FORCE ME TO CHOOSE.
UNDERSTOOD, SIR.
IT SO HAPPENS THAT I AGREE WITH YOU.
AN ATTACK LIKE THIS MUST BE ANSWERED. AND WE MUST BE SEEN TO ANSWER IT.
THEN LET ME USE THE MINDERS TO...
ANSWERING IT DOES NOT MEAN MURDER.
DAVID KINNEY WILL BE IN YOUR OFFICE IN TEN MINUTES.
I EXPECT YOU TO COOPERATE WITH HIM.
I MEAN IT, PAUL.
YES, SIR.

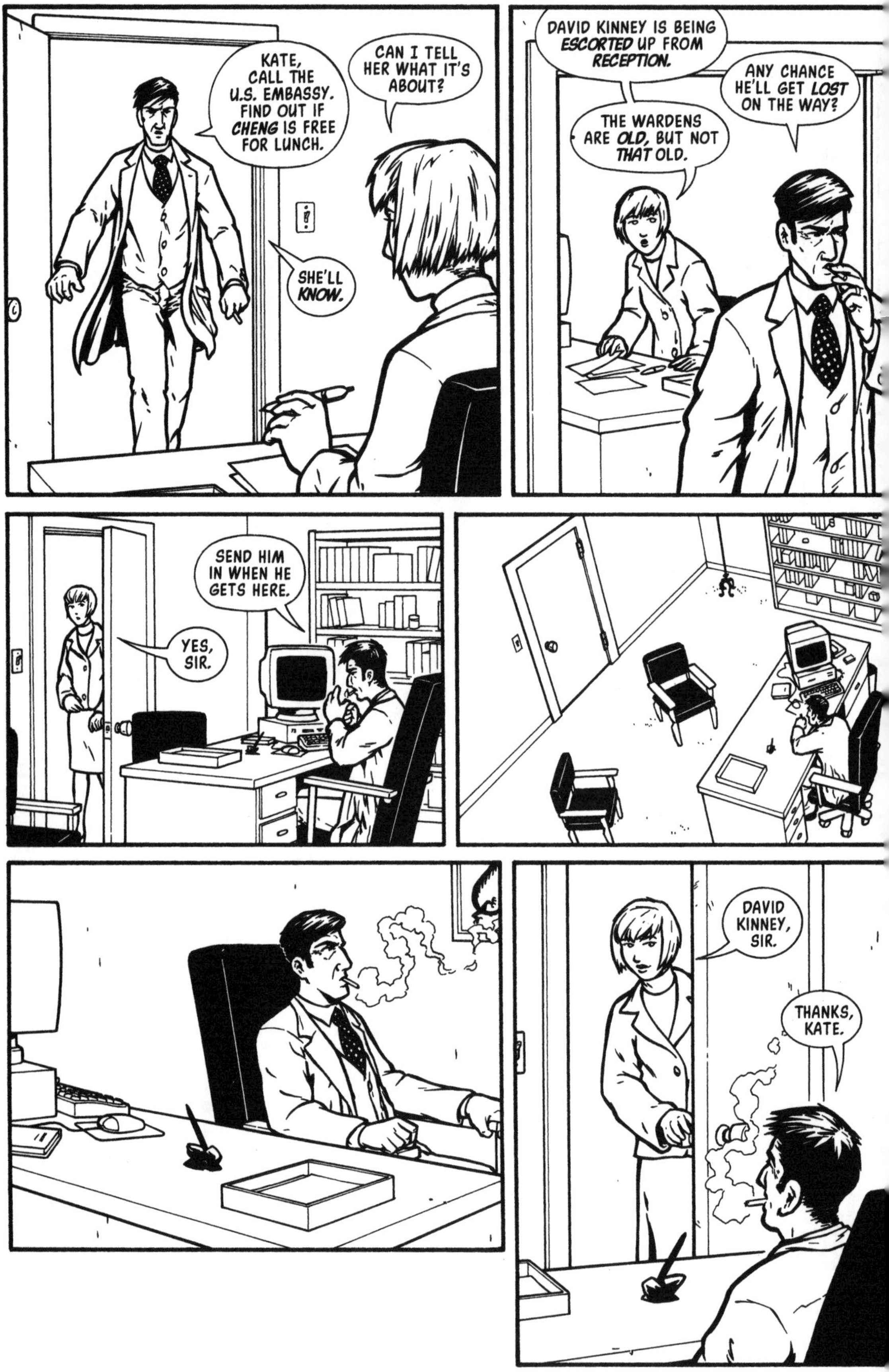
KATE, CALL THE U.S. EMBASSY. FIND OUT IF CHENG IS FREE FOR LUNCH.
CAN I TELL HER WHAT IT'S ABOUT?
SHE'LL KNOW.
DAVID KINNEY IS BEING ESCORTED UP FROM RECEPTION.
THE WARDENS ARE OLD, BUT NOT THAT OLD.
ANY CHANCE HE'LL GET LOST ON THE WAY?
SEND HIM IN WHEN HE GETS HERE.
YES, SIR.
DAVID KINNEY, SIR.
THANKS, KATE.

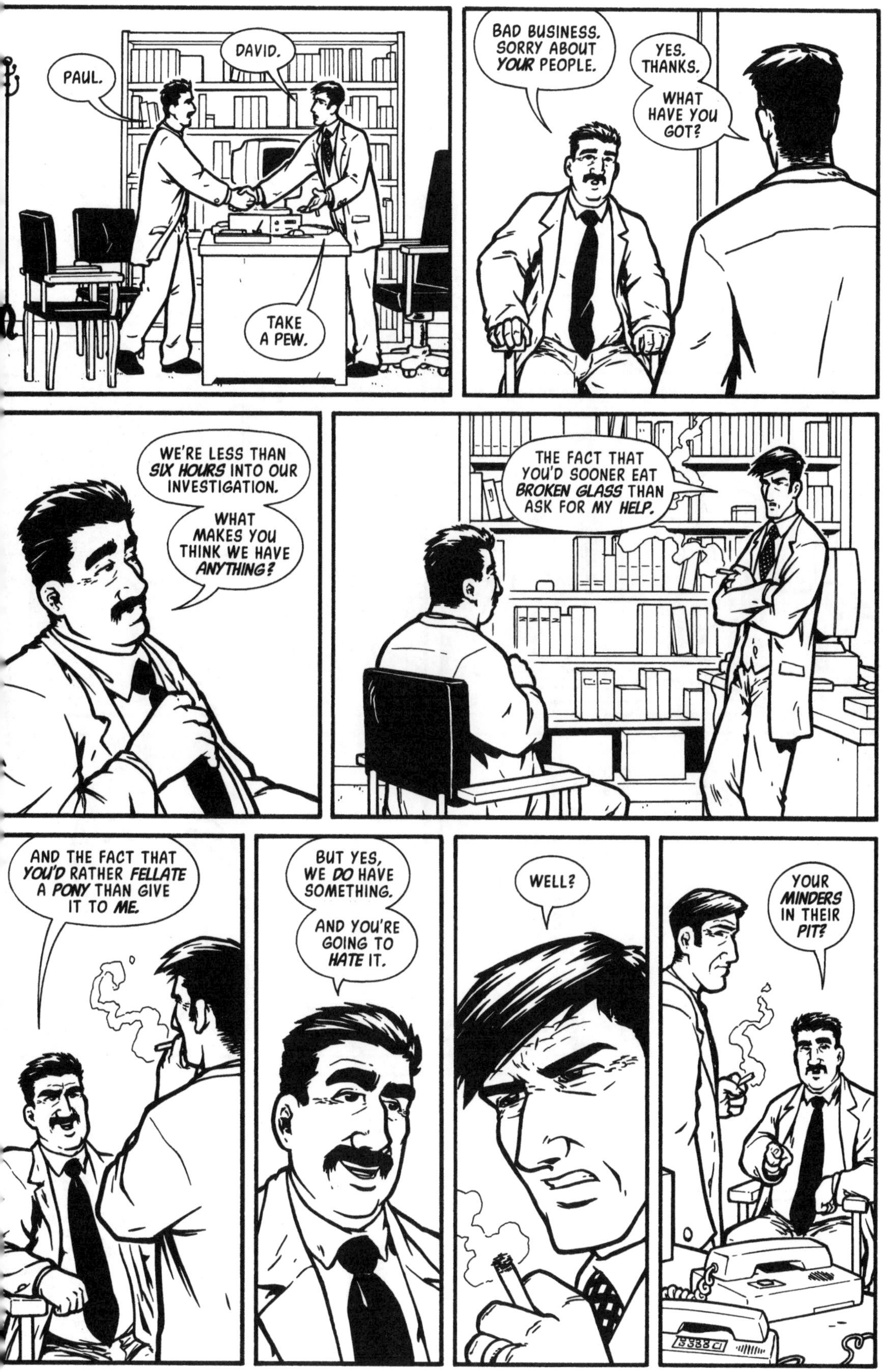
PAUL.
DAVID.
TAKE A PEW.
BAD BUSINESS. SORRY ABOUT YOUR PEOPLE.
YES. THANKS.
WHAT HAVE YOU GOT?
WE'RE LESS THAN SIX HOURS INTO OUR INVESTIGATION.
WHAT MAKES YOU THINK WE HAVE ANYTHING?
THE FACT THAT YOU'D SOONER EAT BROKEN GLASS THAN ASK FOR MY HELP.
AND THE FACT THAT YOU'D RATHER FELLATE A PONY THAN GIVE IT TO ME.
BUT YES, WE DO HAVE SOMETHING.
AND YOU'RE GOING TO HATE IT.
WELL?
YOUR MINDERS IN THEIR PIT?

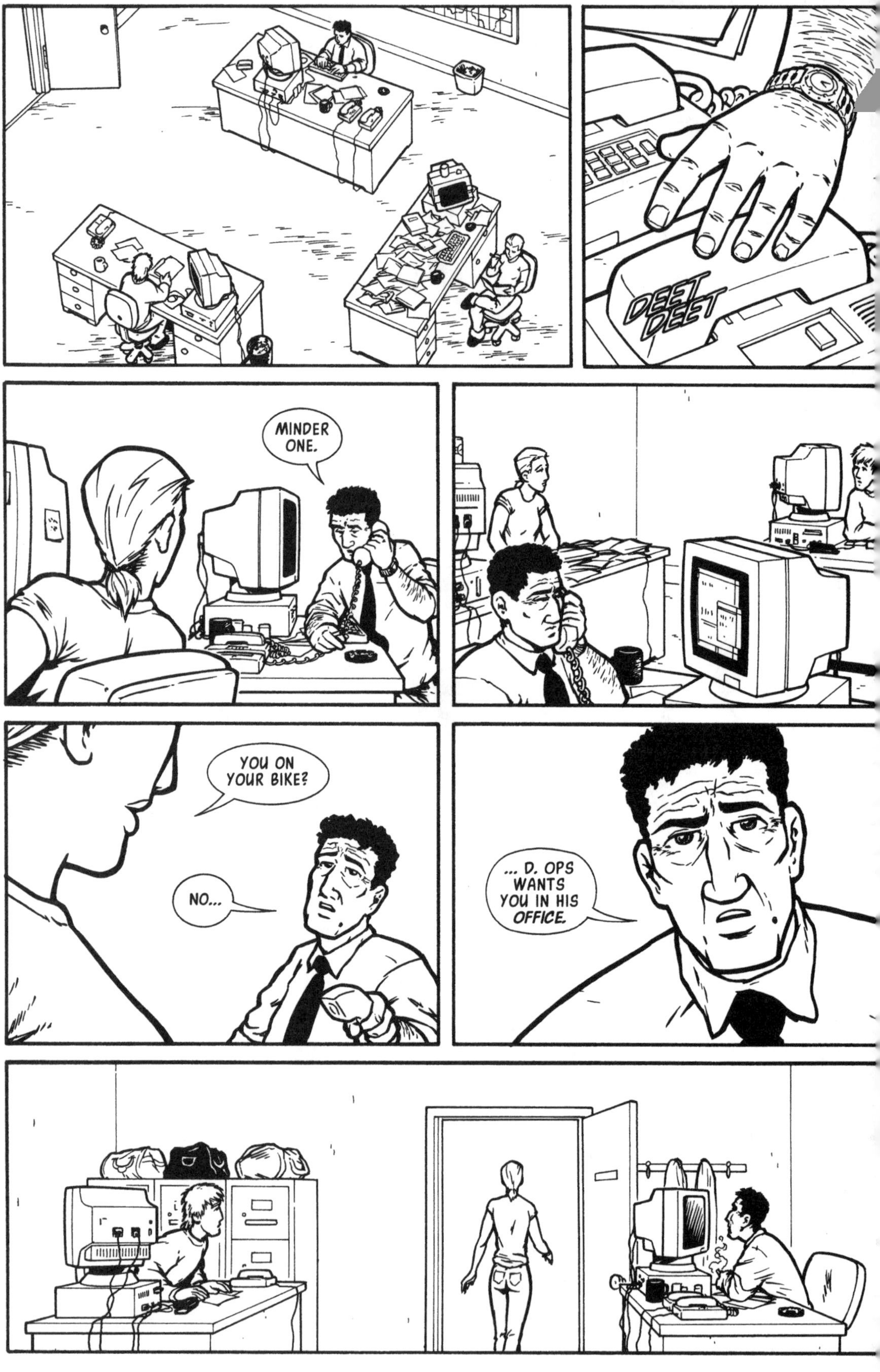
DEET DEET
MINDER ONE.
YOU ON YOUR BIKE?
NO...
... D. OPS WANTS YOU IN HIS OFFICE.

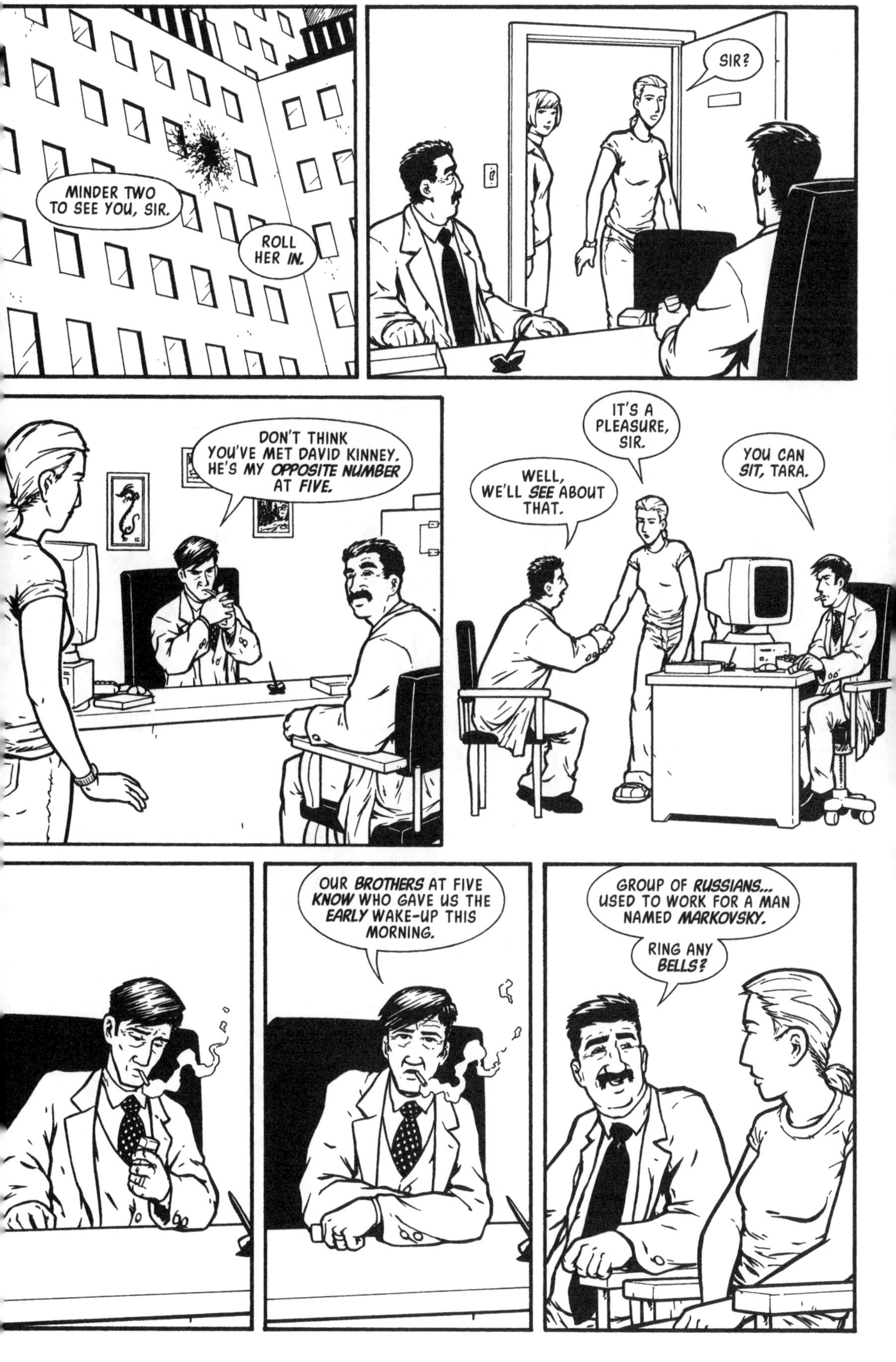
MINDER TWO TO SEE YOU, SIR.
ROLL HER IN.
SIR?
DON'T THINK YOU'VE MET DAVID KINNEY. HE'S MY OPPOSITE NUMBER AT FIVE.
WELL, WE'LL SEE ABOUT THAT.
IT'S A PLEASURE, SIR.
YOU CAN SIT, TARA.
OUR BROTHERS AT FIVE KNOW WHO GAVE US THE EARLY WAKE-UP THIS MORNING.
GROUP OF RUSSIANS... USED TO WORK FOR A MAN NAMED MARKOVSKY.
RING ANY BELLS?

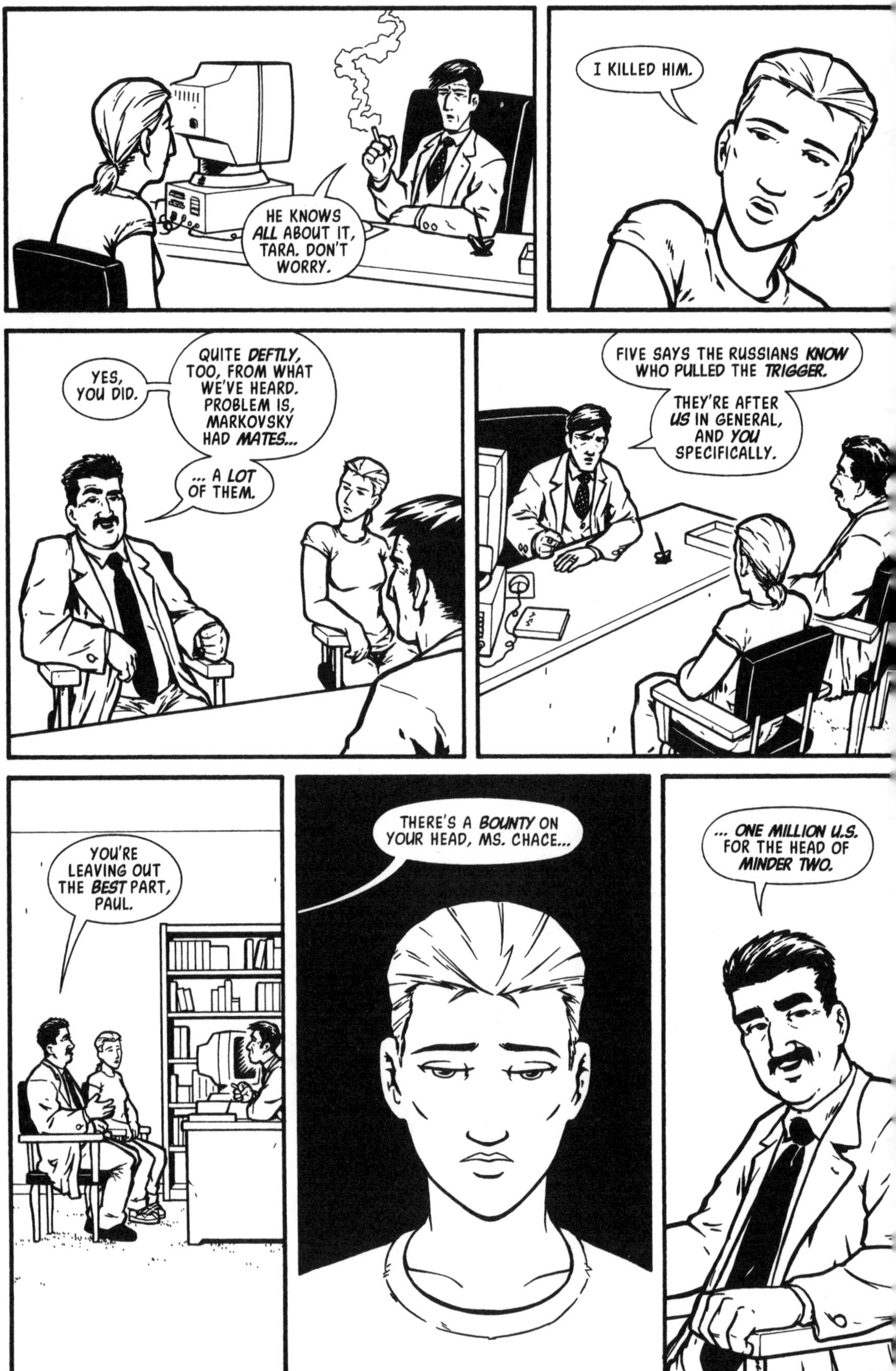
HE KNOWS ALL ABOUT IT, TARA. DON'T WORRY.
I KILLED HIM.
YES, YOU DID.
QUITE DEFTLY, TOO, FROM WHAT WE'VE HEARD. PROBLEM IS, MARKOVSKY HAD MATES...
... A LOT OF THEM.
FIVE SAYS THE RUSSIANS KNOW WHO PULLED THE TRIGGER.
THEY'RE AFTER US IN GENERAL, AND YOU SPECIFICALLY.
YOU'RE LEAVING OUT THE BEST PART, PAUL.
THERE'S A BOUNTY ON YOUR HEAD, MS. CHACE...
... ONE MILLION U.S. FOR THE HEAD OF MINDER TWO.

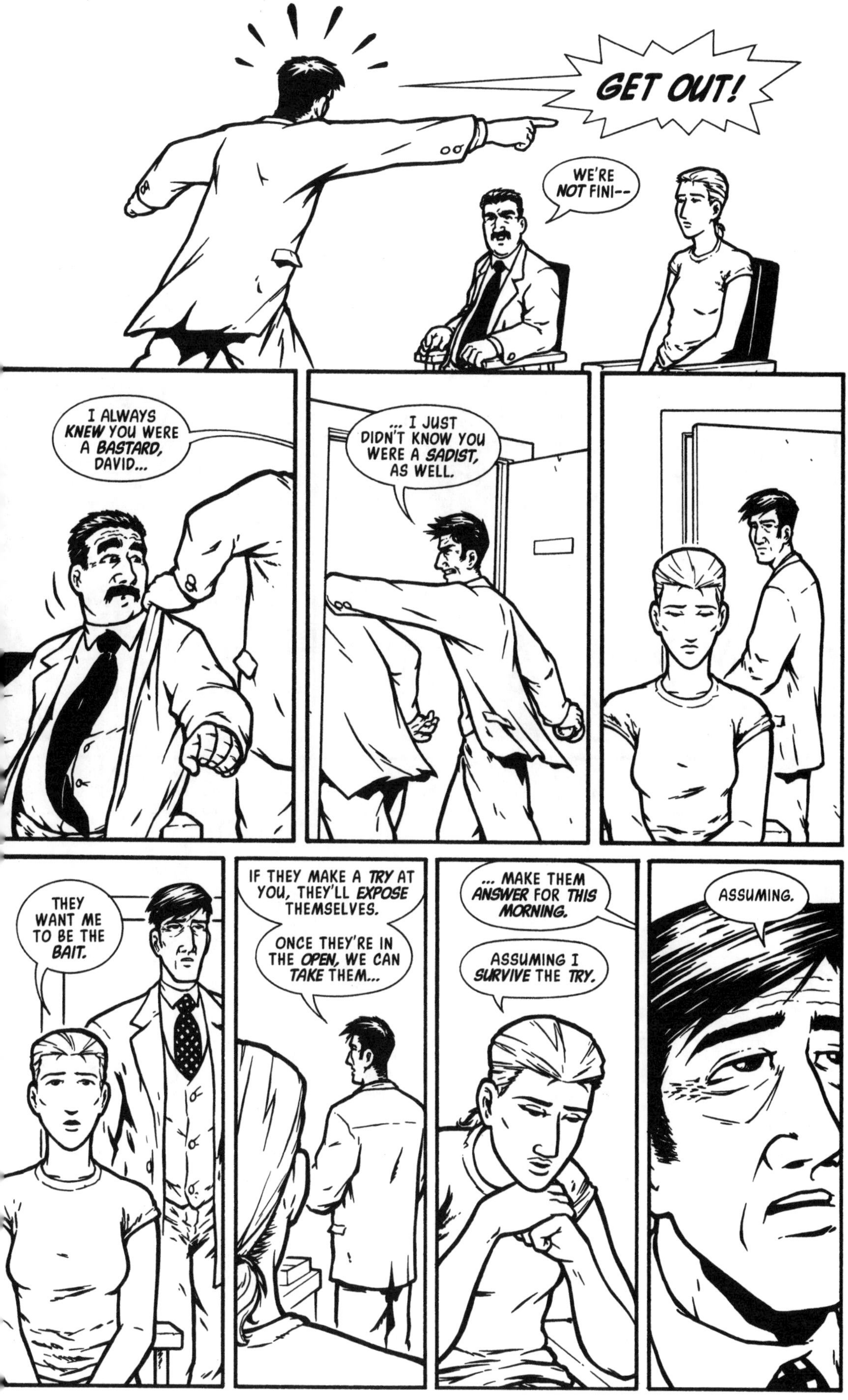
GET OUT!
WE'RE NOT FINI--
I ALWAYS KNEW YOU WERE A BASTARD, DAVID...
... I JUST DIDN'T KNOW YOU WERE A SADIST, AS WELL.
THEY WANT ME TO BE THE BAIT.
IF THEY MAKE A TRY AT YOU, THEY'LL EXPOSE THEMSELVES.
ONCE THEY'RE IN THE OPEN, WE CAN TAKE THEM...
... MAKE THEM ANSWER FOR THIS MORNING.
ASSUMING I SURVIVE THE TRY.
ASSUMING.

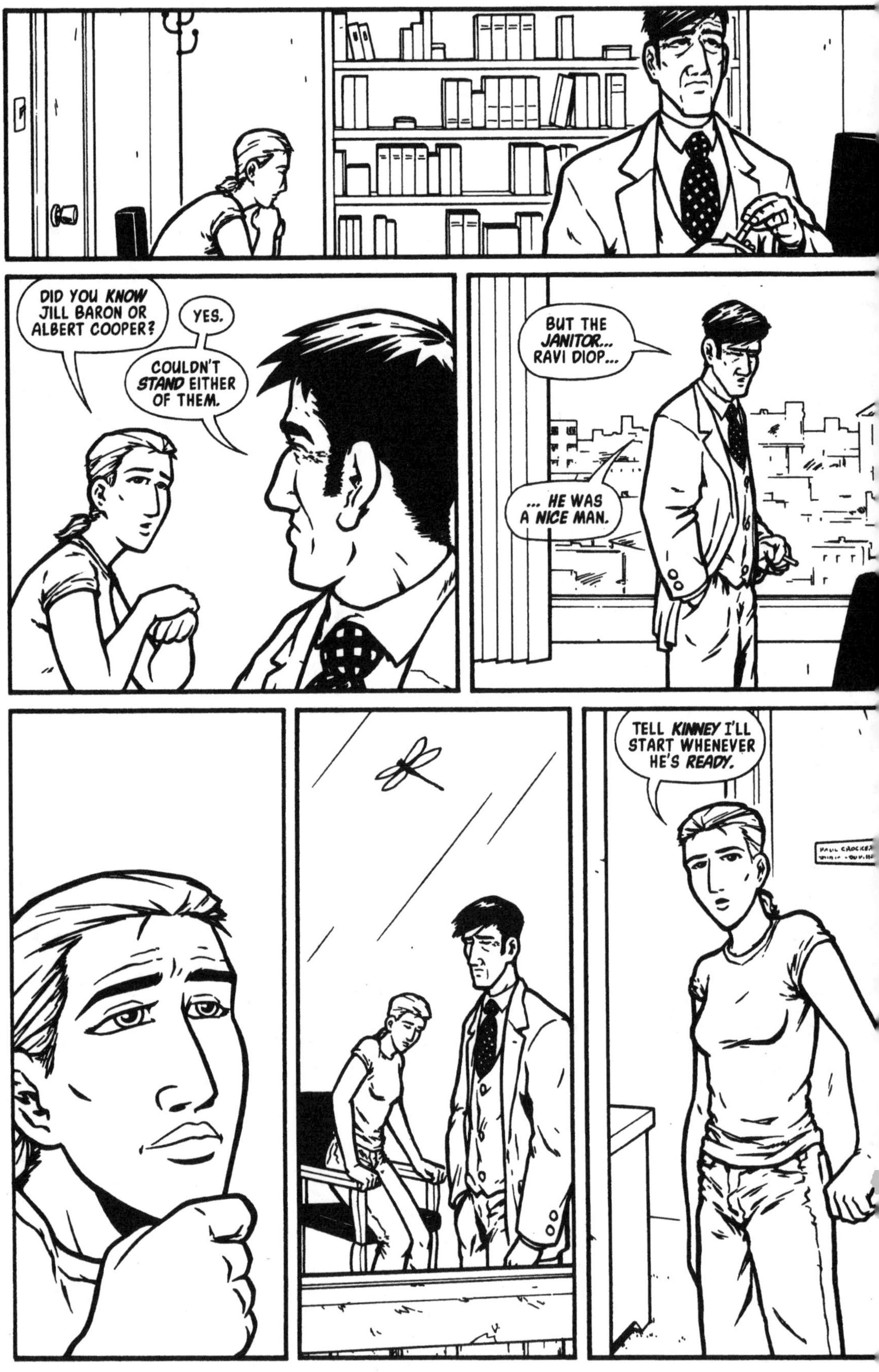
DID YOU KNOW JILL BARON OR ALBERT COOPER?
YES.
COULDN'T STAND EITHER OF THEM.
BUT THE JANITOR... RAVI DIOP...
... HE WAS A NICE MAN.
TELL KINNEY I'LL START WHENEVER HE'S READY.

CHAPTER 3

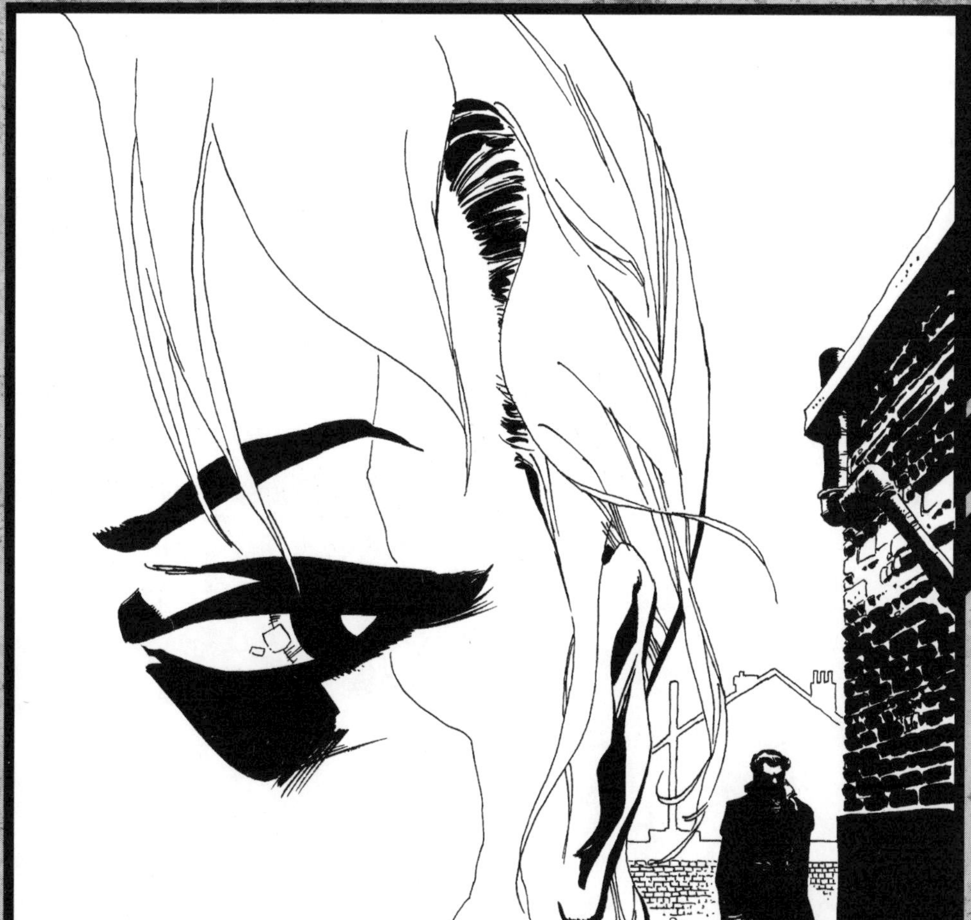
TS
01

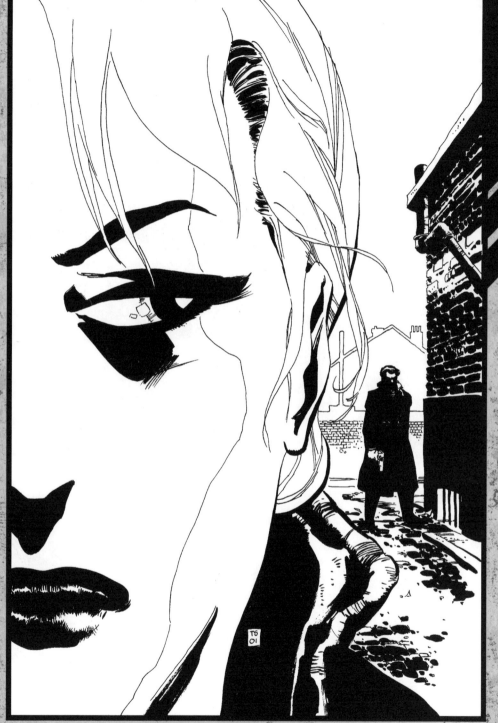

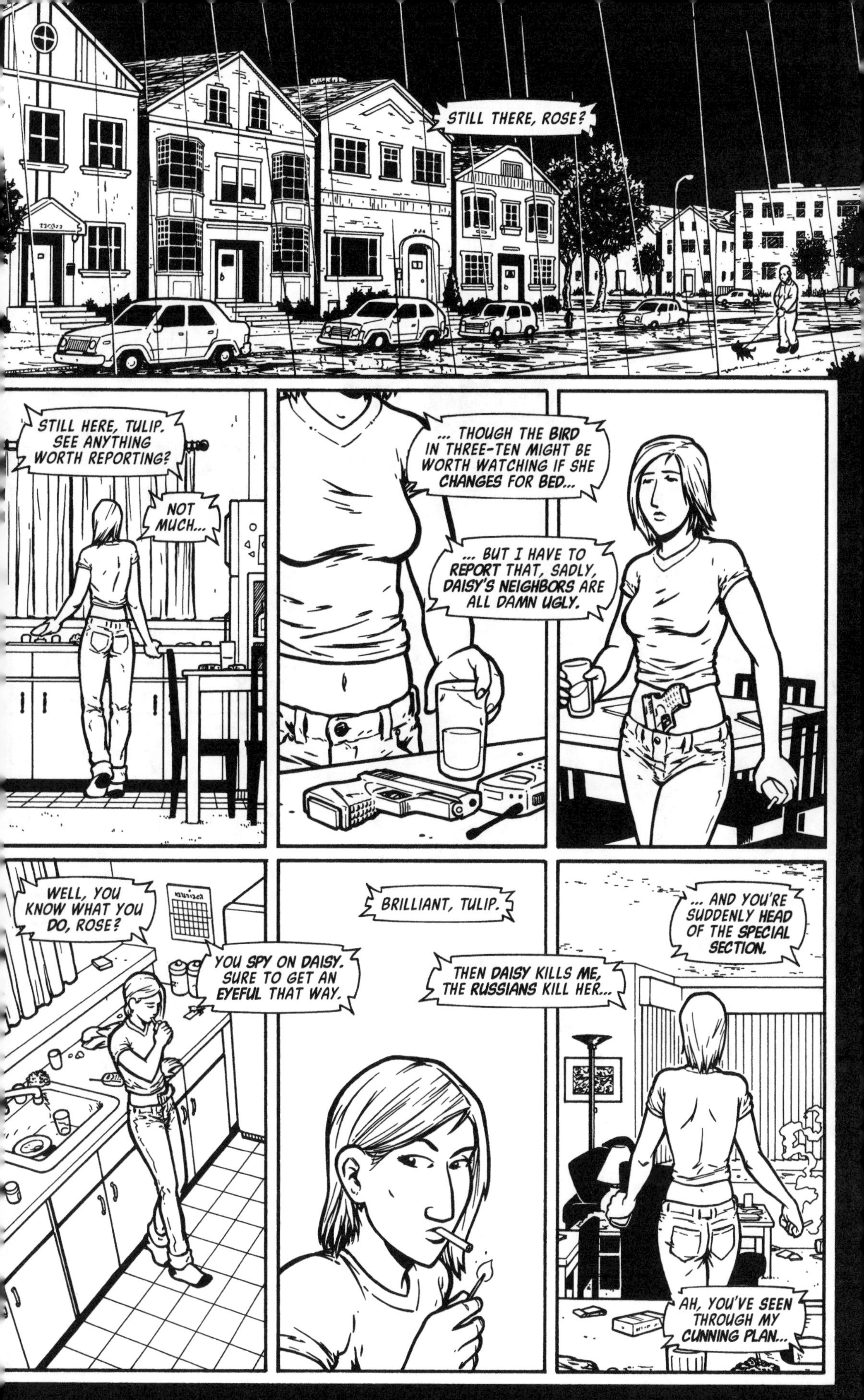
STILL THERE, ROSE?
STILL HERE, TULIP. SEE ANYTHING WORTH REPORTING?
NOT MUCH...
... THOUGH THE BIRD IN THREE-TEN MIGHT BE WORTH WATCHING IF SHE CHANGES FOR BED...
... BUT I HAVE TO REPORT THAT, SADLY, DAISY'S NEIGHBORS ARE ALL DAMN UGLY.
WELL, YOU KNOW WHAT YOU DO, ROSE?
YOU SPY ON DAISY. SURE TO GET AN EYEFUL THAT WAY.
BRILLIANT, TULIP.
THEN DAISY KILLS ME, THE RUSSIANS KILL HER...
... AND YOU'RE SUDDENLY HEAD OF THE SPECIAL SECTION.
AH, YOU'VE SEEN THROUGH MY CUNNING PLAN...

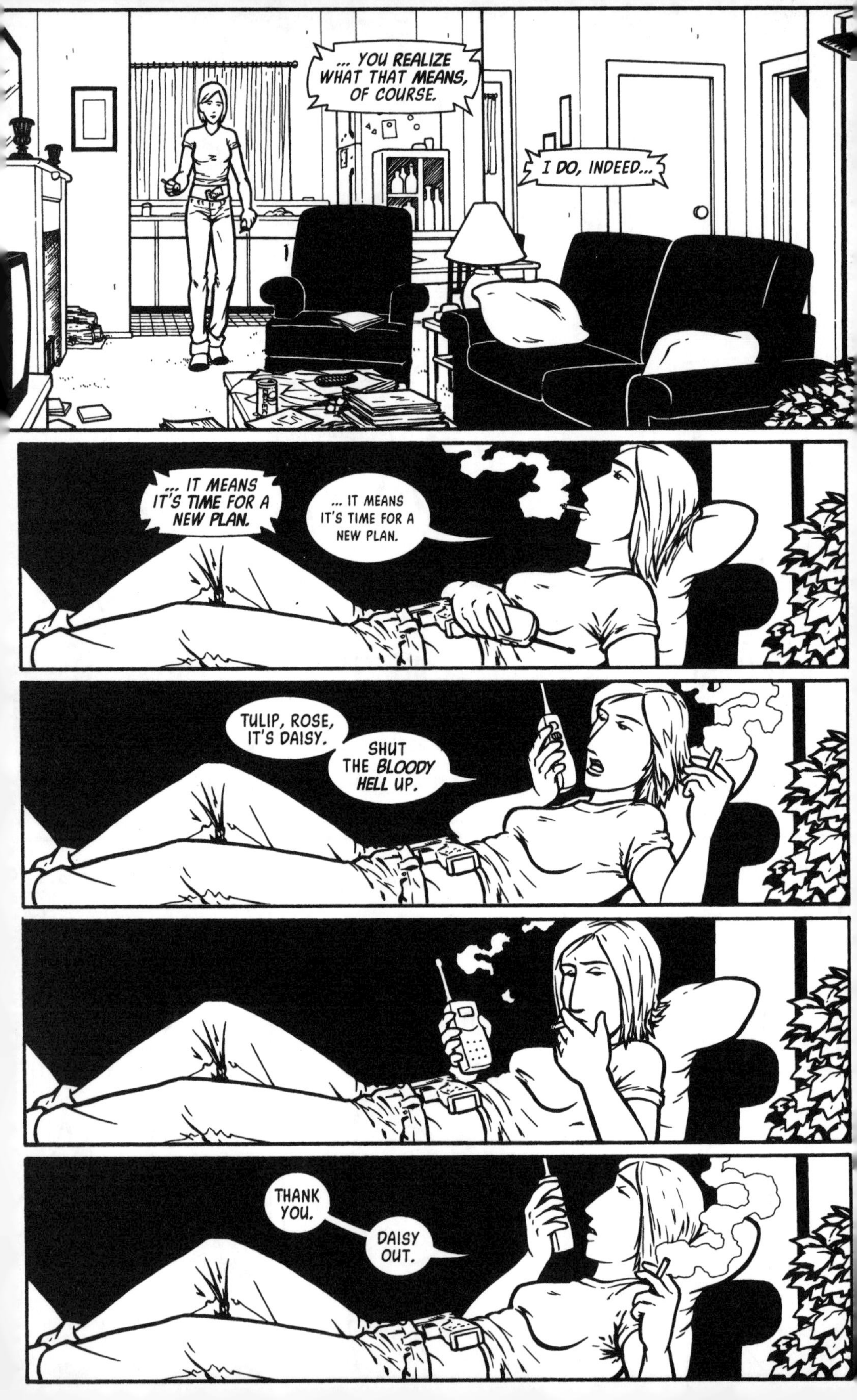
... YOU REALIZE WHAT THAT MEANS, OF COURSE.
I DO, INDEED...
... IT MEANS IT'S TIME FOR A NEW PLAN.
... IT MEANS IT'S TIME FOR A NEW PLAN.
TULIP, ROSE, IT'S DAISY.
SHUT THE BLOODY HELL UP.
THANK YOU.
DAISY OUT.

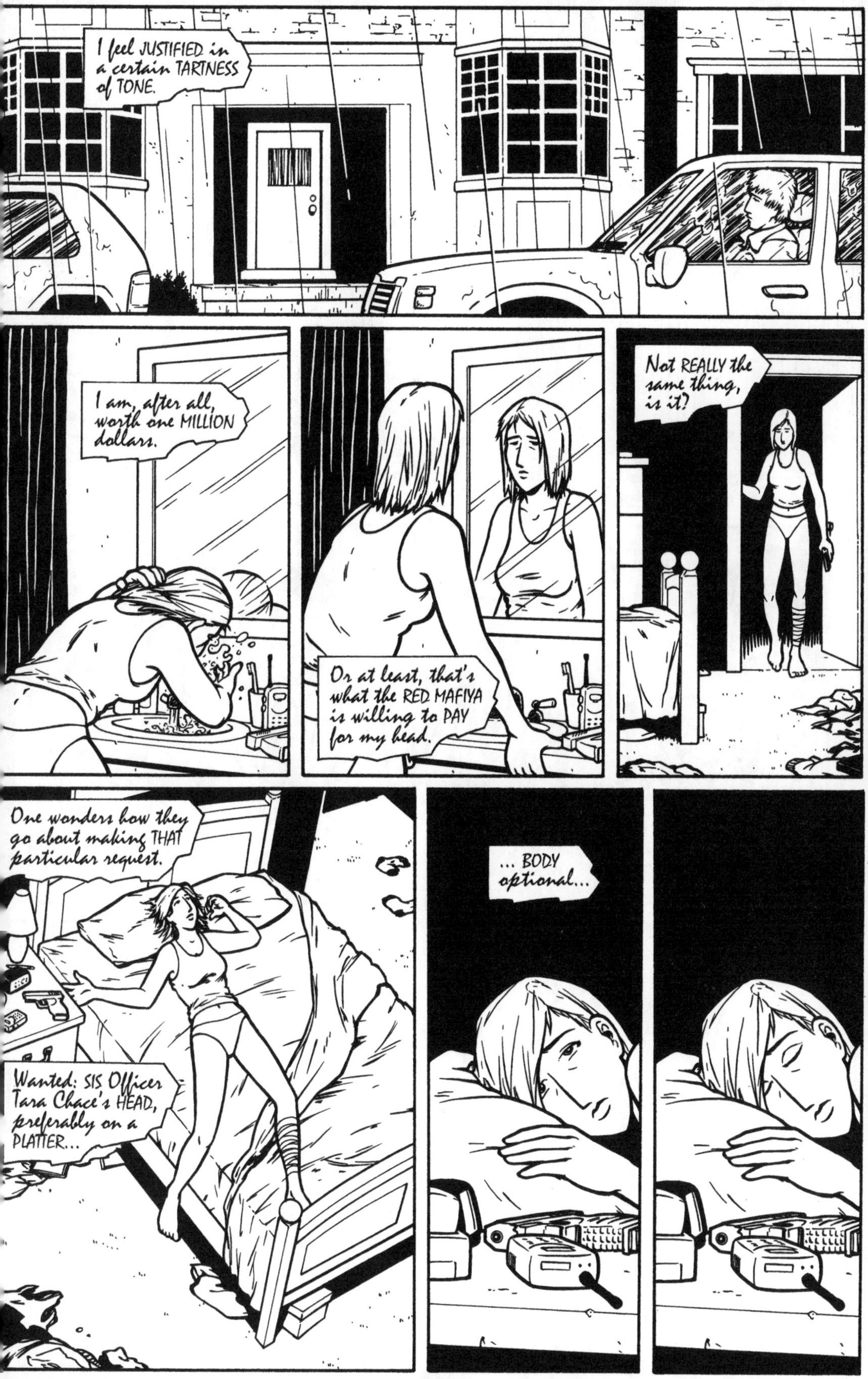
I feel JUSTIFIED in a certain TARTNESS of TONE.
I am, after all, worth one MILLION dollars.
Or at least, that's what the RED MAFIYA is willing to PAY for my head.
Not REALLY the same thing, is it?
One wonders how they go about making THAT particular request.
Wanted: SIS Officer Tara Chace's HEAD, preferably on a PLATTER...
... BODY optional...

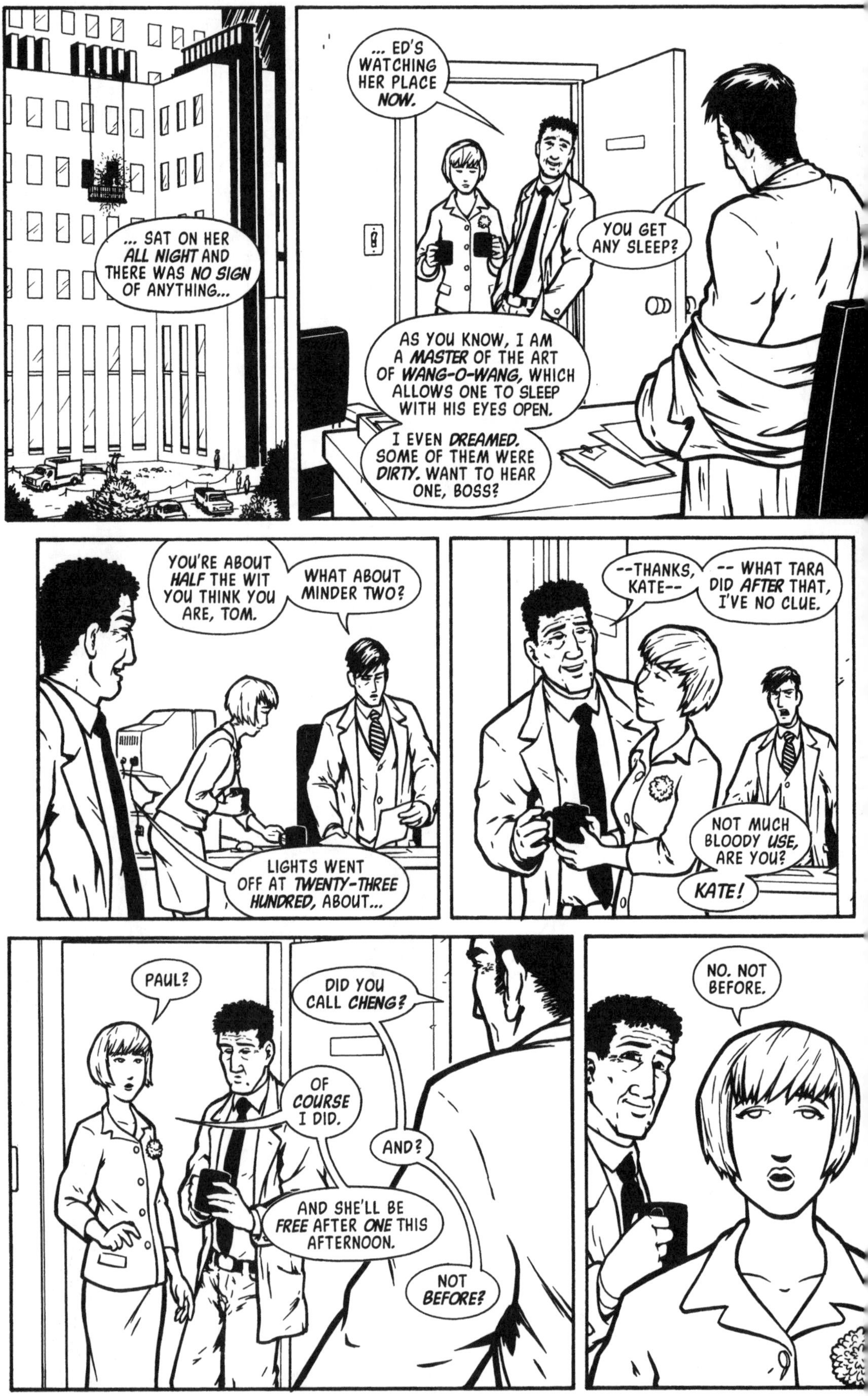
... SAT ON HER ALL NIGHT AND THERE WAS NO SIGN OF ANYTHING...
... ED'S WATCHING HER PLACE NOW.
YOU GET ANY SLEEP?
AS YOU KNOW, I AM A MASTER OF THE ART OF WANG-O-WANG, WHICH ALLOWS ONE TO SLEEP WITH HIS EYES OPEN.
I EVEN DREAMED. SOME OF THEM WERE DIRTY. WANT TO HEAR ONE, BOSS?
YOU'RE ABOUT HALF THE WIT YOU THINK YOU ARE, TOM.
WHAT ABOUT MINDER TWO?
LIGHTS WENT OFF AT TWENTY-THREE HUNDRED, ABOUT...
--THANKS, KATE--
-- WHAT TARA DID AFTER THAT, I'VE NO CLUE.
NOT MUCH BLOODY USE, ARE YOU?
KATE!
PAUL?
DID YOU CALL CHENG?
OF COURSE I DID.
AND?
AND SHE'LL BE FREE AFTER ONE THIS AFTERNOON.
NOT BEFORE?
NO. NOT BEFORE.

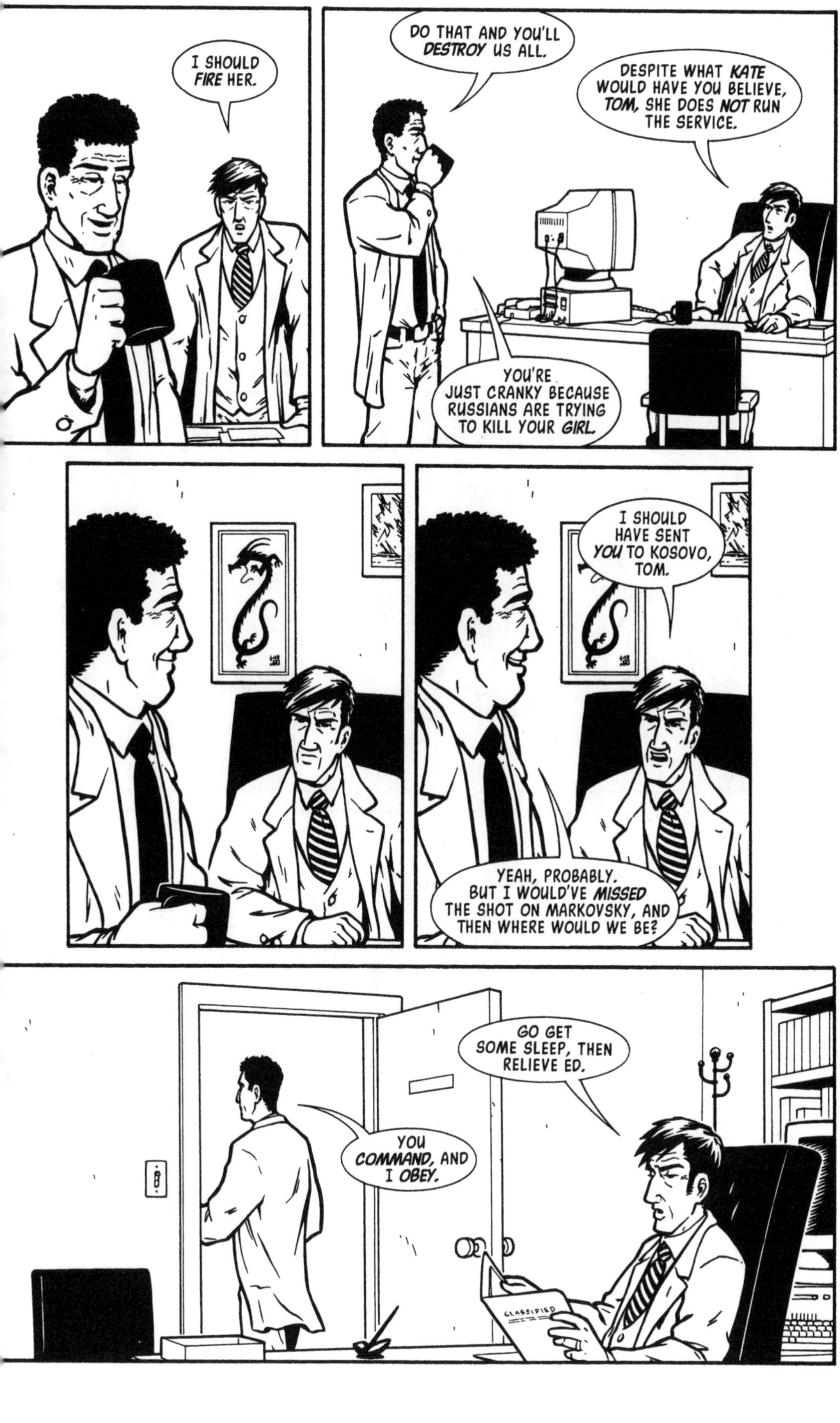
I SHOULD FIRE HER.
DO THAT AND YOU'LL DESTROY US ALL.
DESPITE WHAT KATE WOULD HAVE YOU BELIEVE, TOM, SHE DOES NOT RUN THE SERVICE.
YOU'RE JUST CRANKY BECAUSE RUSSIANS ARE TRYING TO KILL YOUR GIRL.
I SHOULD HAVE SENT YOU TO KOSOVO, TOM.
YEAH, PROBABLY. BUT I WOULD'VE MISSED THE SHOT ON MARKOVSKY, AND THEN WHERE WOULD WE BE?
GO GET SOME SLEEP, THEN RELIEVE ED.
YOU COMMAND, AND I OBEY.
CLASSIFIED

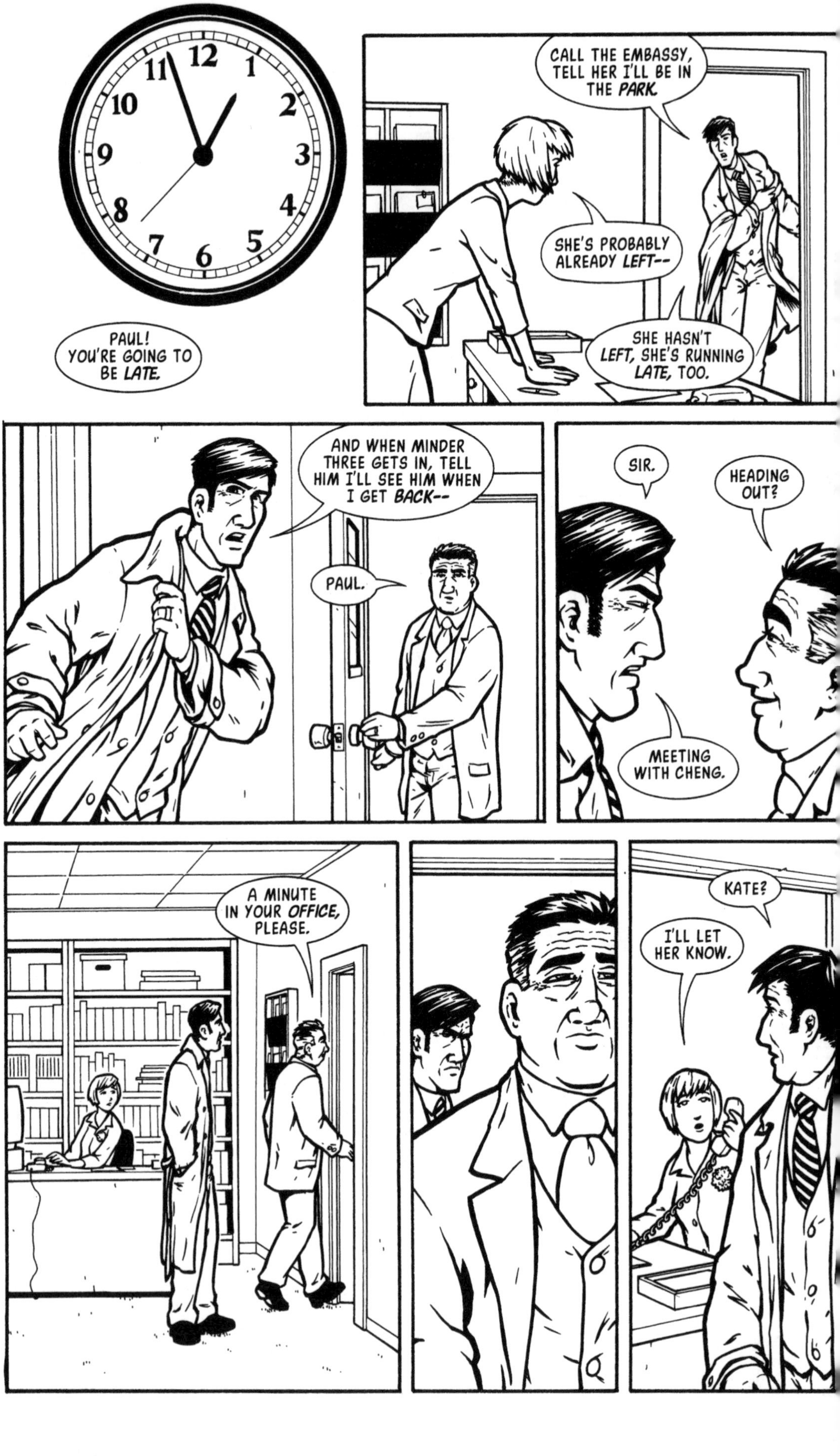

12
1
2
3
4
5
6
7
8
9
10
11
PAUL! YOU'RE GOING TO BE LATE.
CALL THE EMBASSY, TELL HER I'LL BE IN THE PARK.
SHE'S PROBABLY ALREADY LEFT--
SHE HASN'T LEFT, SHE'S RUNNING LATE, TOO.
AND WHEN MINDER THREE GETS IN, TELL HIM I'LL SEE HIM WHEN I GET BACK--
PAUL.
SIR.
HEADING OUT?
MEETING WITH CHENG.
A MINUTE IN YOUR OFFICE, PLEASE.
KATE?
I'LL LET HER KNOW.

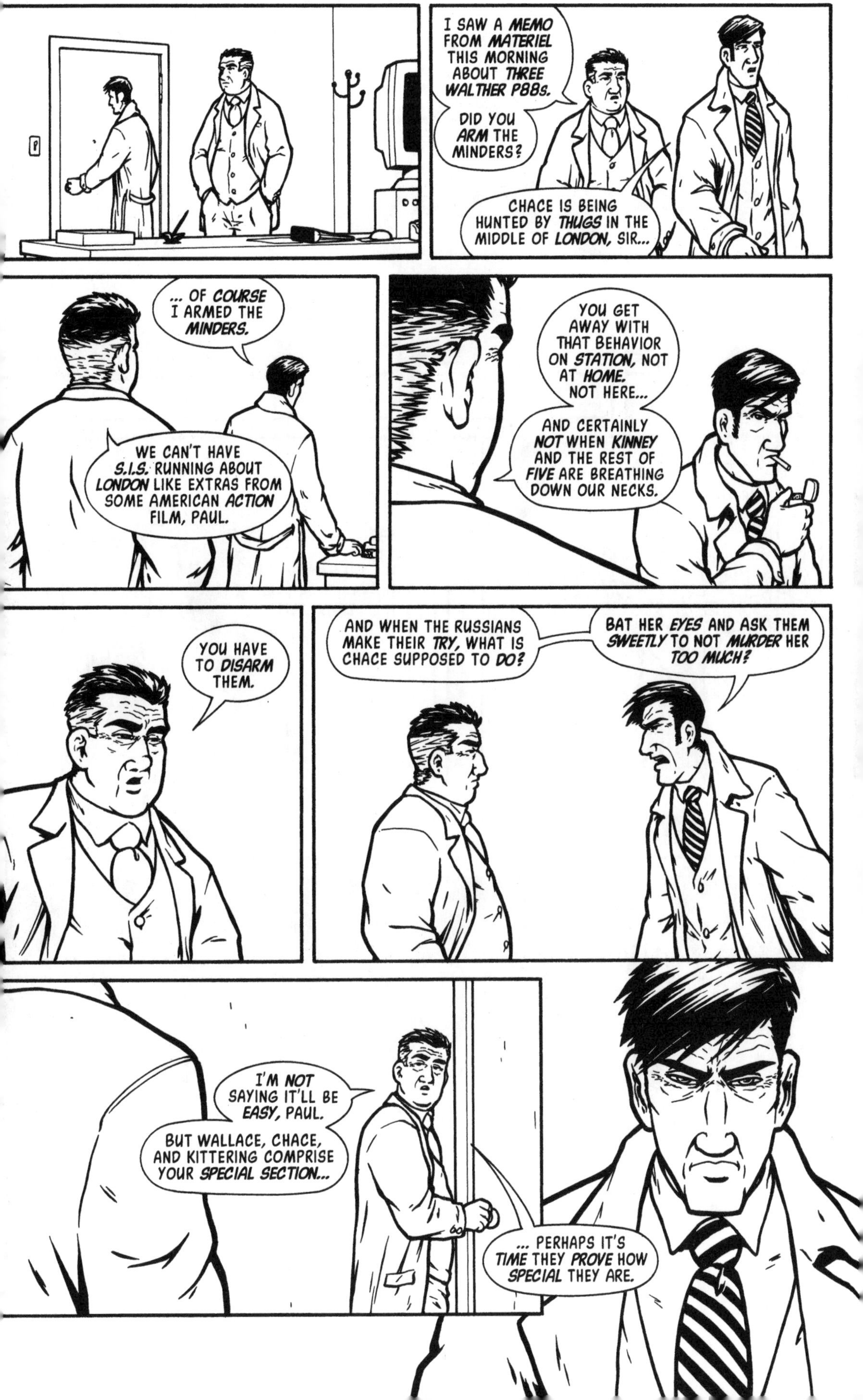
I SAW A MEMO FROM MATERIEL THIS MORNING ABOUT THREE WALTHER P88s.
DID YOU ARM THE MINDERS?
CHACE IS BEING HUNTED BY THUGS IN THE MIDDLE OF LONDON, SIR...
... OF COURSE I ARMED THE MINDERS.
WE CAN'T HAVE S.I.S. RUNNING ABOUT LONDON LIKE EXTRAS FROM SOME AMERICAN ACTION FILM, PAUL.
YOU GET AWAY WITH THAT BEHAVIOR ON STATION, NOT AT HOME. NOT HERE...
AND CERTAINLY NOT WHEN KINNEY AND THE REST OF FIVE ARE BREATHING DOWN OUR NECKS.
YOU HAVE TO DISARM THEM.
AND WHEN THE RUSSIANS MAKE THEIR TRY, WHAT IS CHACE SUPPOSED TO DO?
BAT HER EYES AND ASK THEM SWEETLY TO NOT MURDER HER TOO MUCH?
I'M NOT SAYING IT'LL BE EASY, PAUL.
BUT WALLACE, CHACE, AND KITTERING COMPRISE YOUR SPECIAL SECTION...
... PERHAPS IT'S TIME THEY PROVE HOW SPECIAL THEY ARE.

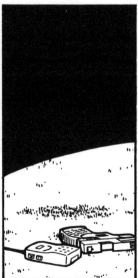

DAISY? IT'S TULIP...

... YOUR PHONE IS ABOUT TO RING.

BRRT *BRRT*

BRRT

THAT WAS VERY CLEVER, TULIP.

CAN YOU TELL ME WHAT HAPPENS NEXT WEEK ON CASUALTY?

SORRY?

CHACE.

TARA? IT'S PAUL.

YES, SIR?

I JUST HAD A MEETING WITH THE DEPUTY CHIEF.

HE'S ORDERED THE MINDERS TO TURN IN THEIR WEAPONS.

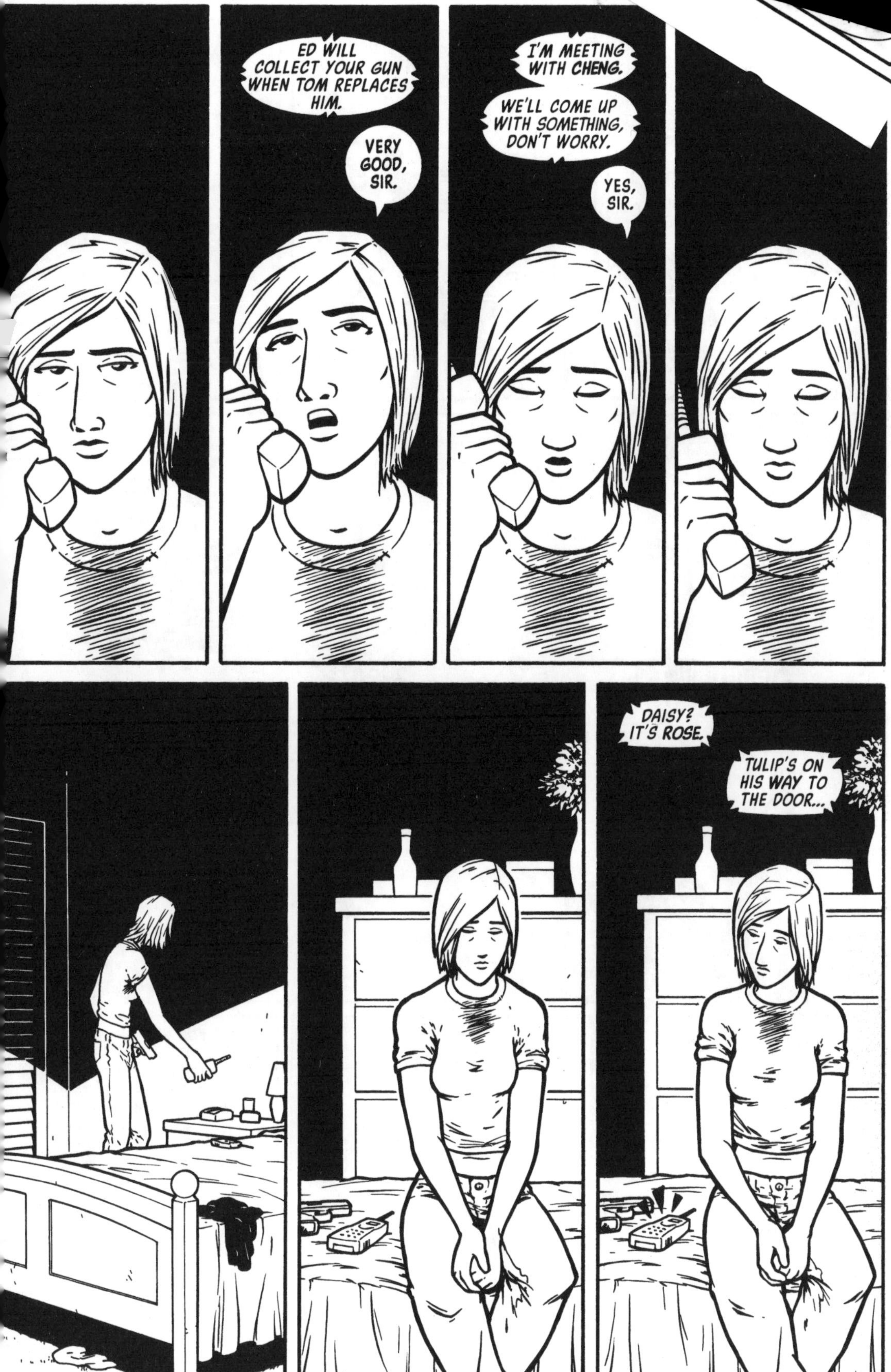
ED WILL COLLECT YOUR GUN WHEN TOM REPLACES HIM.
VERY GOOD, SIR.
I'M MEETING WITH CHENG.
WE'LL COME UP WITH SOMETHING, DON'T WORRY.
YES, SIR.
DAISY? IT'S ROSE.
TULIP'S ON HIS WAY TO THE DOOR...

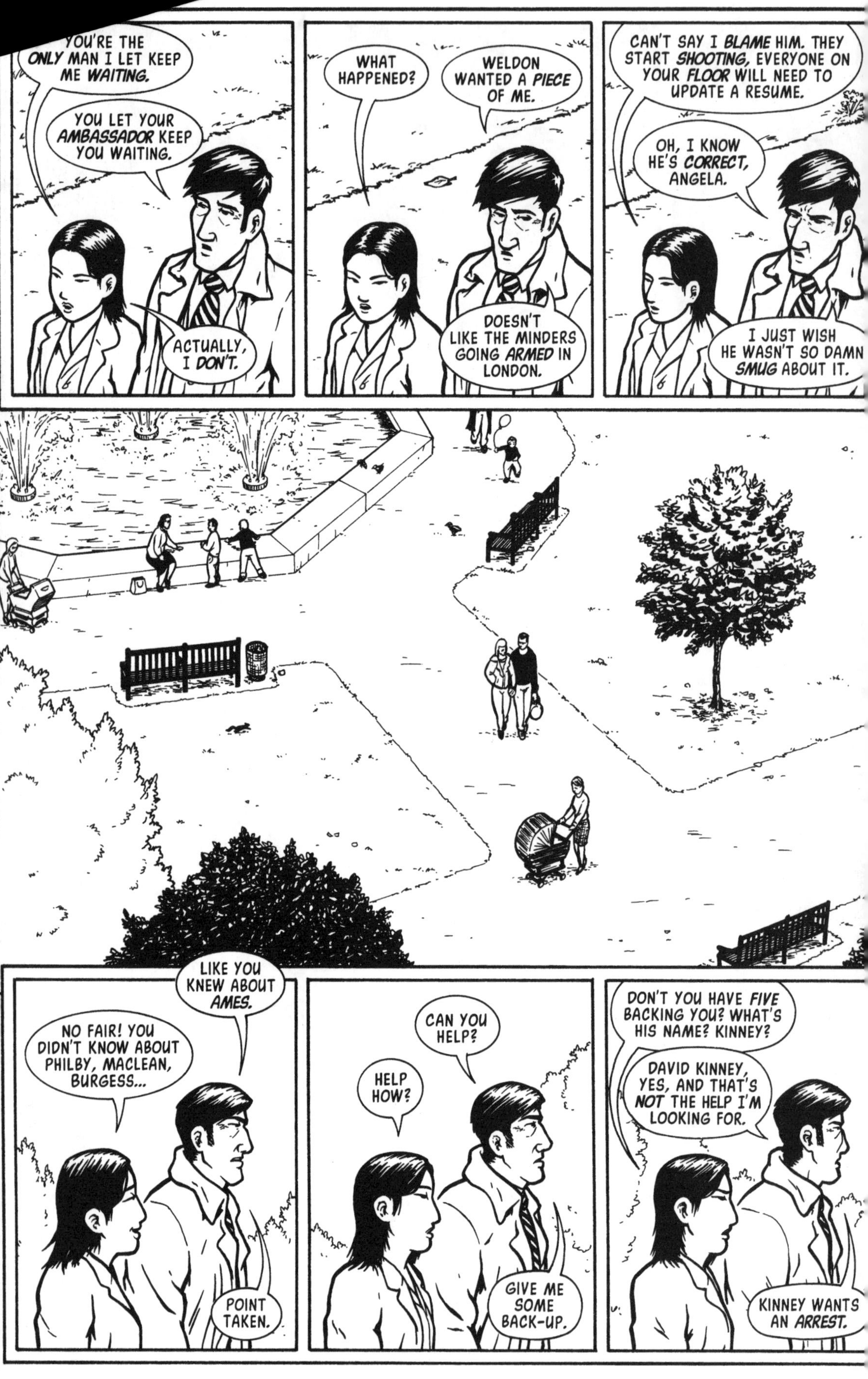
YOU'RE THE ONLY MAN I LET KEEP ME WAITING.
YOU LET YOUR AMBASSADOR KEEP YOU WAITING.
ACTUALLY, I DON'T.
WHAT HAPPENED?
WELDON WANTED A PIECE OF ME.
DOESN'T LIKE THE MINDERS GOING ARMED IN LONDON.
CAN'T SAY I BLAME HIM. THEY START SHOOTING, EVERYONE ON YOUR FLOOR WILL NEED TO UPDATE A RESUME.
OH, I KNOW HE'S CORRECT, ANGELA.
I JUST WISH HE WASN'T SO DAMN SMUG ABOUT IT.
NO FAIR! YOU DIDN'T KNOW ABOUT PHILBY, MACLEAN, BURGESS...
LIKE YOU KNEW ABOUT AMES.
POINT TAKEN.
CAN YOU HELP?
HELP HOW?
GIVE ME SOME BACK-UP.
DON'T YOU HAVE FIVE BACKING YOU? WHAT'S HIS NAME? KINNEY?
DAVID KINNEY, YES, AND THAT'S NOT THE HELP I'M LOOKING FOR.
KINNEY WANTS AN ARREST.

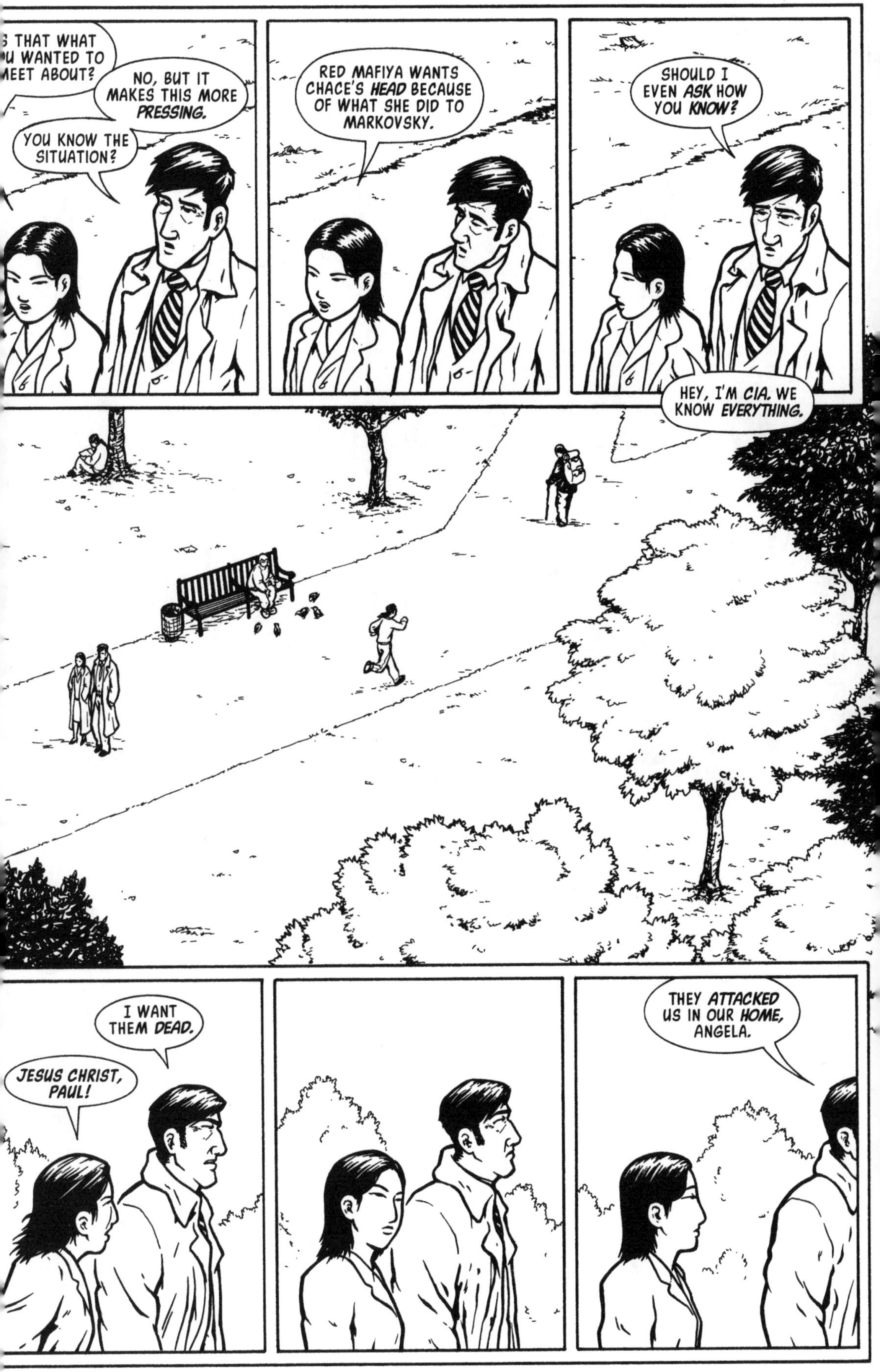

S THAT WHAT
U WANTED TO
MEET ABOUT?
NO, BUT IT MAKES THIS MORE PRESSING.
YOU KNOW THE SITUATION?
RED MAFIYA WANTS CHACE'S HEAD BECAUSE OF WHAT SHE DID TO MARKOVSKY.
SHOULD I EVEN ASK HOW YOU KNOW?
HEY, I'M CIA. WE KNOW EVERYTHING.
I WANT THEM DEAD.
JESUS CHRIST, PAUL!
THEY ATTACKED US IN OUR HOME, ANGELA.

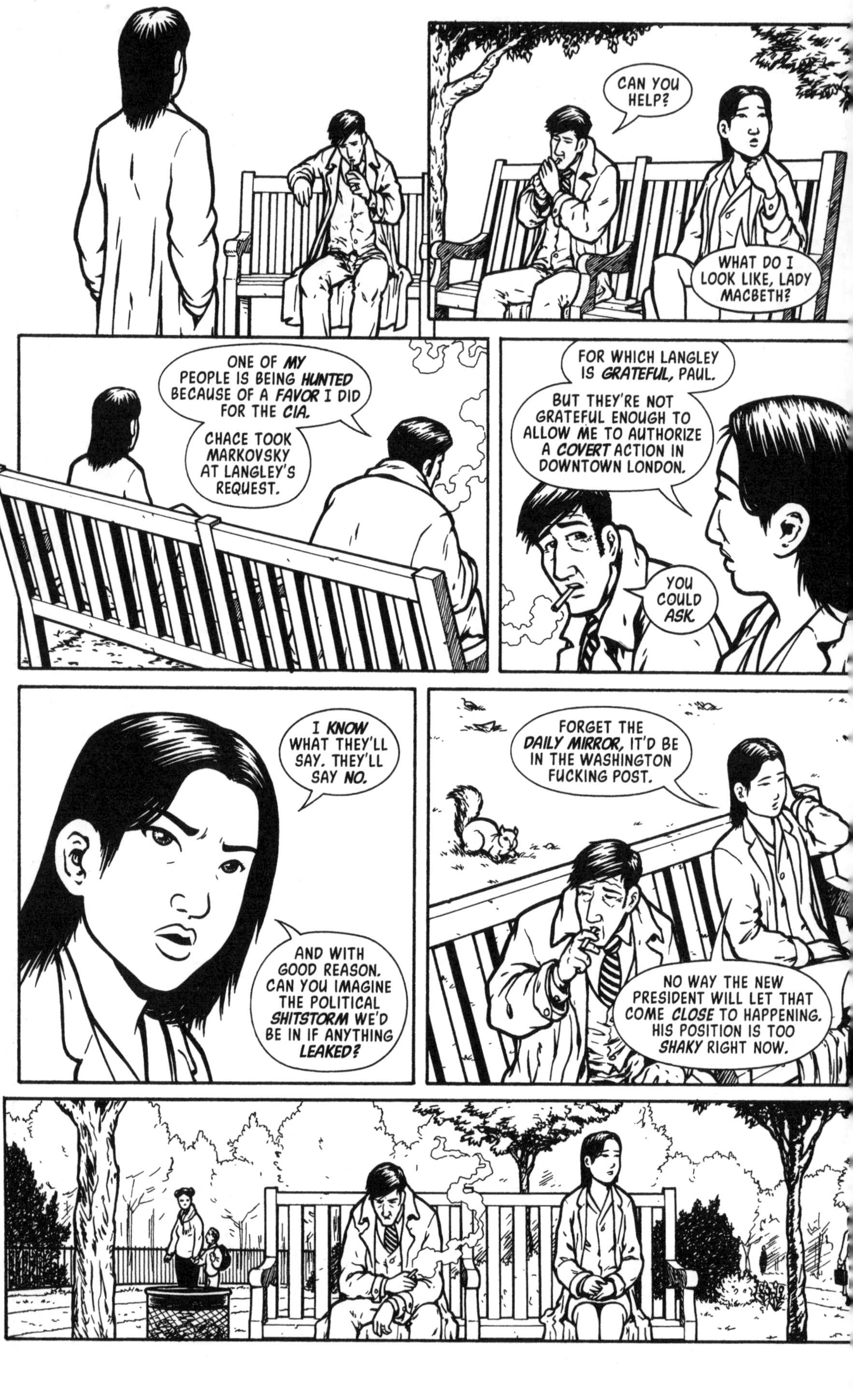
CAN YOU HELP?
WHAT DO I LOOK LIKE, LADY MACBETH?
ONE OF MY PEOPLE IS BEING HUNTED BECAUSE OF A FAVOR I DID FOR THE CIA.
CHACE TOOK MARKOVSKY AT LANGLEY'S REQUEST.
FOR WHICH LANGLEY IS GRATEFUL, PAUL.
BUT THEY'RE NOT GRATEFUL ENOUGH TO ALLOW ME TO AUTHORIZE A COVERT ACTION IN DOWNTOWN LONDON.
YOU COULD ASK.
I KNOW WHAT THEY'LL SAY. THEY'LL SAY NO.
AND WITH GOOD REASON. CAN YOU IMAGINE THE POLITICAL SHITSTORM WE'D BE IN IF ANYTHING LEAKED?
FORGET THE DAILY MIRROR, IT'D BE IN THE WASHINGTON FUCKING POST.
NO WAY THE NEW PRESIDENT WILL LET THAT COME CLOSE TO HAPPENING. HIS POSITION IS TOO SHAKY RIGHT NOW.

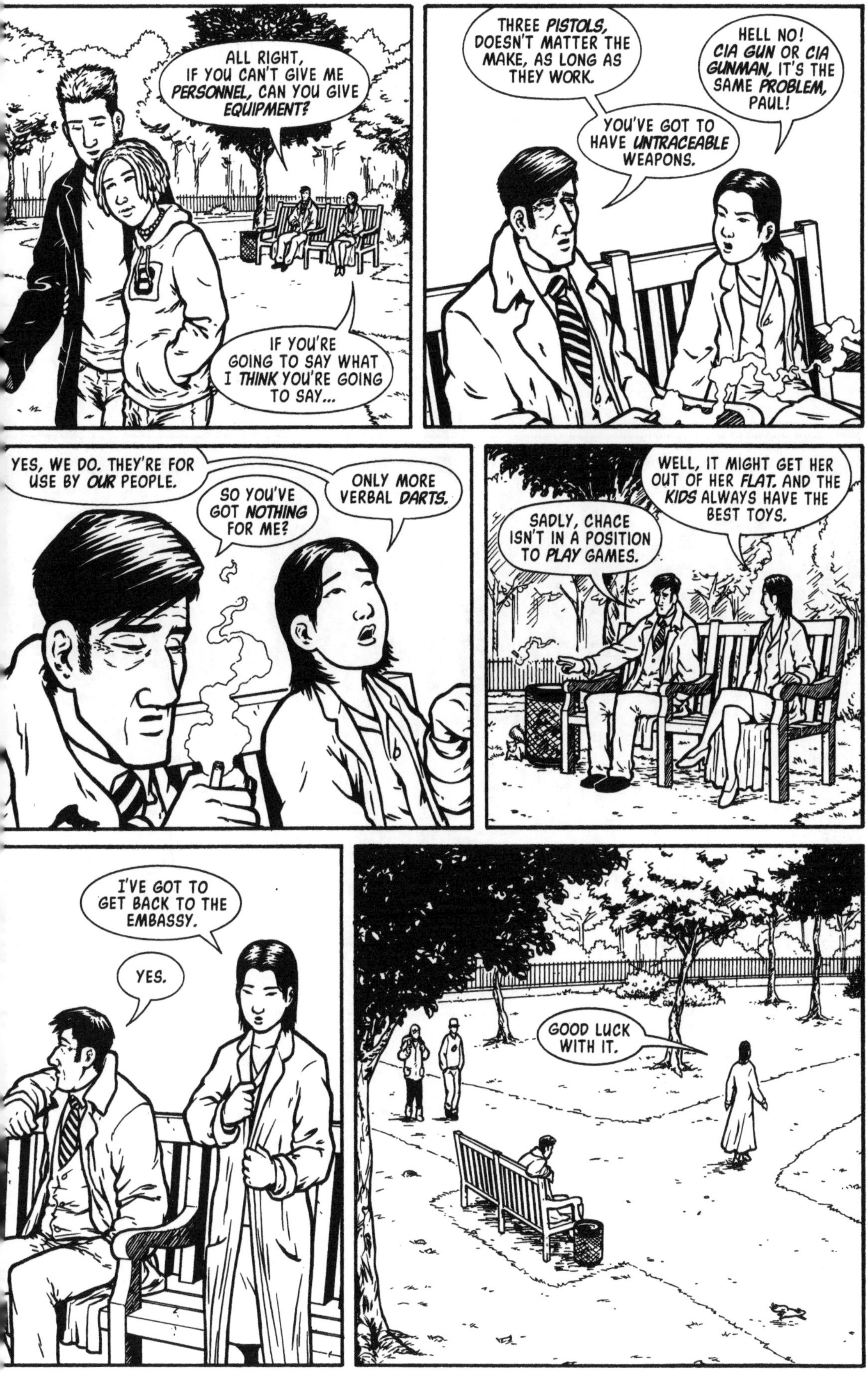
ALL RIGHT, IF YOU CAN'T GIVE ME PERSONNEL, CAN YOU GIVE EQUIPMENT?
IF YOU'RE GOING TO SAY WHAT I THINK YOU'RE GOING TO SAY...
THREE PISTOLS, DOESN'T MATTER THE MAKE, AS LONG AS THEY WORK.
YOU'VE GOT TO HAVE UNTRACEABLE WEAPONS.
HELL NO! CIA GUN OR CIA GUNMAN, IT'S THE SAME PROBLEM, PAUL!
YES, WE DO. THEY'RE FOR USE BY OUR PEOPLE.
SO YOU'VE GOT NOTHING FOR ME?
ONLY MORE VERBAL DARTS.
SADLY, CHACE ISN'T IN A POSITION TO PLAY GAMES.
WELL, IT MIGHT GET HER OUT OF HER FLAT. AND THE KIDS ALWAYS HAVE THE BEST TOYS.
I'VE GOT TO GET BACK TO THE EMBASSY.
YES.
GOOD LUCK WITH IT.

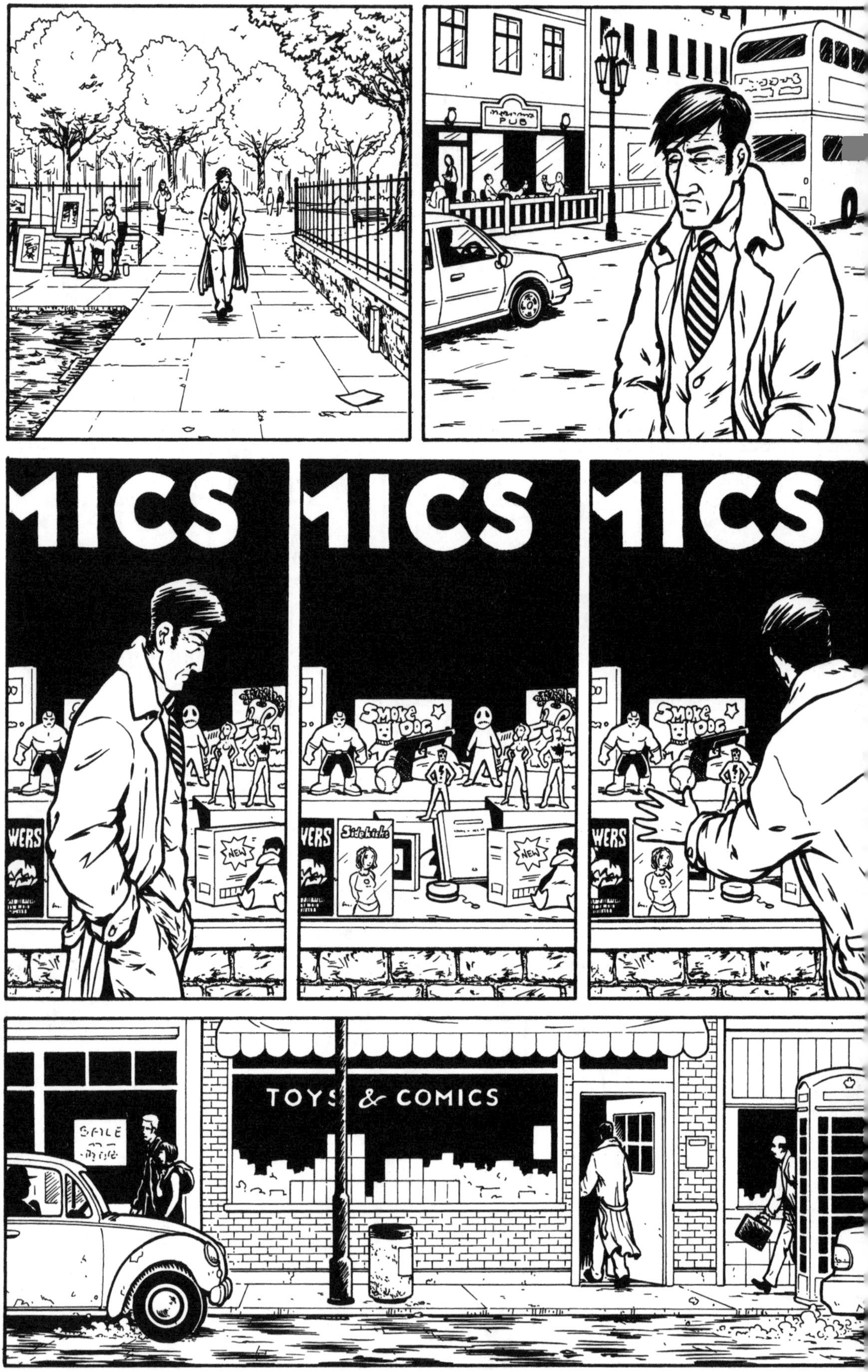
PUB
MICS
WERS
NEW
MICS
SMOKE DOG
WERS
Sidekicks
NEW
MICS
SMOKE DOG
WERS
SALE
TOYS & COMICS

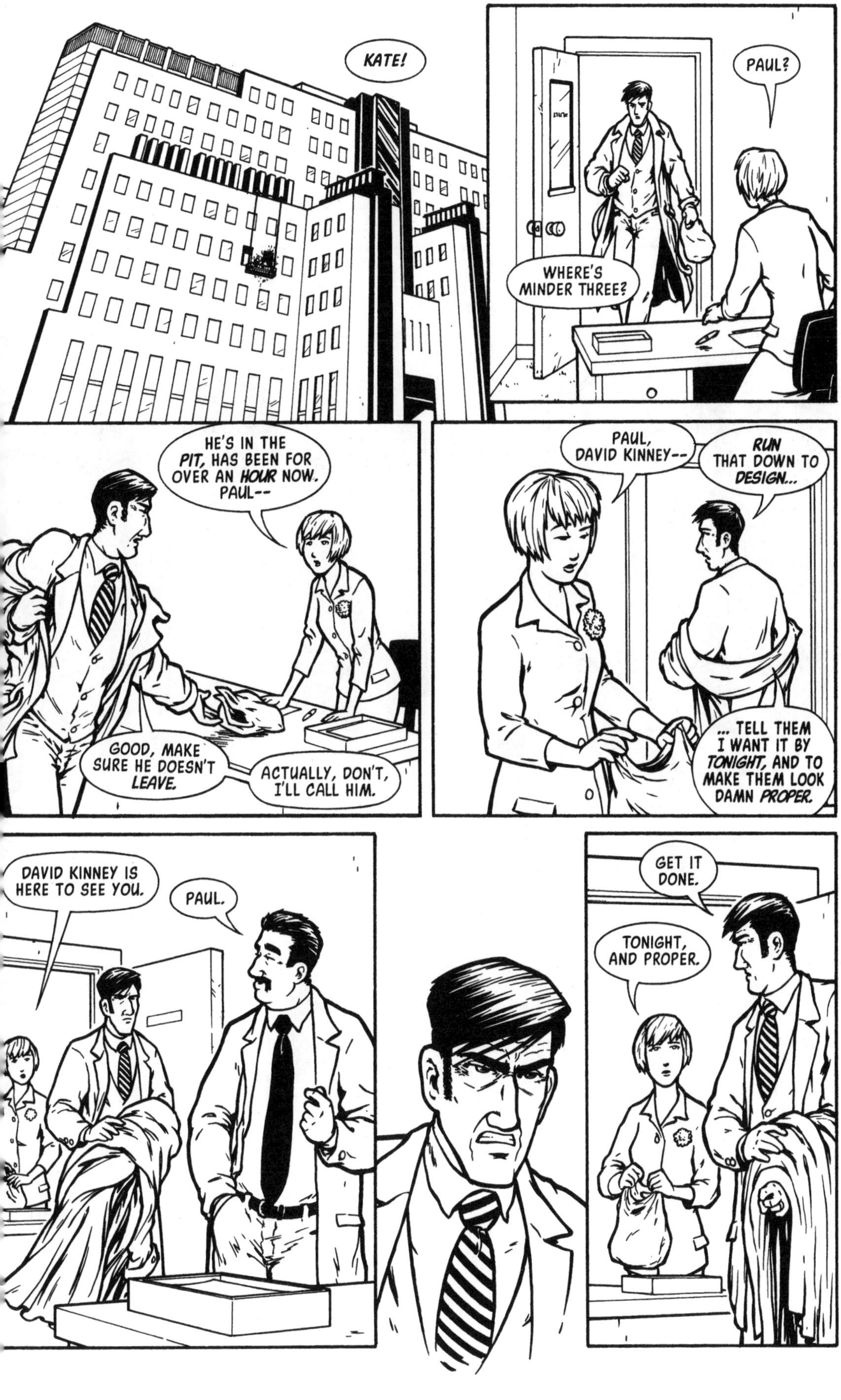
KATE!
PAUL?
WHERE'S MINDER THREE?
HE'S IN THE *PIT,* HAS BEEN FOR OVER AN *HOUR* NOW. PAUL--
GOOD, MAKE SURE HE DOESN'T *LEAVE.*
ACTUALLY, DON'T, I'LL CALL HIM.
PAUL, DAVID KINNEY--
RUN THAT DOWN TO *DESIGN...*
... TELL THEM I WANT IT BY *TONIGHT,* AND TO MAKE THEM LOOK DAMN *PROPER.*
DAVID KINNEY IS HERE TO SEE YOU.
PAUL.
GET IT DONE.
TONIGHT, AND PROPER.

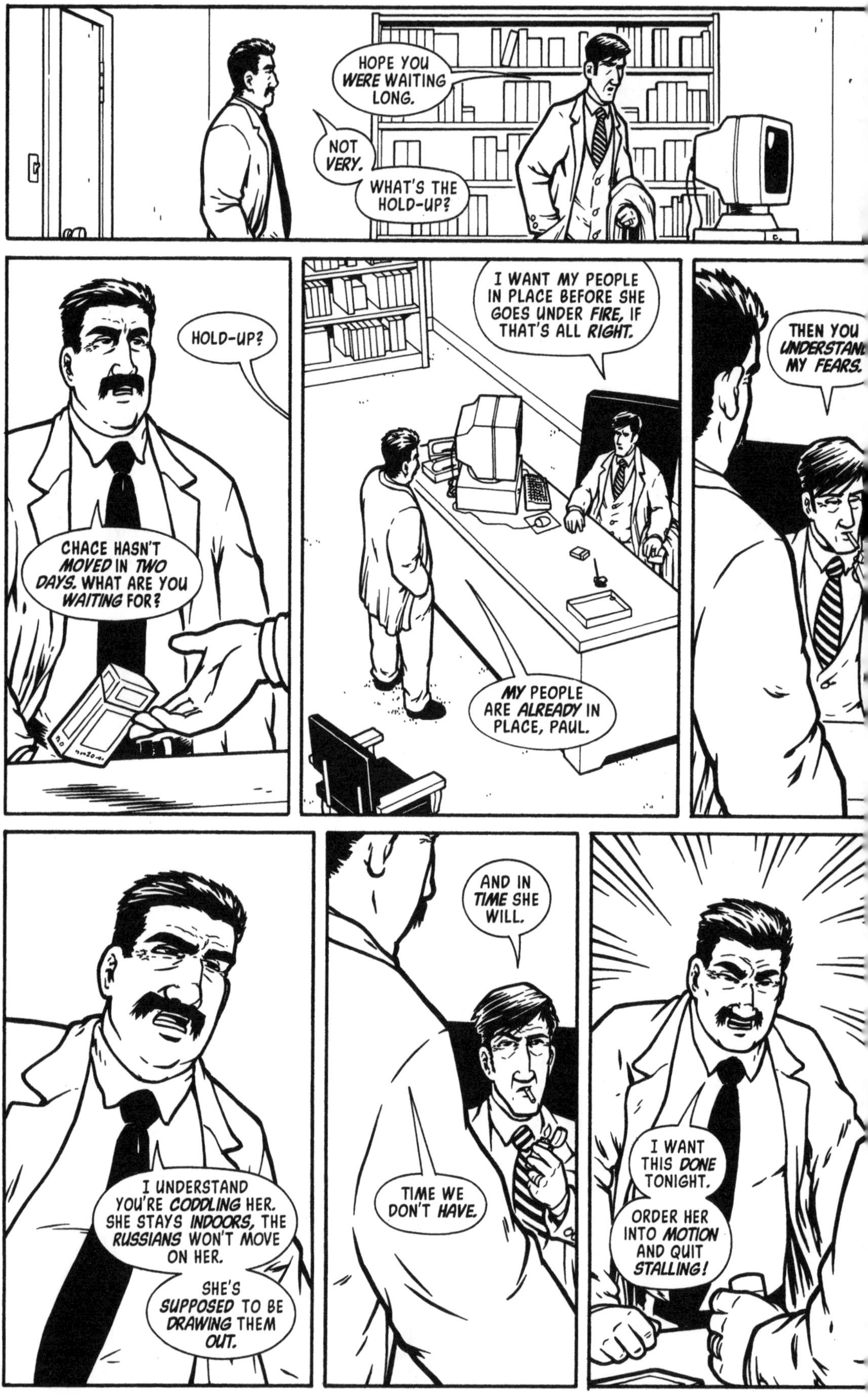
HOPE YOU WERE WAITING LONG.
NOT VERY.
WHAT'S THE HOLD-UP?
HOLD-UP?
CHACE HASN'T MOVED IN TWO DAYS. WHAT ARE YOU WAITING FOR?
I WANT MY PEOPLE IN PLACE BEFORE SHE GOES UNDER FIRE, IF THAT'S ALL RIGHT.
MY PEOPLE ARE ALREADY IN PLACE, PAUL.
THEN YOU UNDERSTAND MY FEARS.
I UNDERSTAND YOU'RE CODDLING HER. SHE STAYS INDOORS, THE RUSSIANS WON'T MOVE ON HER.
SHE'S SUPPOSED TO BE DRAWING THEM OUT.
AND IN TIME SHE WILL.
TIME WE DON'T HAVE.
I WANT THIS DONE TONIGHT.
ORDER HER INTO MOTION AND QUIT STALLING!

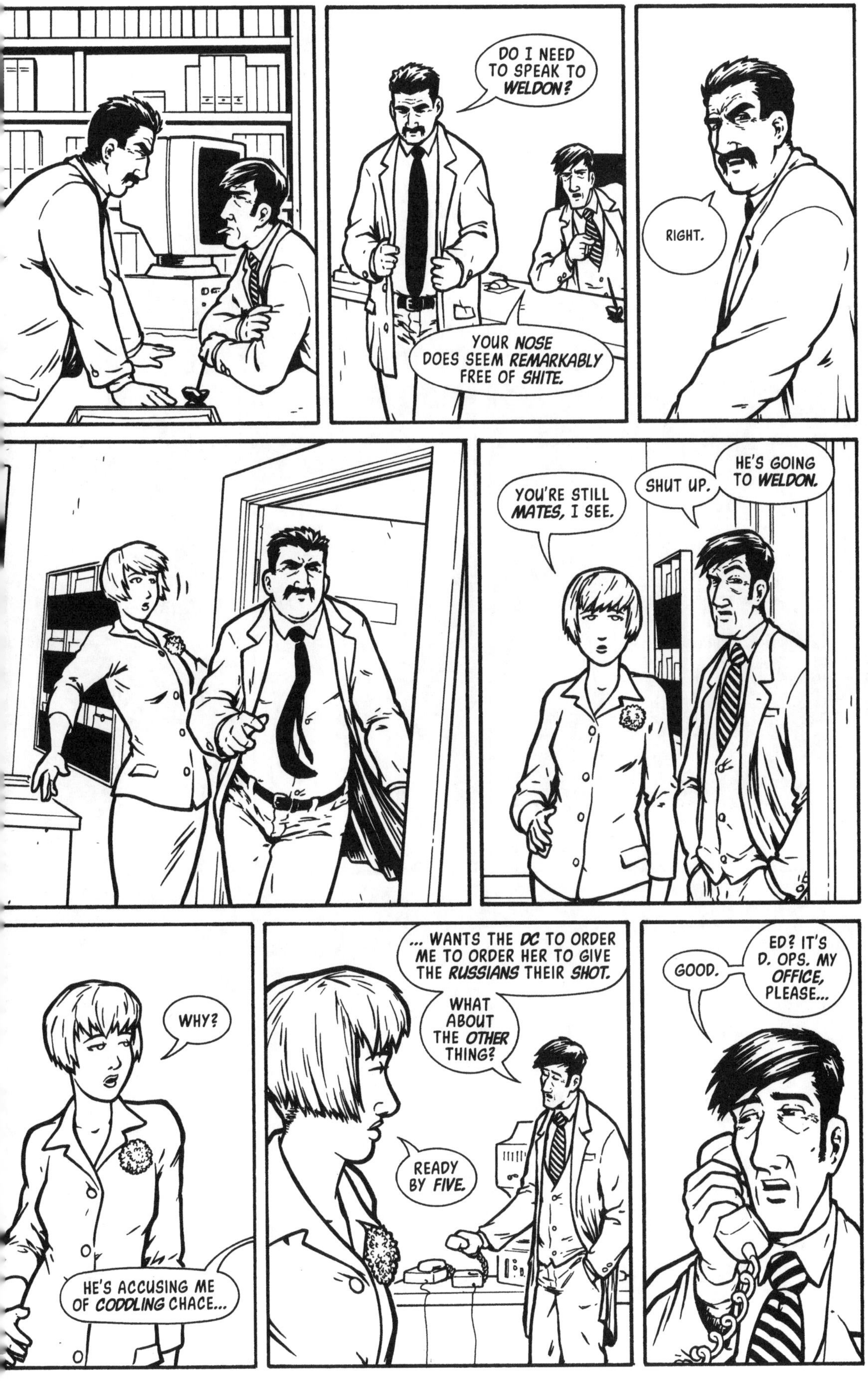
DO I NEED TO SPEAK TO WELDON?
YOUR NOSE DOES SEEM REMARKABLY FREE OF SHITE.
RIGHT.
YOU'RE STILL MATES, I SEE.
SHUT UP.
HE'S GOING TO WELDON.
WHY?
HE'S ACCUSING ME OF CODDLING CHACE...
... WANTS THE DC TO ORDER ME TO ORDER HER TO GIVE THE RUSSIANS THEIR SHOT.
WHAT ABOUT THE OTHER THING?
READY BY FIVE.
GOOD.
ED? IT'S D. OPS. MY OFFICE, PLEASE...

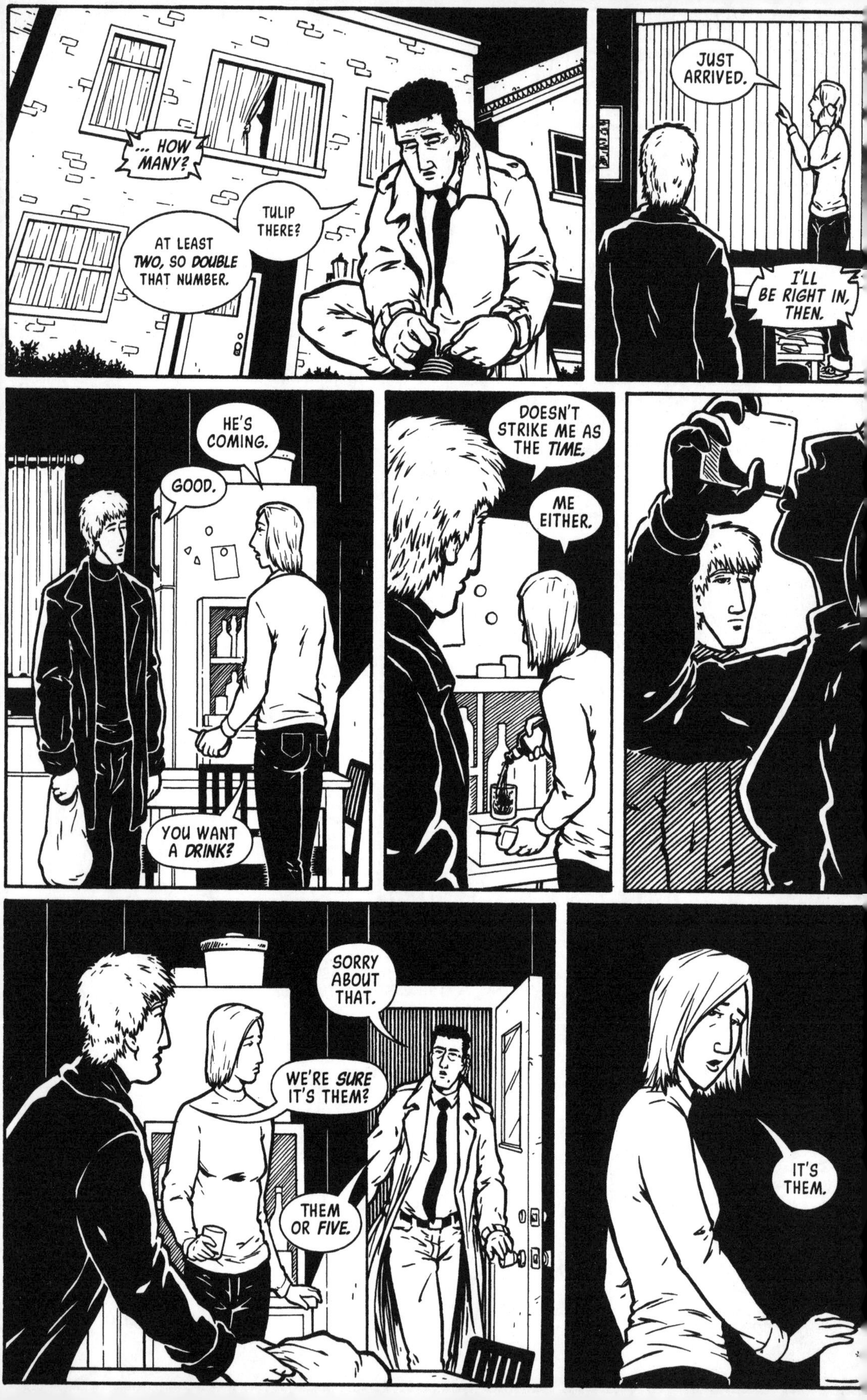
... HOW MANY?
TULIP THERE?
AT LEAST TWO, SO DOUBLE THAT NUMBER.
JUST ARRIVED.
I'LL BE RIGHT IN, THEN.
HE'S COMING.
GOOD.
YOU WANT A DRINK?
DOESN'T STRIKE ME AS THE TIME.
ME EITHER.
SORRY ABOUT THAT.
WE'RE SURE IT'S THEM?
THEM OR FIVE.
IT'S THEM.

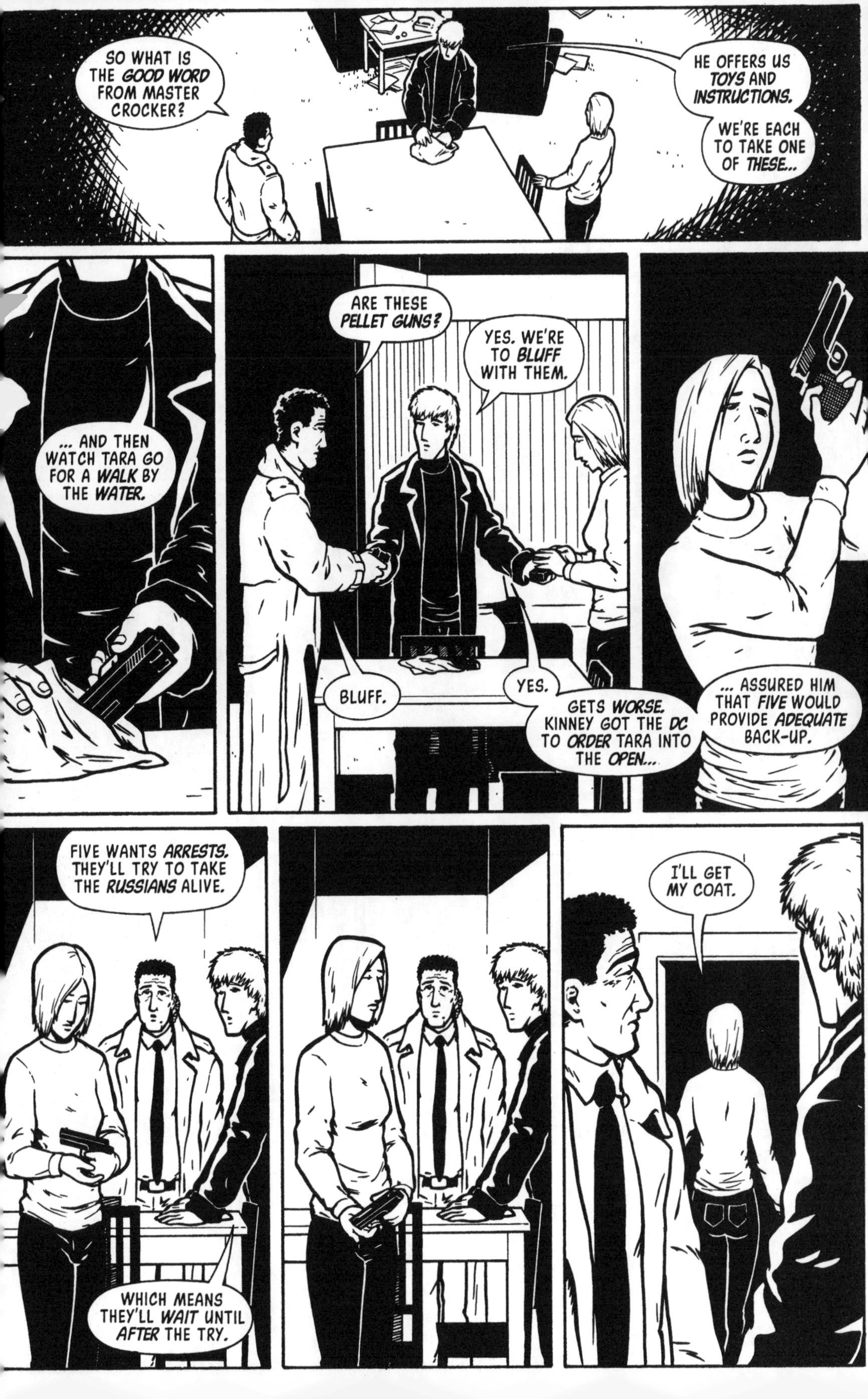
SO WHAT IS THE GOOD WORD FROM MASTER CROCKER?
HE OFFERS US TOYS AND INSTRUCTIONS.
WE'RE EACH TO TAKE ONE OF THESE...
... AND THEN WATCH TARA GO FOR A WALK BY THE WATER.
ARE THESE PELLET GUNS?
YES. WE'RE TO BLUFF WITH THEM.
BLUFF.
YES.
GETS WORSE. KINNEY GOT THE DC TO ORDER TARA INTO THE OPEN...
... ASSURED HIM THAT FIVE WOULD PROVIDE ADEQUATE BACK-UP.
FIVE WANTS ARRESTS. THEY'LL TRY TO TAKE THE RUSSIANS ALIVE.
WHICH MEANS THEY'LL WAIT UNTIL AFTER THE TRY.
I'LL GET MY COAT.

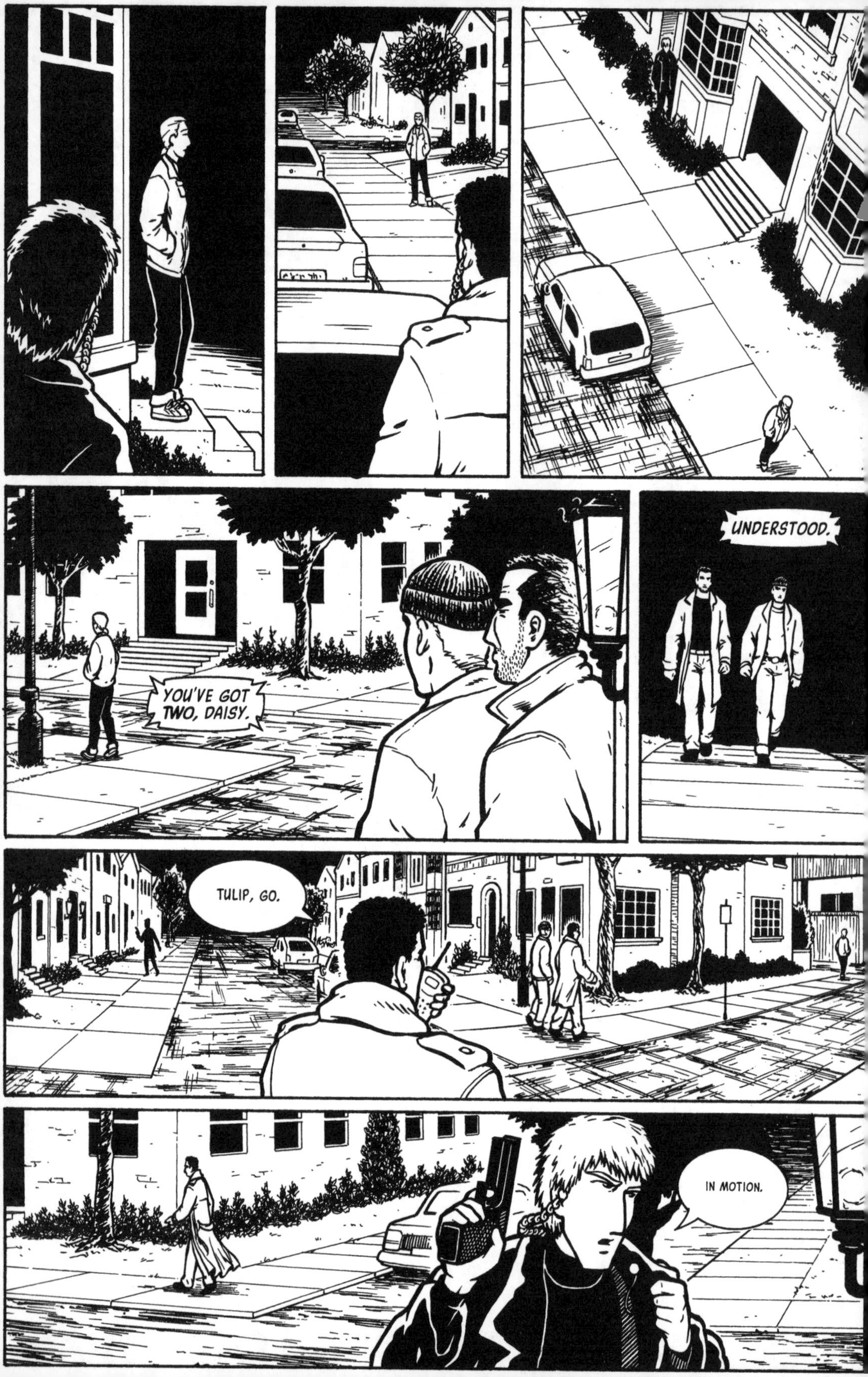
YOU'VE GOT TWO, DAISY.
UNDERSTOOD.
TULIP, GO.
IN MOTION.

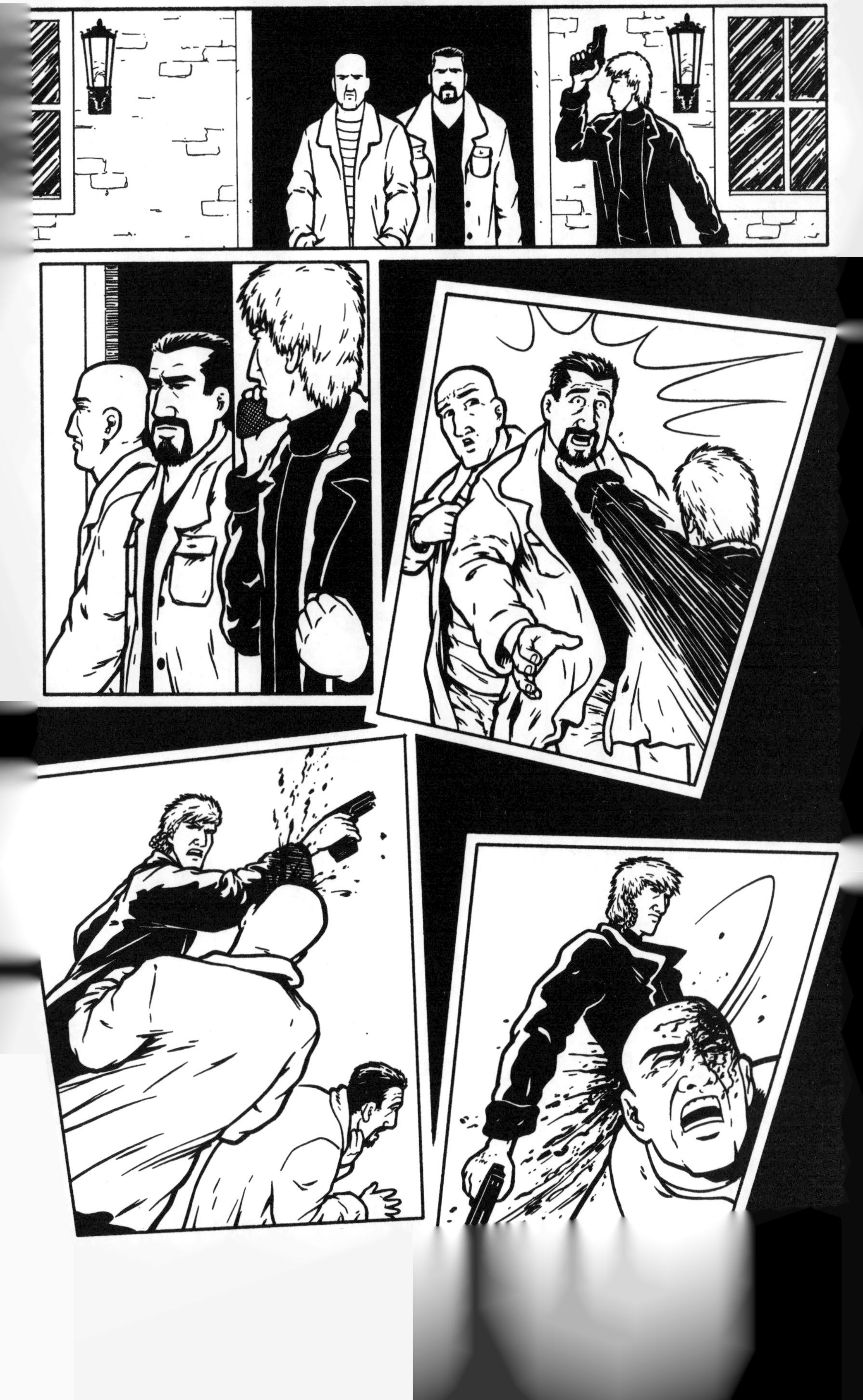

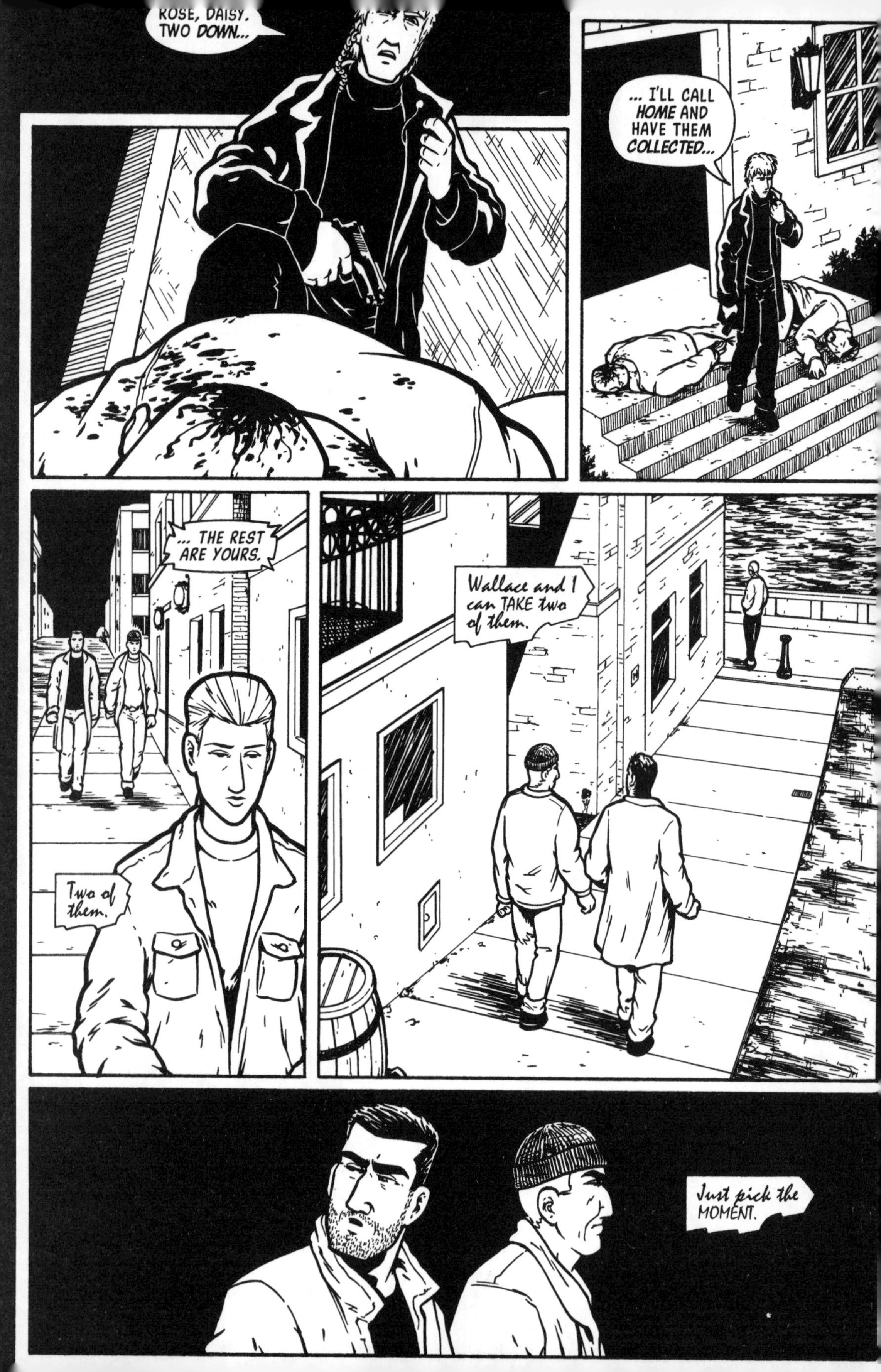
ROSE, DAISY. TWO DOWN...
... I'LL CALL HOME AND HAVE THEM COLLECTED...
... THE REST ARE YOURS.
Two of them.
Wallace and I can TAKE two of them.
Just pick the MOMENT.

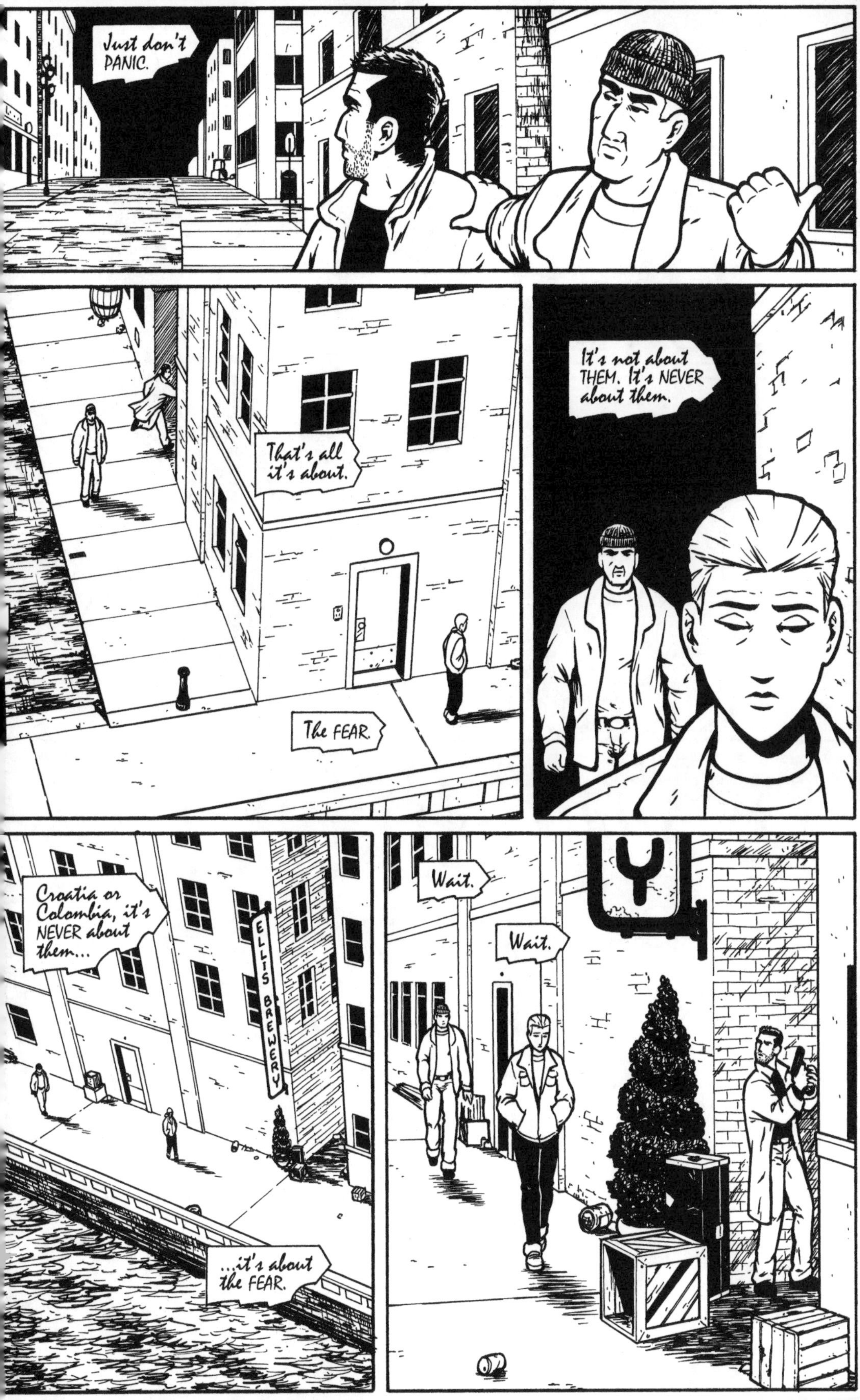
Just don't PANIC.
That's all it's about.
The FEAR.
It's not about THEM. It's NEVER about them.
Croatia or Colombia, it's NEVER about them...
ELLIS BREWERY
...it's about the FEAR.
Wait.
Wait.

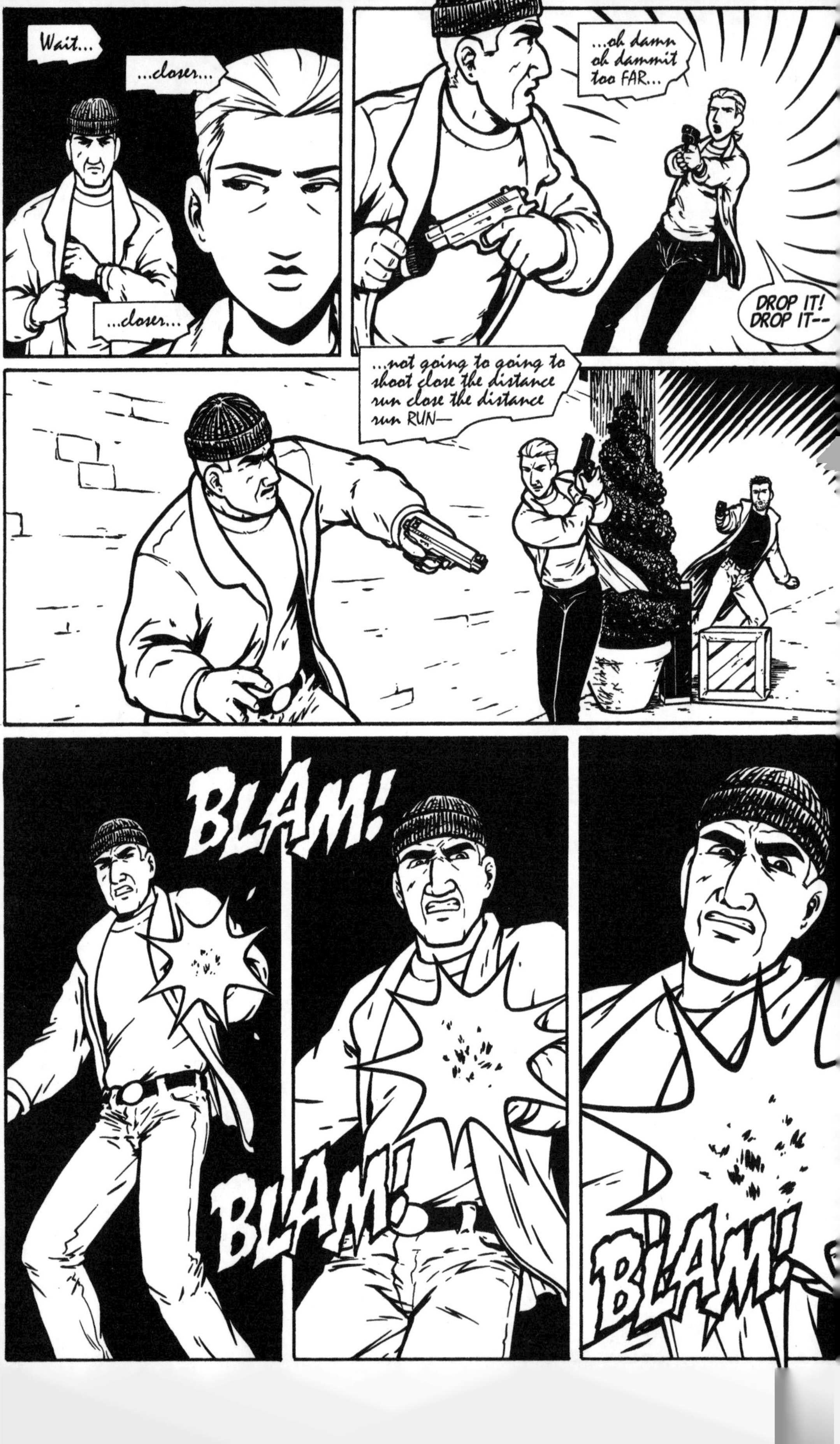
Wait...
...closer...
...closer...
...oh damn
oh dammit
too FAR...
DROP IT!
DROP IT--
...not going to going to
shoot close the distance
run close the distance
run RUN—
BLAM!
BLAM!
BLAM!

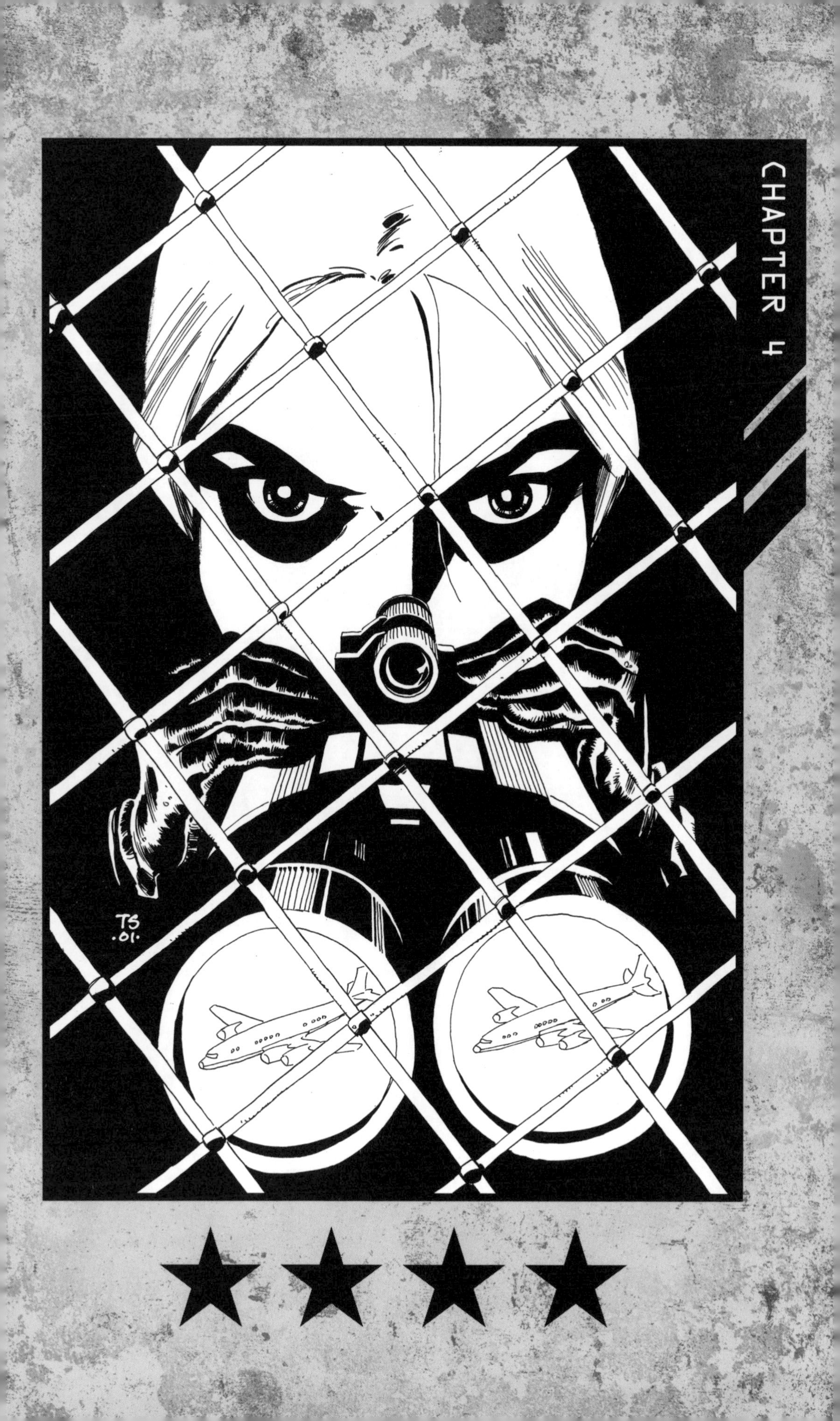

CHAPTER 4

★★★★

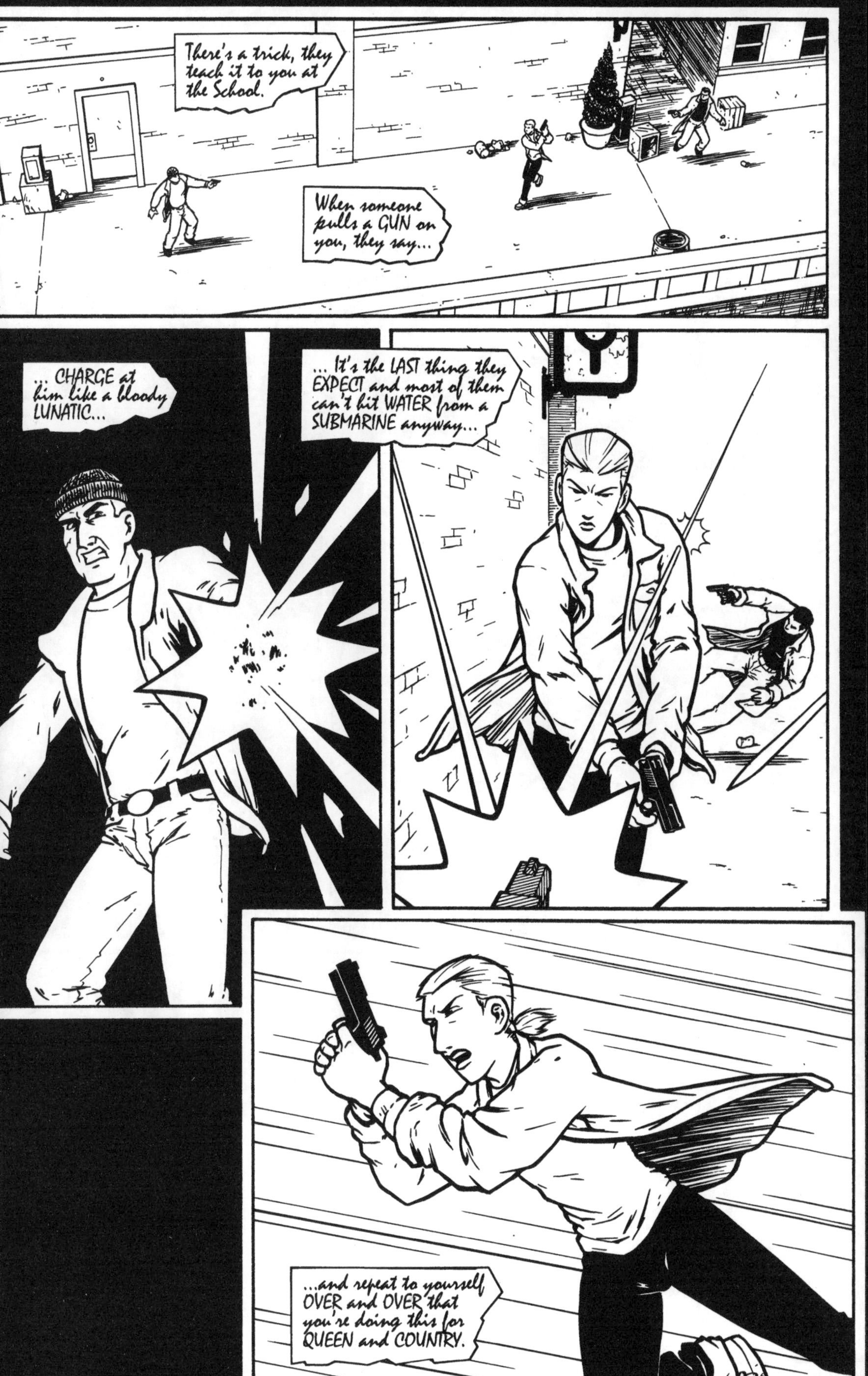
There's a trick, they teach it to you at the School.
When someone pulls a GUN on you, they say...
... CHARGE at him like a bloody LUNATIC...
... It's the LAST thing they EXPECT and most of them can't hit WATER from a SUBMARINE anyway...
...and repeat to yourself OVER and OVER that you're doing this for QUEEN and COUNTRY.

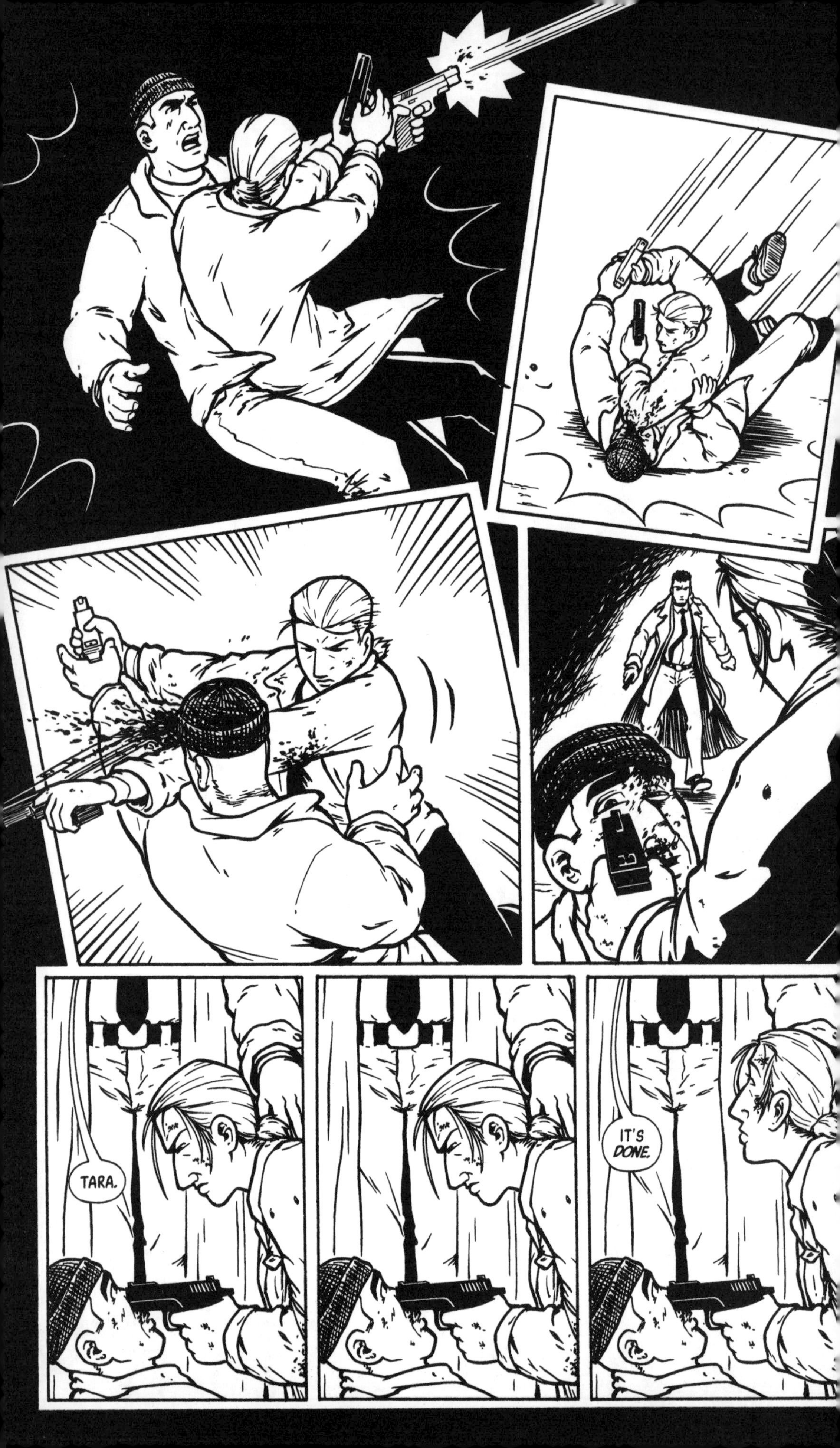
TARA.
IT'S *DONE.*

THERE WAS *ONE MORE*.

YEAH, HE'S *NOT GOING TO BE TROUBLE*.

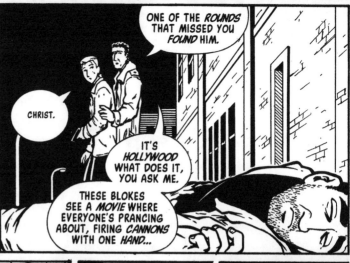

ONE OF THE *ROUNDS* THAT MISSED YOU *FOUND HIM*.

CHRIST.

IT'S *HOLLYWOOD* WHAT DOES IT, YOU ASK ME.

THESE BLOKES SEE A *MOVIE* WHERE EVERYONE'S PRANCING ABOUT, FIRING *CANNONS* WITH ONE *HAND*...

... THEY'RE MORE CONCERNED WITH LOOKING *GOOD* DURING A GUNFIGHT THAN WITH *LIVING* THROUGH THE DAMN THING.

WHAT THEY DON'T *REALIZE*, YOU SEE, IS THAT *EVERY* BULLET *HAS* TO GO *SOMEWHERE*.

HEY-- TOM?

YES, LOVE?

... NOTHING.

NEVER MIND.

AH, GOOD MASTER KINNEY AND ETCETERA HAVE *ARRIVED*.

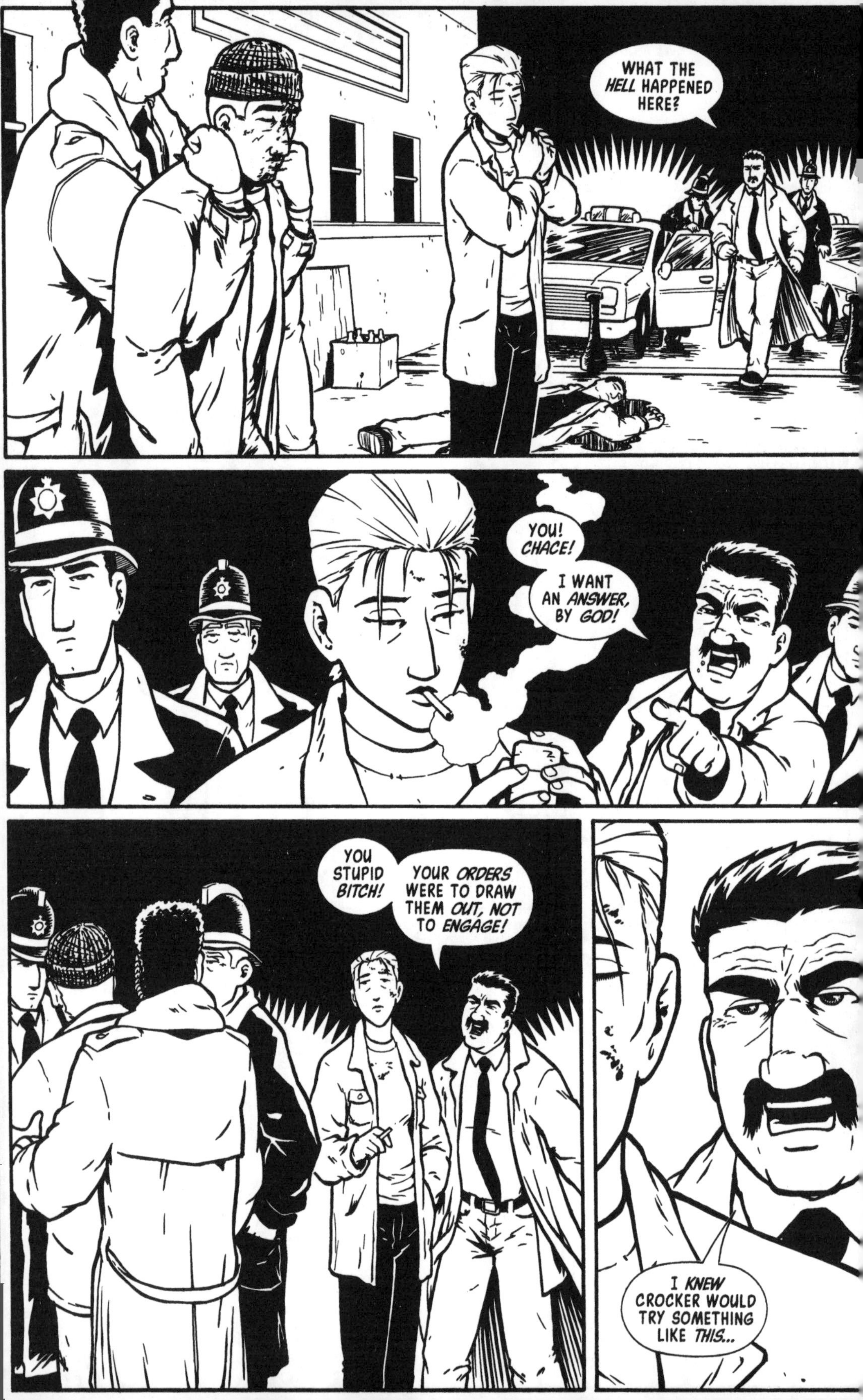
WHAT THE *HELL* HAPPENED HERE?
YOU! *CHACE!*
I WANT AN *ANSWER,* BY *GOD!*
YOU STUPID *BITCH!*
YOUR *ORDERS* WERE TO DRAW THEM *OUT,* NOT TO *ENGAGE!*
I *KNEW* CROCKER WOULD TRY SOMETHING LIKE *THIS...*

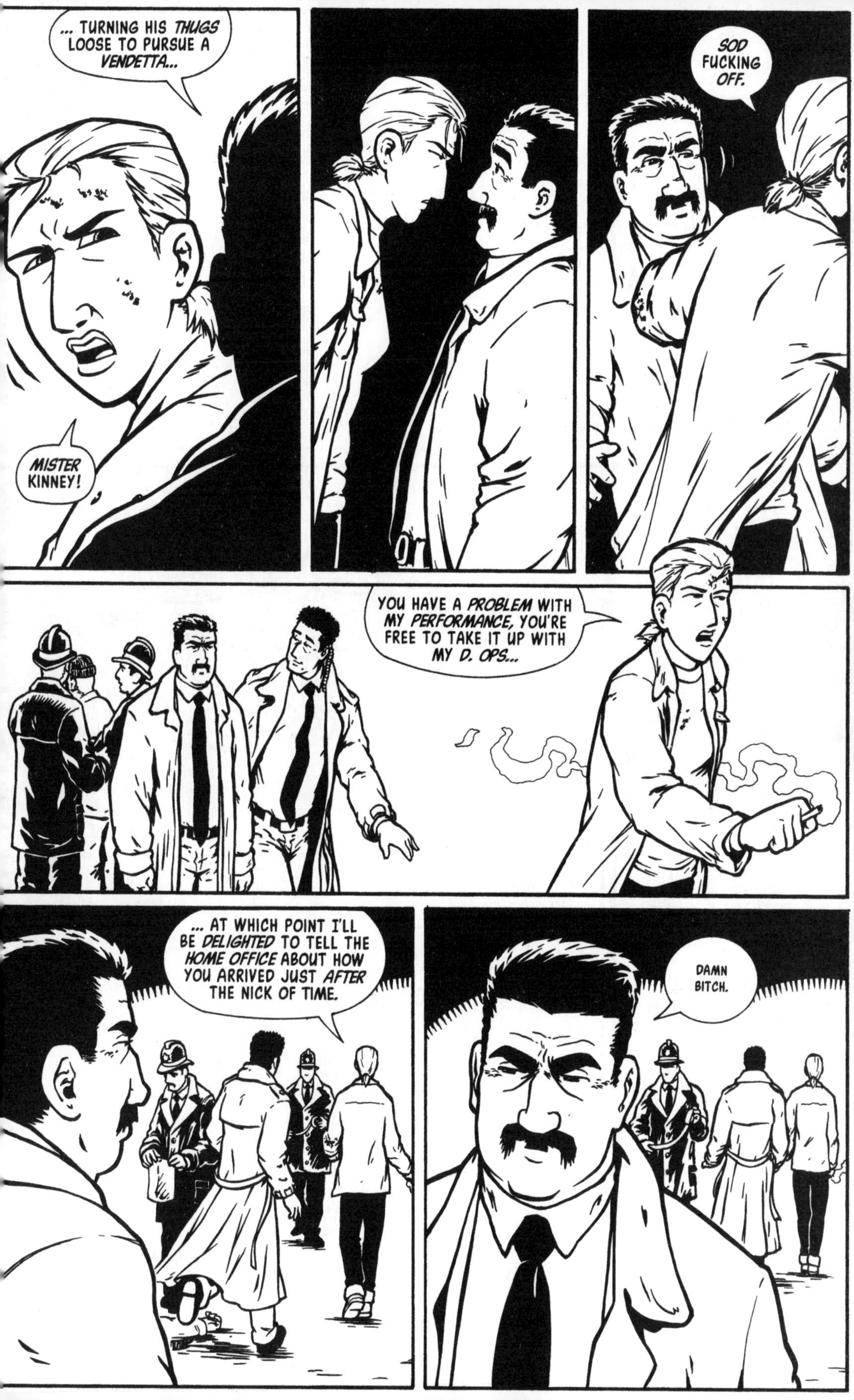
... TURNING HIS THUGS LOOSE TO PURSUE A VENDETTA...
MISTER KINNEY!
SOD FUCKING OFF.
YOU HAVE A PROBLEM WITH MY PERFORMANCE, YOU'RE FREE TO TAKE IT UP WITH MY D. OPS...
... AT WHICH POINT I'LL BE DELIGHTED TO TELL THE HOME OFFICE ABOUT HOW YOU ARRIVED JUST AFTER THE NICK OF TIME.
DAMN BITCH.

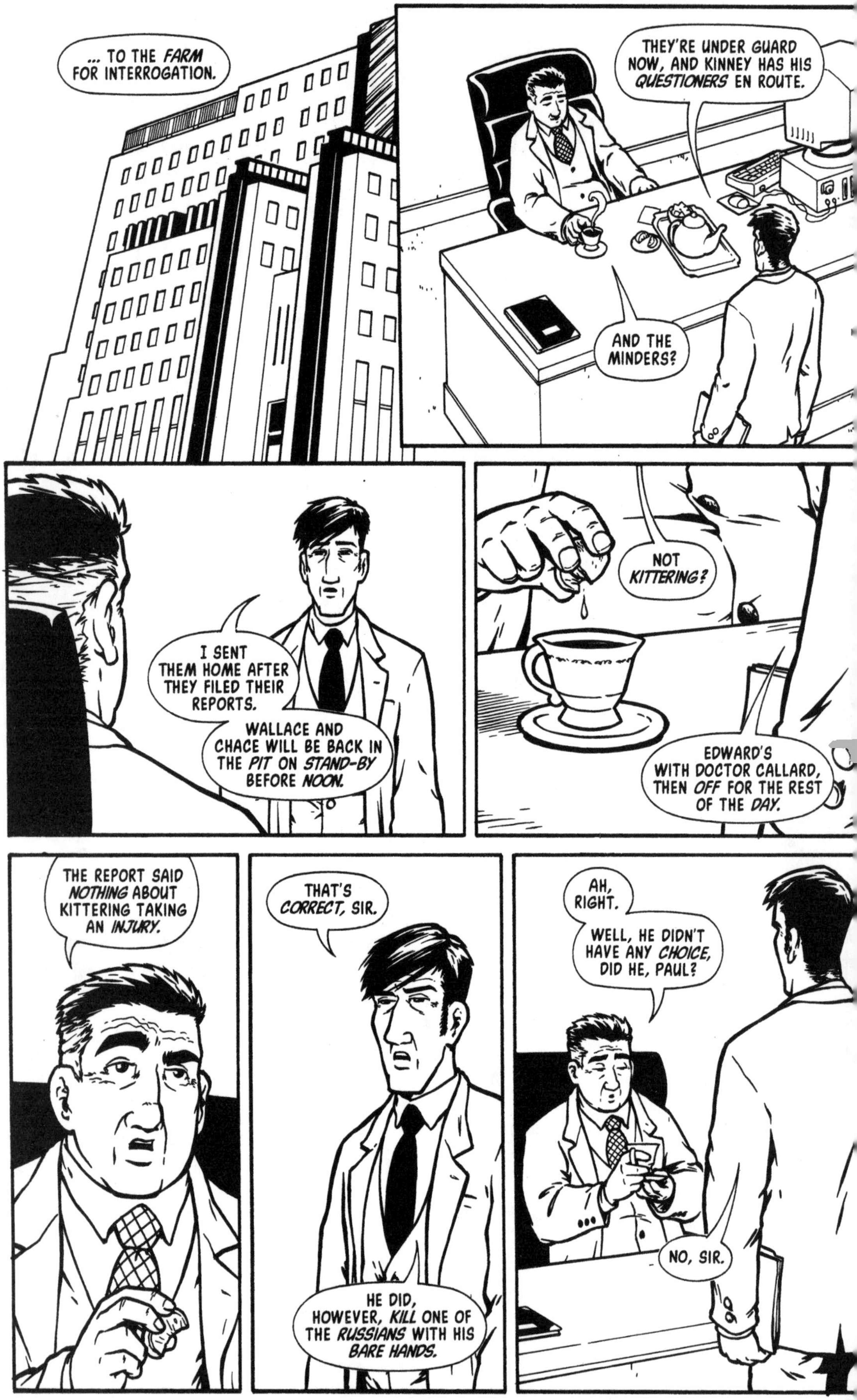
... TO THE FARM FOR INTERROGATION.
THEY'RE UNDER GUARD NOW, AND KINNEY HAS HIS QUESTIONERS EN ROUTE.
AND THE MINDERS?
I SENT THEM HOME AFTER THEY FILED THEIR REPORTS.
WALLACE AND CHACE WILL BE BACK IN THE PIT ON STAND-BY BEFORE NOON.
NOT KITTERING?
EDWARD'S WITH DOCTOR CALLARD, THEN OFF FOR THE REST OF THE DAY.
THE REPORT SAID NOTHING ABOUT KITTERING TAKING AN INJURY.
THAT'S CORRECT, SIR.
HE DID, HOWEVER, KILL ONE OF THE RUSSIANS WITH HIS BARE HANDS.
AH, RIGHT.
WELL, HE DIDN'T HAVE ANY CHOICE, DID HE, PAUL?
NO, SIR.

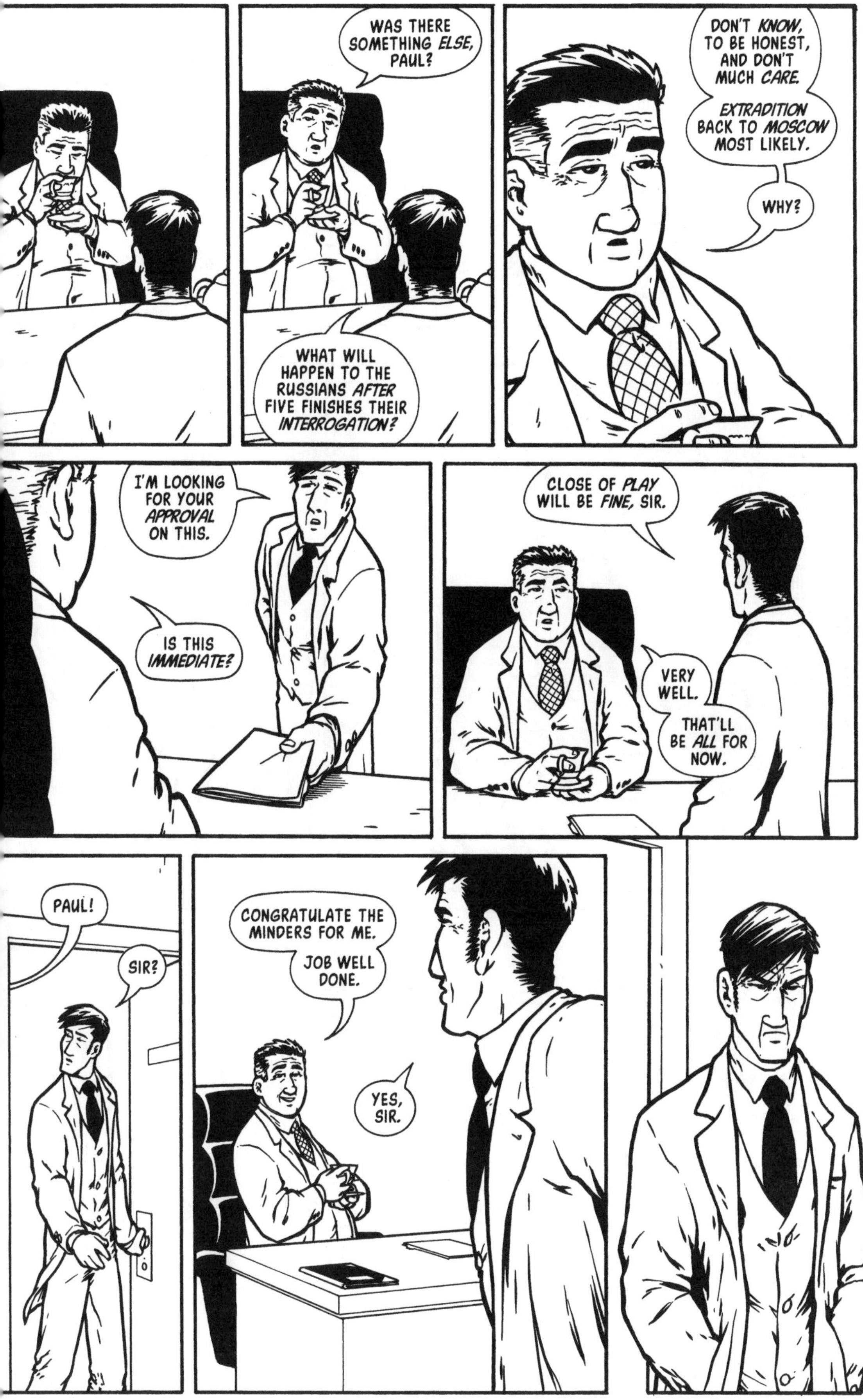
WAS THERE SOMETHING ELSE, PAUL?
WHAT WILL HAPPEN TO THE RUSSIANS AFTER FIVE FINISHES THEIR INTERROGATION?
DON'T KNOW, TO BE HONEST, AND DON'T MUCH CARE.
EXTRADITION BACK TO MOSCOW MOST LIKELY.
WHY?
I'M LOOKING FOR YOUR APPROVAL ON THIS.
IS THIS IMMEDIATE?
CLOSE OF PLAY WILL BE FINE, SIR.
VERY WELL.
THAT'LL BE ALL FOR NOW.
PAUL!
SIR?
CONGRATULATE THE MINDERS FOR ME.
JOB WELL DONE.
YES, SIR.

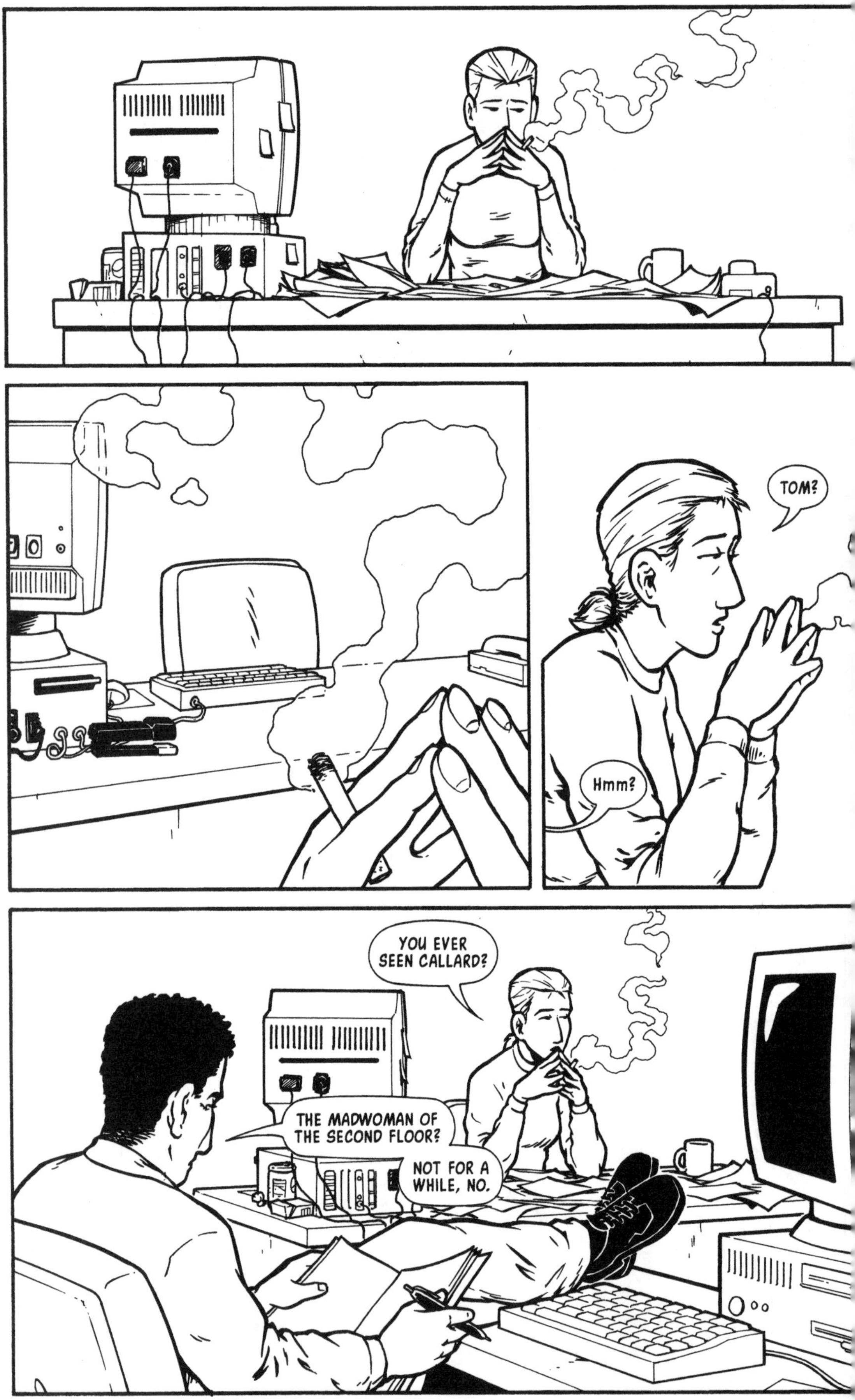
TOM?
Hmm?
YOU EVER SEEN CALLARD?
THE MADWOMAN OF THE SECOND FLOOR?
NOT FOR A WHILE, NO.

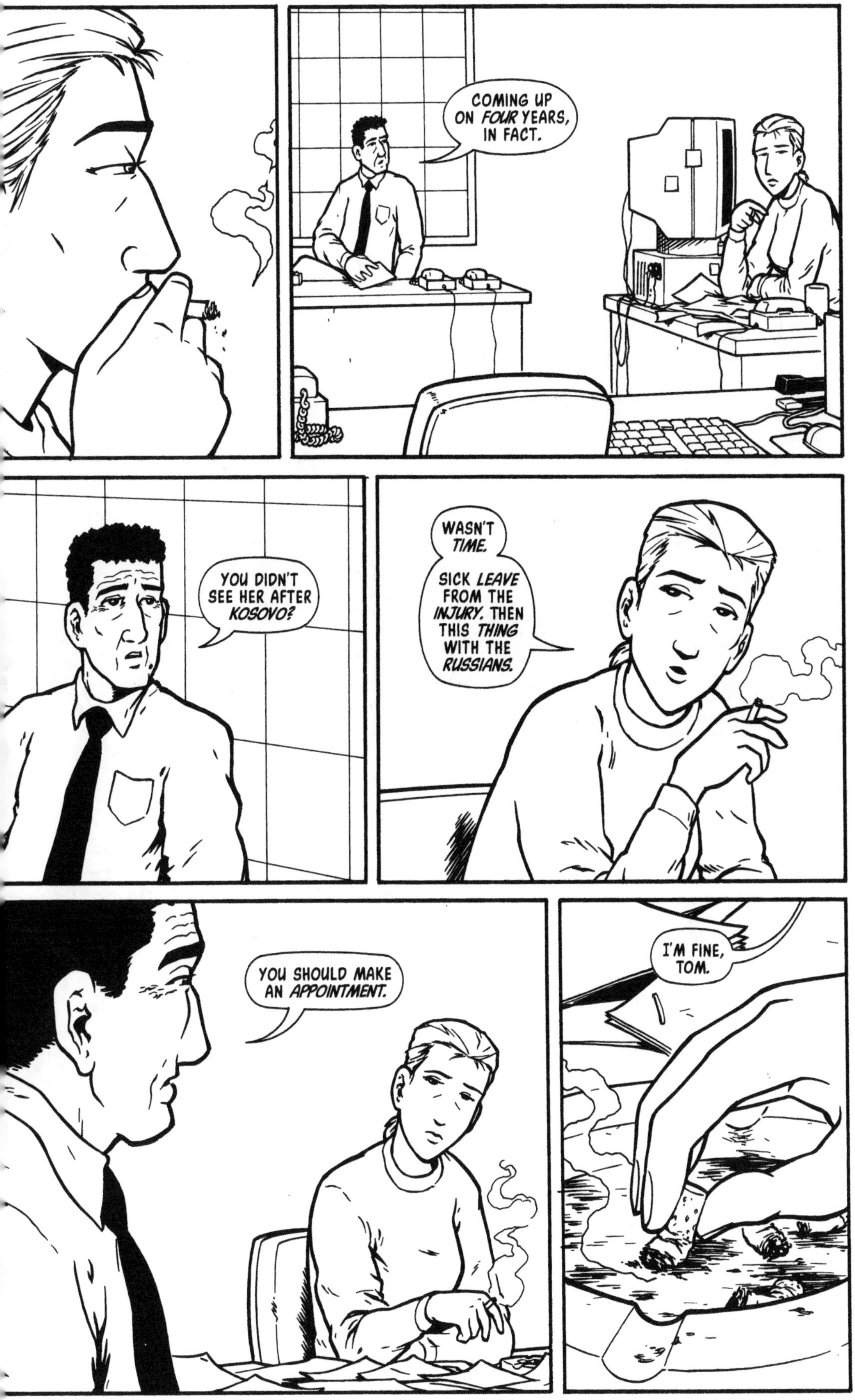
COMING UP ON FOUR YEARS, IN FACT.
YOU DIDN'T SEE HER AFTER KOSOVO?
WASN'T TIME.
SICK LEAVE FROM THE INJURY. THEN THIS THING WITH THE RUSSIANS.
YOU SHOULD MAKE AN APPOINTMENT.
I'M FINE, TOM.

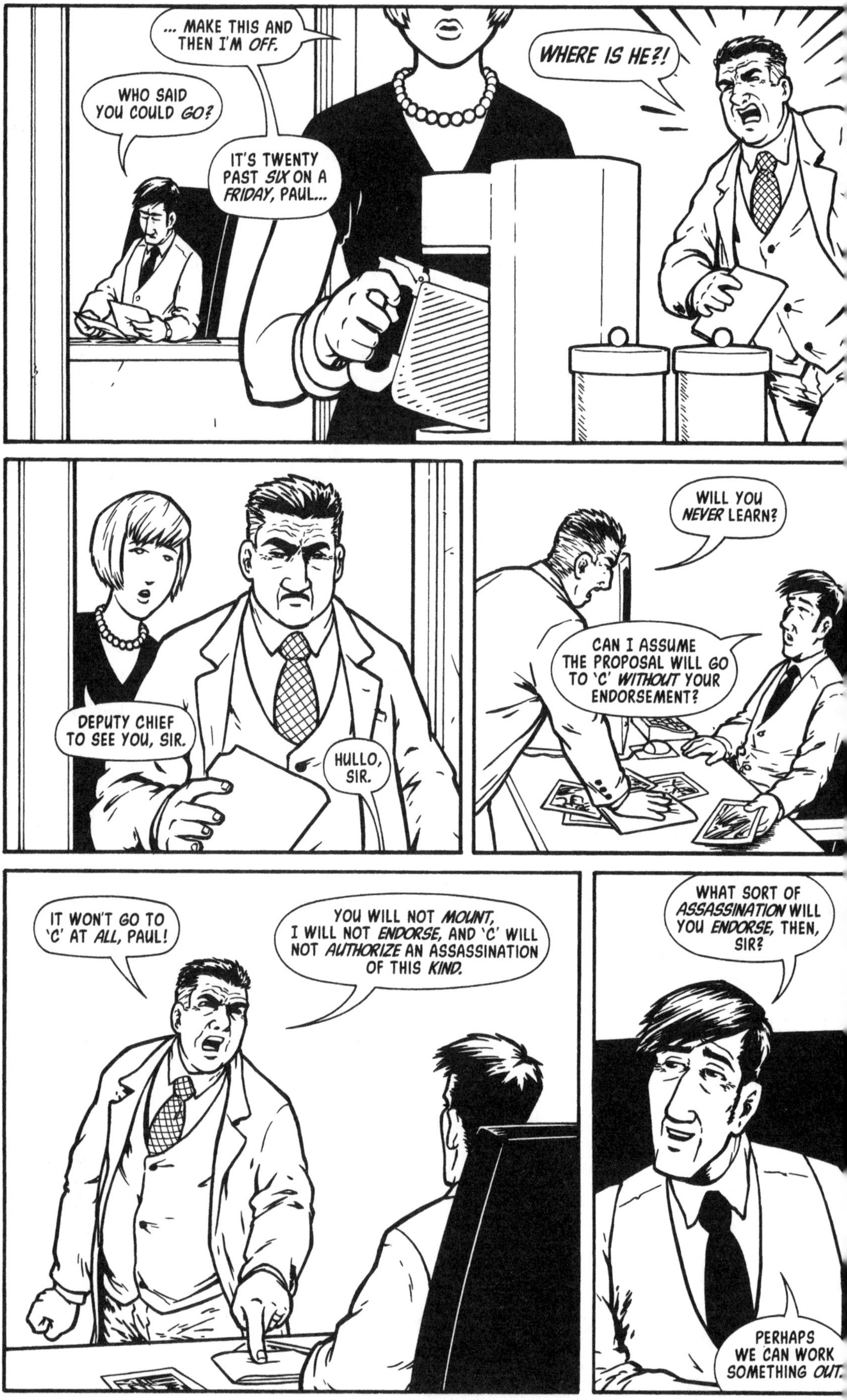
... MAKE THIS AND THEN I'M OFF.
WHO SAID YOU COULD GO?
IT'S TWENTY PAST SIX ON A FRIDAY, PAUL...
WHERE IS HE?!
DEPUTY CHIEF TO SEE YOU, SIR.
HULLO, SIR.
WILL YOU NEVER LEARN?
CAN I ASSUME THE PROPOSAL WILL GO TO 'C' WITHOUT YOUR ENDORSEMENT?
IT WON'T GO TO 'C' AT ALL, PAUL!
YOU WILL NOT MOUNT, I WILL NOT ENDORSE, AND 'C' WILL NOT AUTHORIZE AN ASSASSINATION OF THIS KIND.
WHAT SORT OF ASSASSINATION WILL YOU ENDORSE, THEN, SIR?
PERHAPS WE CAN WORK SOMETHING OUT.

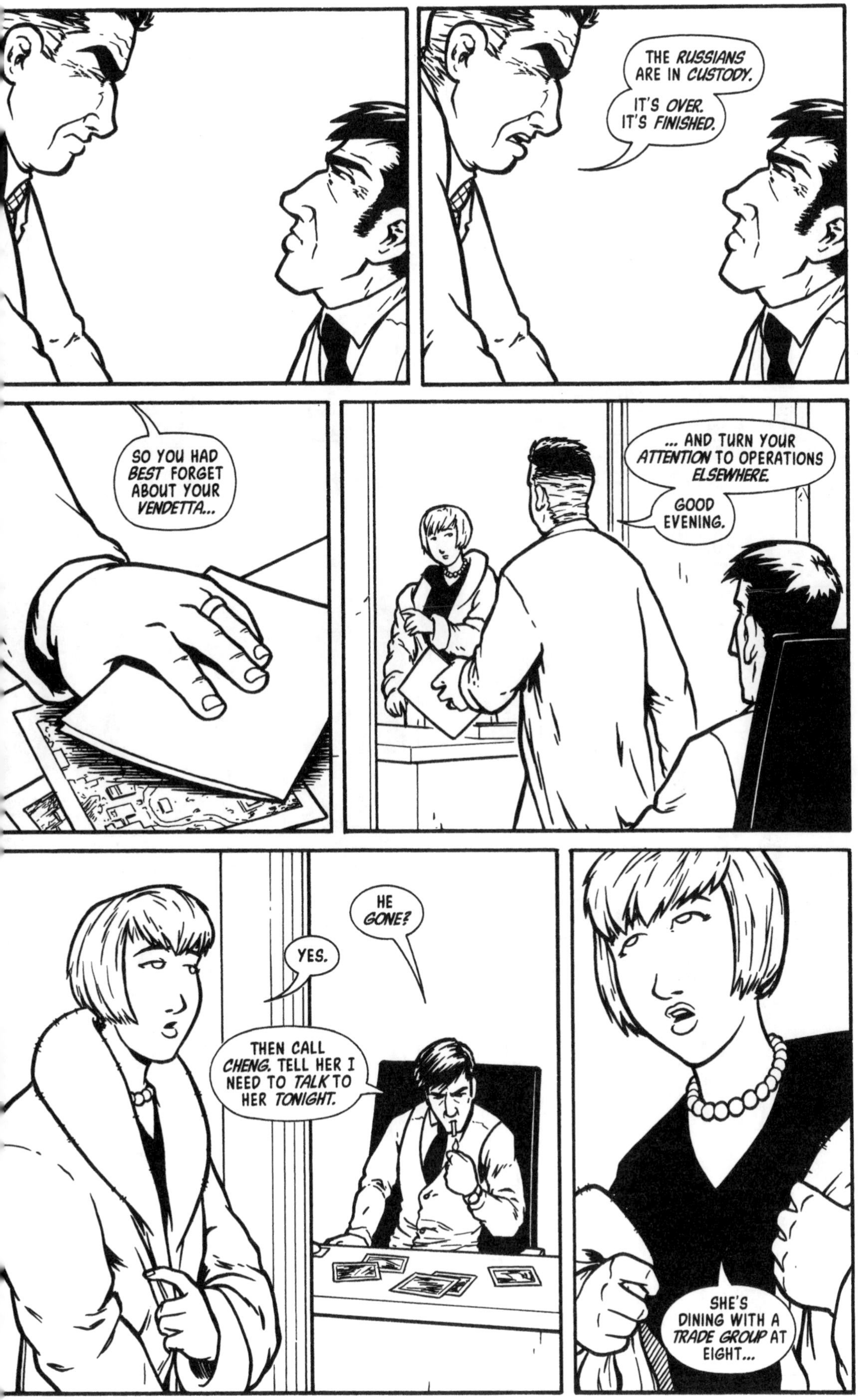
THE *RUSSIANS* ARE IN *CUSTODY*.
IT'S *OVER*. IT'S *FINISHED*.
SO YOU HAD *BEST* FORGET ABOUT YOUR *VENDETTA*...
... AND TURN YOUR *ATTENTION* TO OPERATIONS *ELSEWHERE*.
GOOD EVENING.
HE *GONE*?
YES.
THEN CALL *CHENG*. TELL HER I NEED TO *TALK* TO HER *TONIGHT*.
SHE'S DINING WITH A *TRADE GROUP* AT EIGHT...

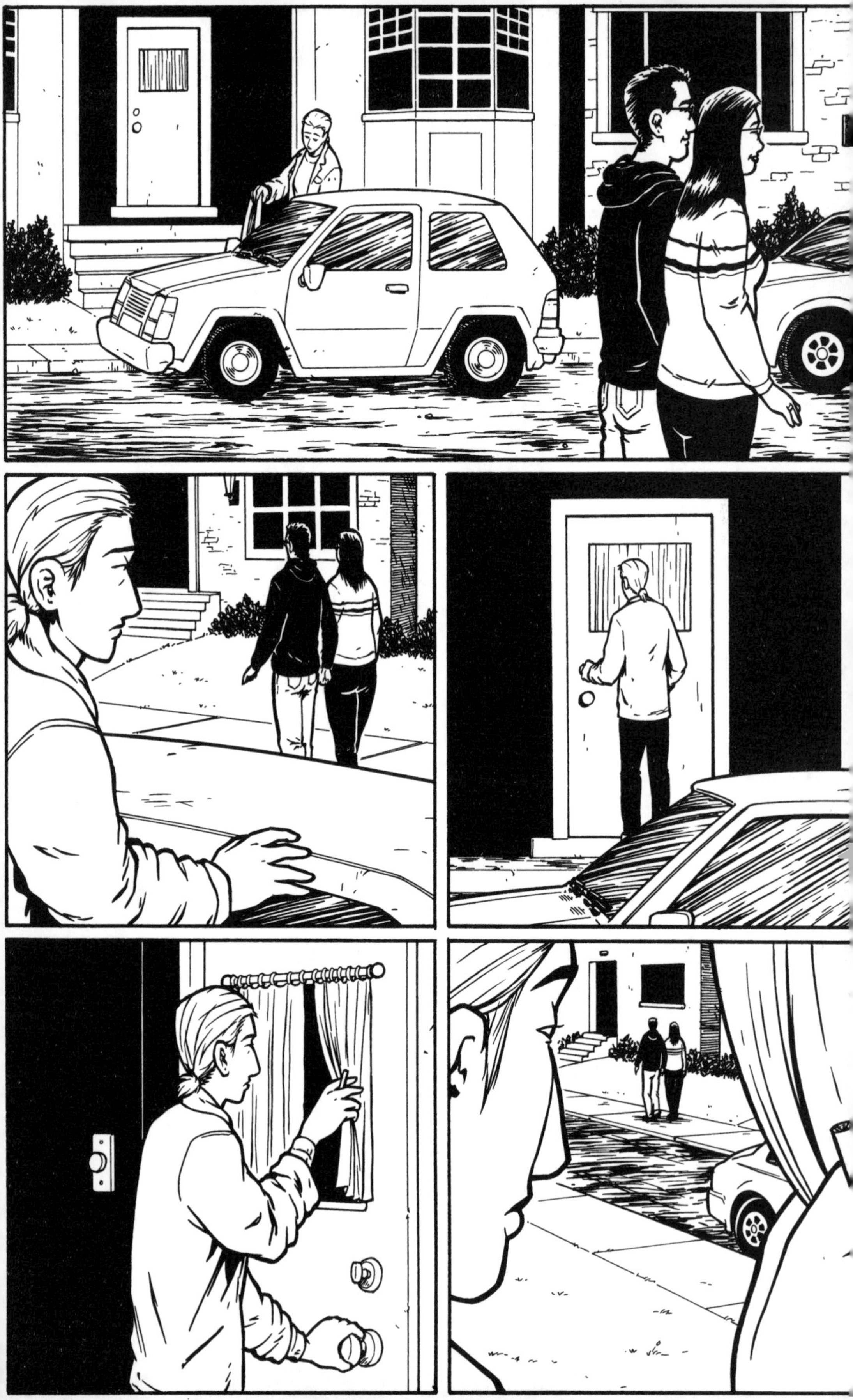

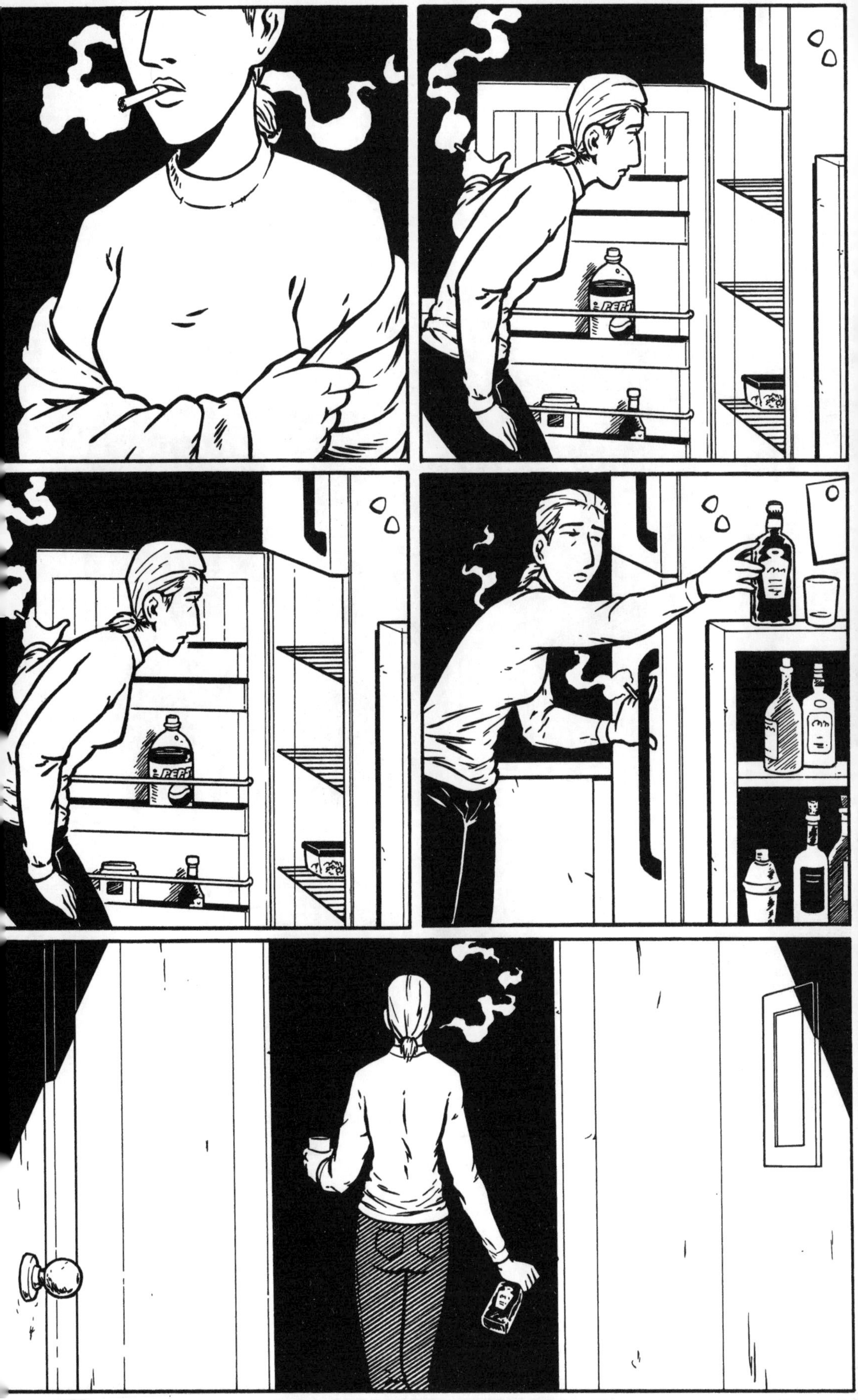

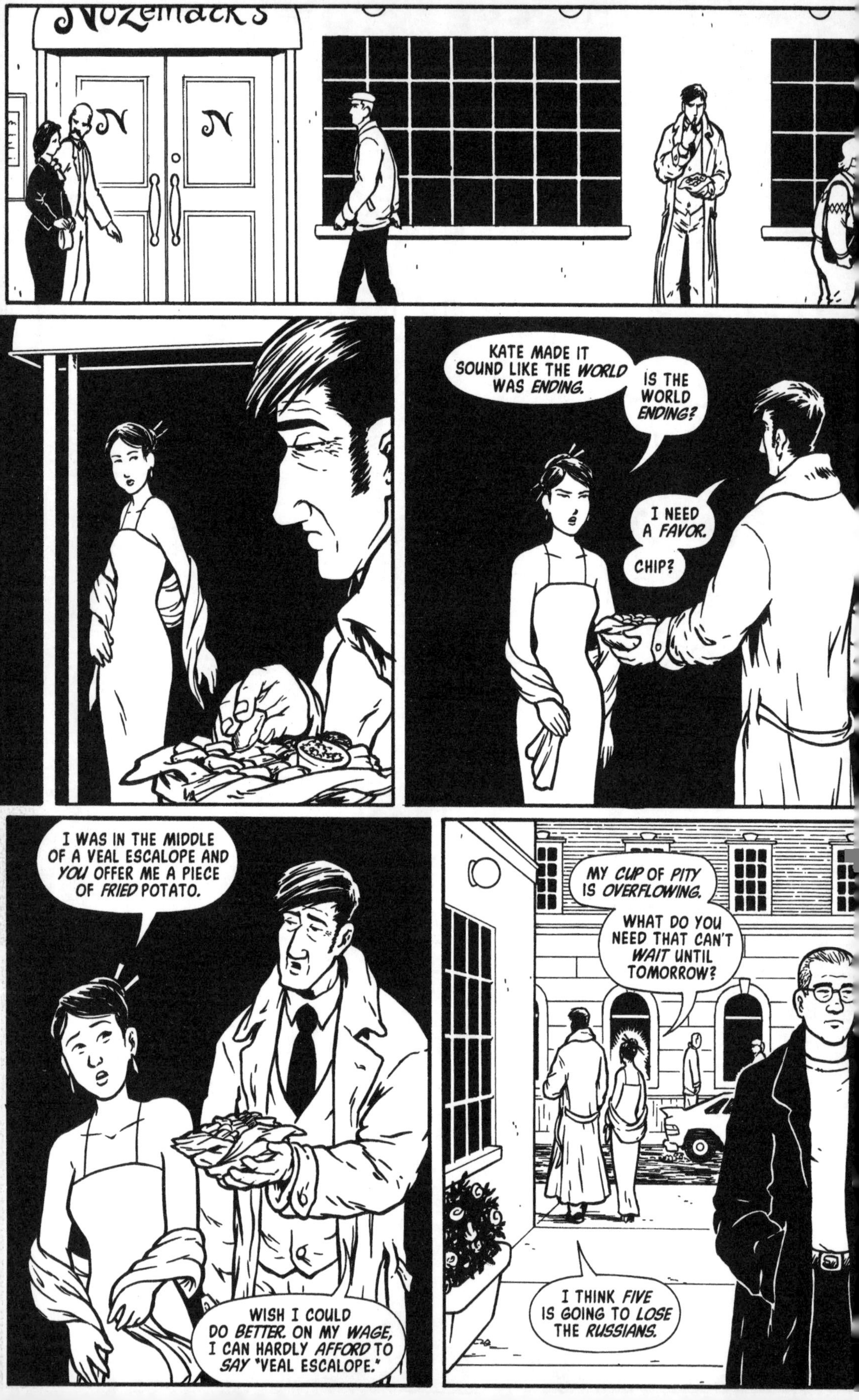
NOZEMACK'S
KATE MADE IT SOUND LIKE THE *WORLD* WAS *ENDING.*
IS THE WORLD *ENDING?*
I NEED A *FAVOR.*
CHIP?
I WAS IN THE MIDDLE OF A VEAL ESCALOPE AND *YOU* OFFER ME A PIECE OF *FRIED* POTATO.
WISH I COULD DO *BETTER.* ON MY *WAGE,* I CAN HARDLY *AFFORD* TO *SAY* "VEAL ESCALOPE."
MY *CUP* OF *PITY* IS *OVERFLOWING.*
WHAT DO YOU NEED THAT CAN'T *WAIT* UNTIL TOMORROW?
I THINK *FIVE* IS GOING TO *LOSE* THE *RUSSIANS.*

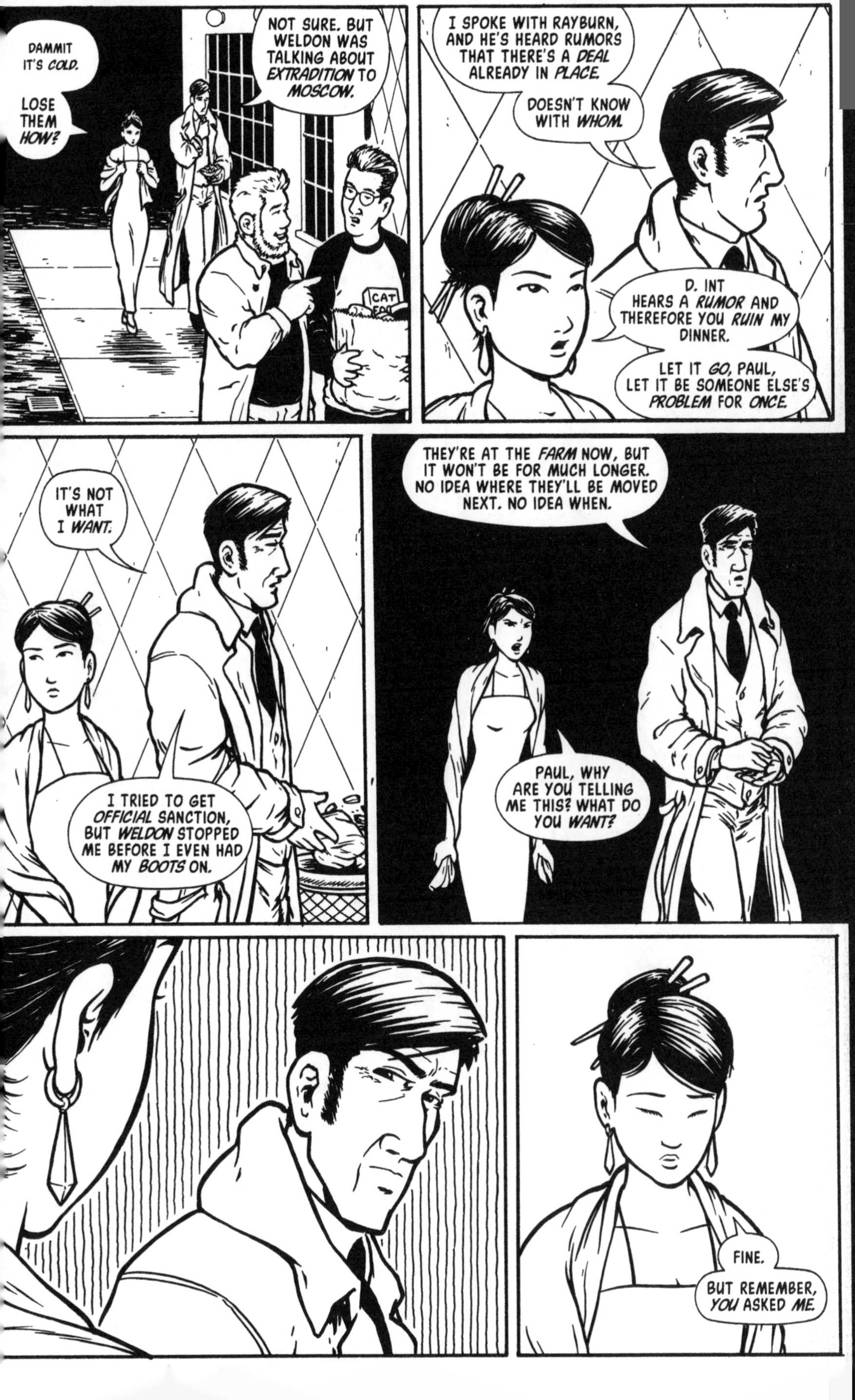
DAMMIT IT'S COLD.
LOSE THEM HOW?
NOT SURE. BUT WELDON WAS TALKING ABOUT EXTRADITION TO MOSCOW.
CAT FOOD
I SPOKE WITH RAYBURN, AND HE'S HEARD RUMORS THAT THERE'S A DEAL ALREADY IN PLACE.
DOESN'T KNOW WITH WHOM.
D. INT HEARS A RUMOR AND THEREFORE YOU RUIN MY DINNER.
LET IT GO, PAUL, LET IT BE SOMEONE ELSE'S PROBLEM FOR ONCE.
IT'S NOT WHAT I WANT.
I TRIED TO GET OFFICIAL SANCTION, BUT WELDON STOPPED ME BEFORE I EVEN HAD MY BOOTS ON.
THEY'RE AT THE FARM NOW, BUT IT WON'T BE FOR MUCH LONGER. NO IDEA WHERE THEY'LL BE MOVED NEXT. NO IDEA WHEN.
PAUL, WHY ARE YOU TELLING ME THIS? WHAT DO YOU WANT?
FINE.
BUT REMEMBER, YOU ASKED ME.

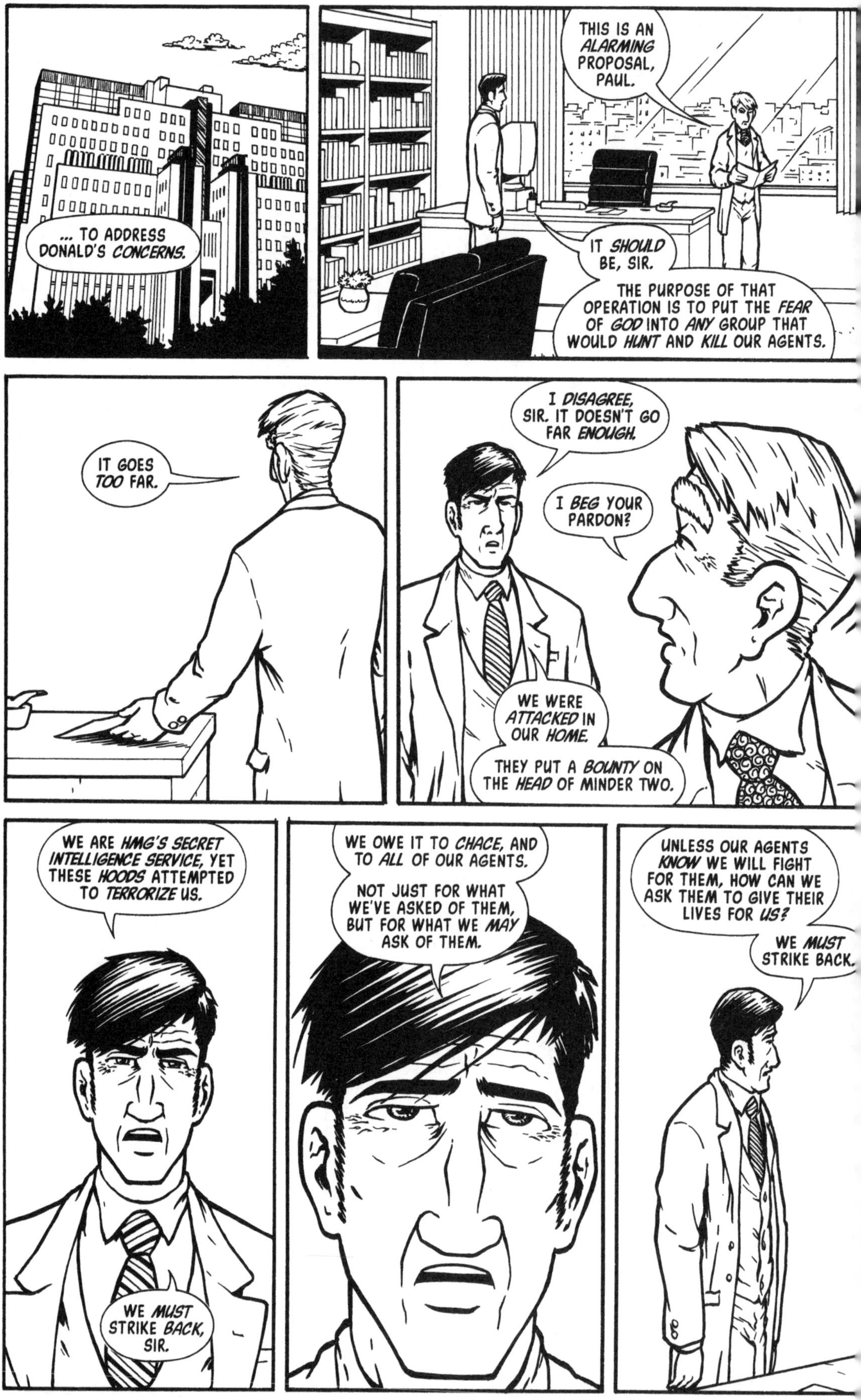
... TO ADDRESS DONALD'S CONCERNS.
THIS IS AN ALARMING PROPOSAL, PAUL.
IT SHOULD BE, SIR.
THE PURPOSE OF THAT OPERATION IS TO PUT THE FEAR OF GOD INTO ANY GROUP THAT WOULD HUNT AND KILL OUR AGENTS.
IT GOES TOO FAR.
I DISAGREE, SIR. IT DOESN'T GO FAR ENOUGH.
I BEG YOUR PARDON?
WE WERE ATTACKED IN OUR HOME.
THEY PUT A BOUNTY ON THE HEAD OF MINDER TWO.
WE ARE HMG'S SECRET INTELLIGENCE SERVICE, YET THESE HOODS ATTEMPTED TO TERRORIZE US.
WE MUST STRIKE BACK, SIR.
WE OWE IT TO CHACE, AND TO ALL OF OUR AGENTS.
NOT JUST FOR WHAT WE'VE ASKED OF THEM, BUT FOR WHAT WE MAY ASK OF THEM.
UNLESS OUR AGENTS KNOW WE WILL FIGHT FOR THEM, HOW CAN WE ASK THEM TO GIVE THEIR LIVES FOR US?
WE MUST STRIKE BACK.

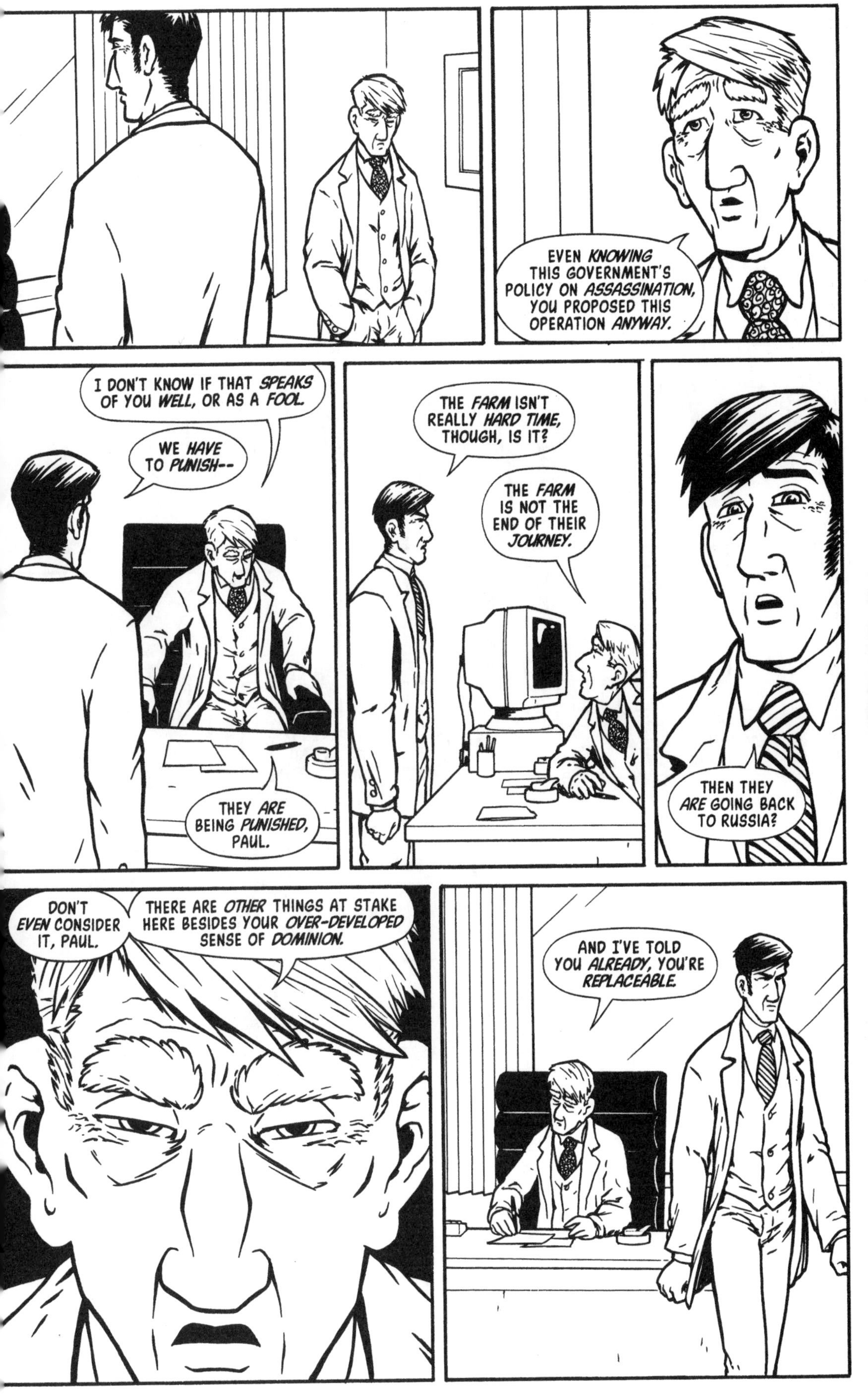
EVEN KNOWING THIS GOVERNMENT'S POLICY ON ASSASSINATION, YOU PROPOSED THIS OPERATION ANYWAY.
I DON'T KNOW IF THAT SPEAKS OF YOU WELL, OR AS A FOOL.
WE HAVE TO PUNISH--
THEY ARE BEING PUNISHED, PAUL.
THE FARM ISN'T REALLY HARD TIME, THOUGH, IS IT?
THE FARM IS NOT THE END OF THEIR JOURNEY.
THEN THEY ARE GOING BACK TO RUSSIA?
DON'T EVEN CONSIDER IT, PAUL.
THERE ARE OTHER THINGS AT STAKE HERE BESIDES YOUR OVER-DEVELOPED SENSE OF DOMINION.
AND I'VE TOLD YOU ALREADY, YOU'RE REPLACEABLE.

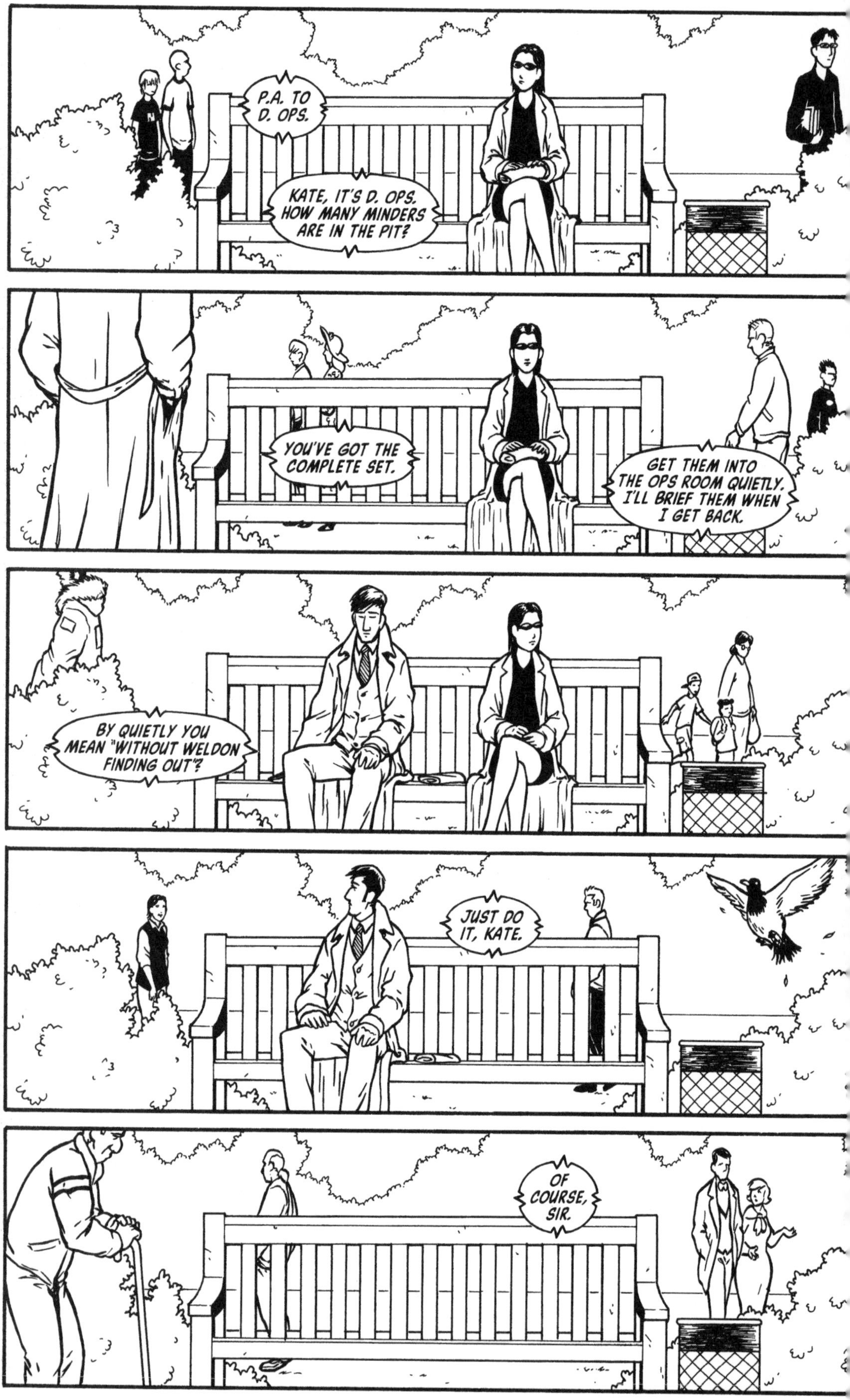
P.A. TO D. OPS.
KATE, IT'S D. OPS. HOW MANY MINDERS ARE IN THE PIT?
YOU'VE GOT THE COMPLETE SET.
GET THEM INTO THE OPS ROOM QUIETLY. I'LL BRIEF THEM WHEN I GET BACK.
BY QUIETLY YOU MEAN "WITHOUT WELDON FINDING OUT"?
JUST DO IT, KATE.
OF COURSE, SIR.

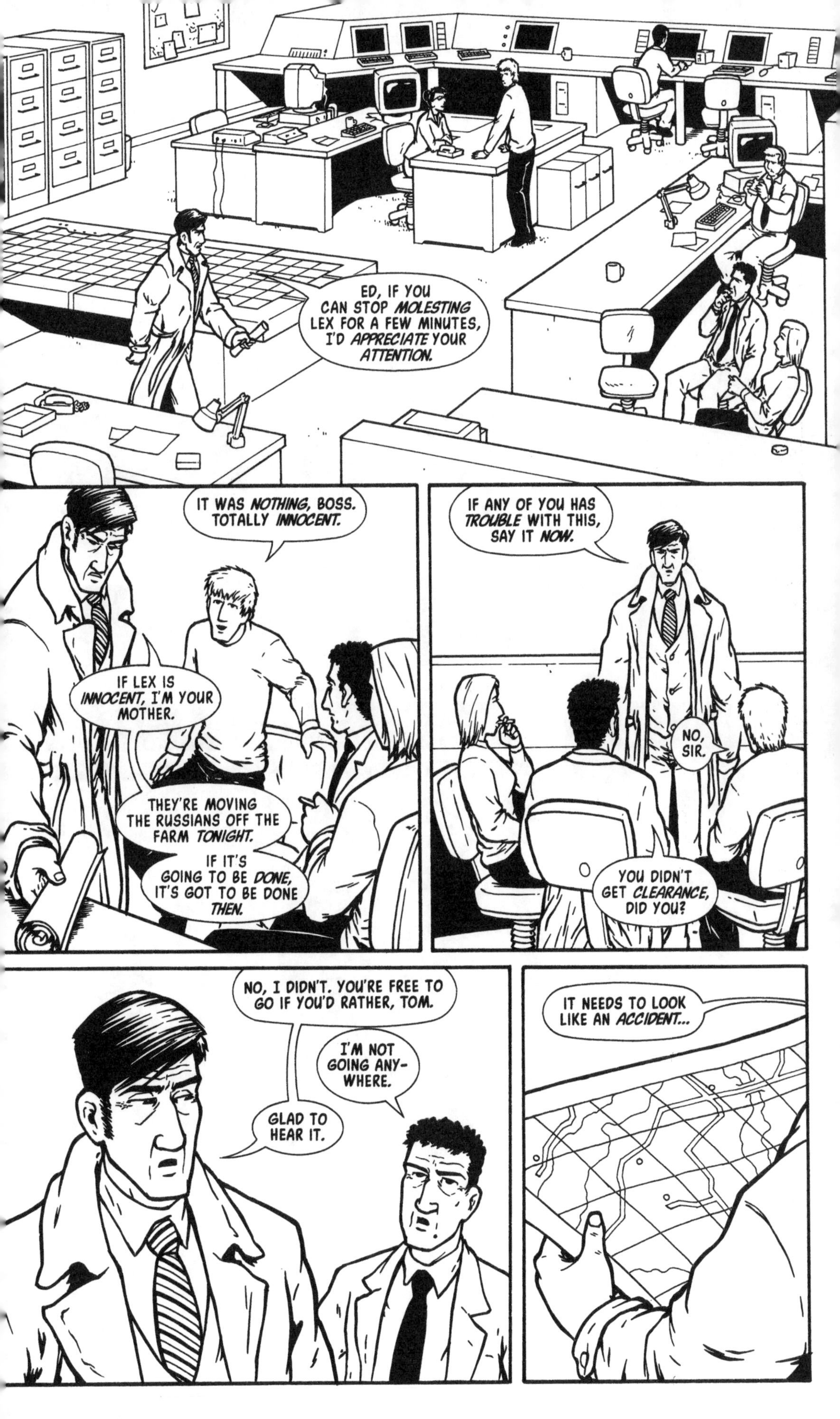
ED, IF YOU CAN STOP *MOLESTING* LEX FOR A FEW MINUTES, I'D *APPRECIATE* YOUR *ATTENTION.*
IT WAS *NOTHING*, BOSS. TOTALLY *INNOCENT.*
IF LEX IS *INNOCENT*, I'M YOUR MOTHER.
THEY'RE *MOVING* THE RUSSIANS OFF THE FARM *TONIGHT.*
IF IT'S GOING TO BE *DONE*, IT'S GOT TO BE DONE *THEN.*
IF ANY OF YOU HAS *TROUBLE* WITH THIS, SAY IT *NOW.*
NO, SIR.
YOU DIDN'T GET *CLEARANCE*, DID YOU?
NO, I DIDN'T. YOU'RE FREE TO GO IF YOU'D RATHER, TOM.
I'M NOT GOING ANY-WHERE.
GLAD TO HEAR IT.
IT NEEDS TO LOOK LIKE AN *ACCIDENT...*

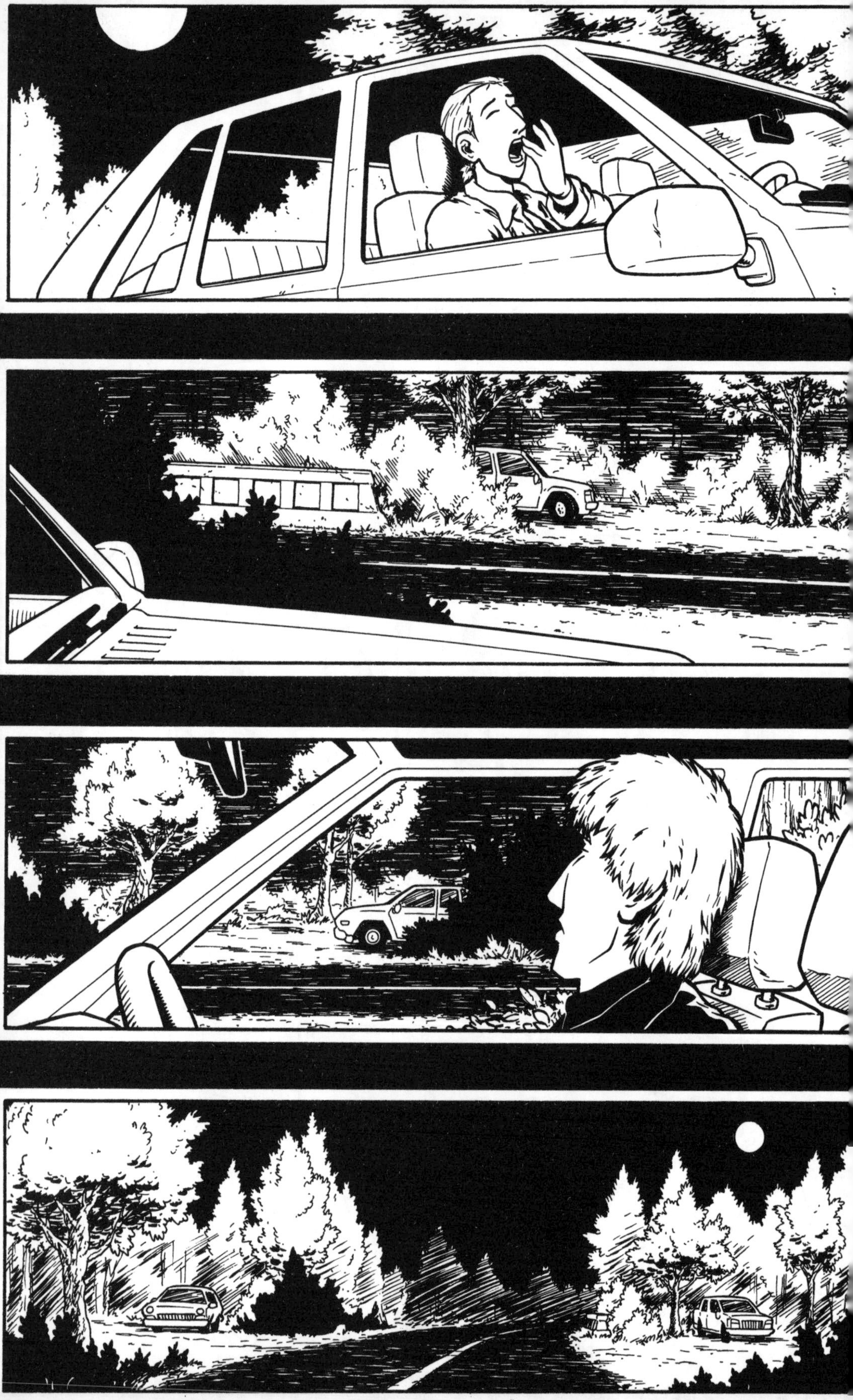

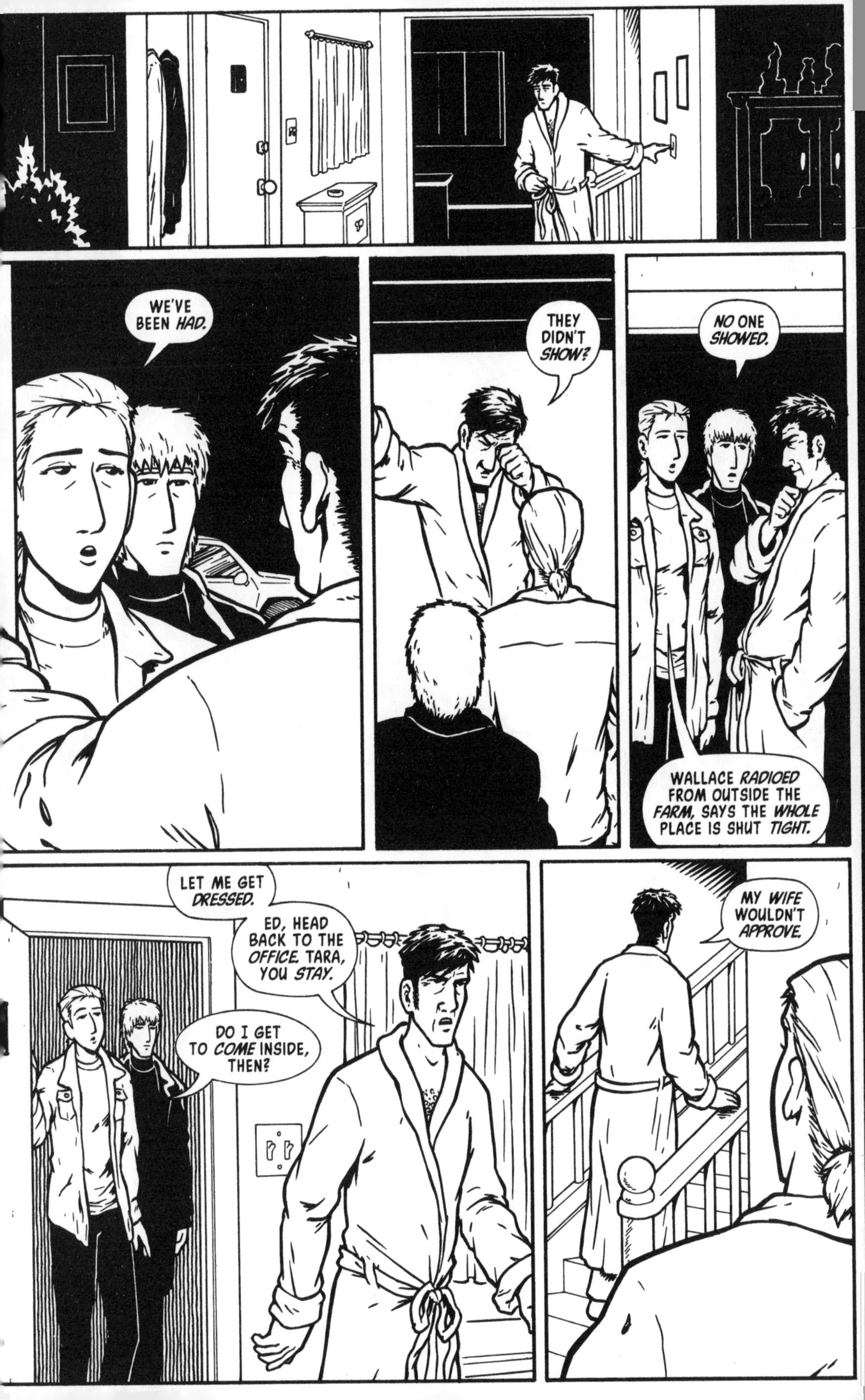

WE'VE BEEN *HAD.*
THEY DIDN'T *SHOW?*
NO ONE SHOWED.
WALLACE *RADIOED* FROM OUTSIDE THE *FARM,* SAYS THE *WHOLE* PLACE IS SHUT *TIGHT.*
LET ME GET *DRESSED.*
ED, HEAD BACK TO THE *OFFICE.* TARA, YOU *STAY.*
DO I GET TO *COME* INSIDE, THEN?
MY *WIFE* WOULDN'T *APPROVE.*

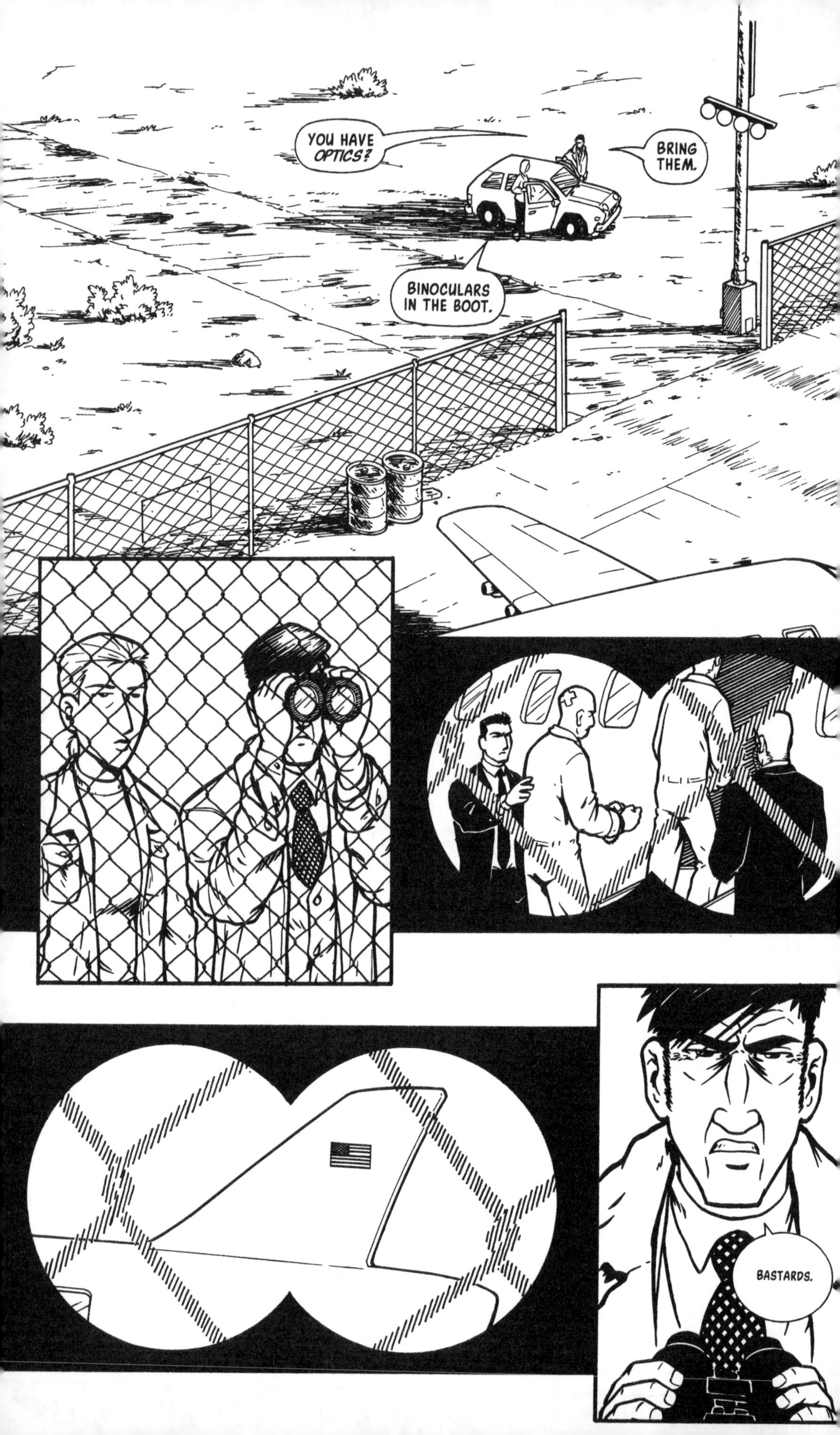
YOU HAVE OPTICS?
BRING THEM.
BINOCULARS IN THE BOOT.
BASTARDS.

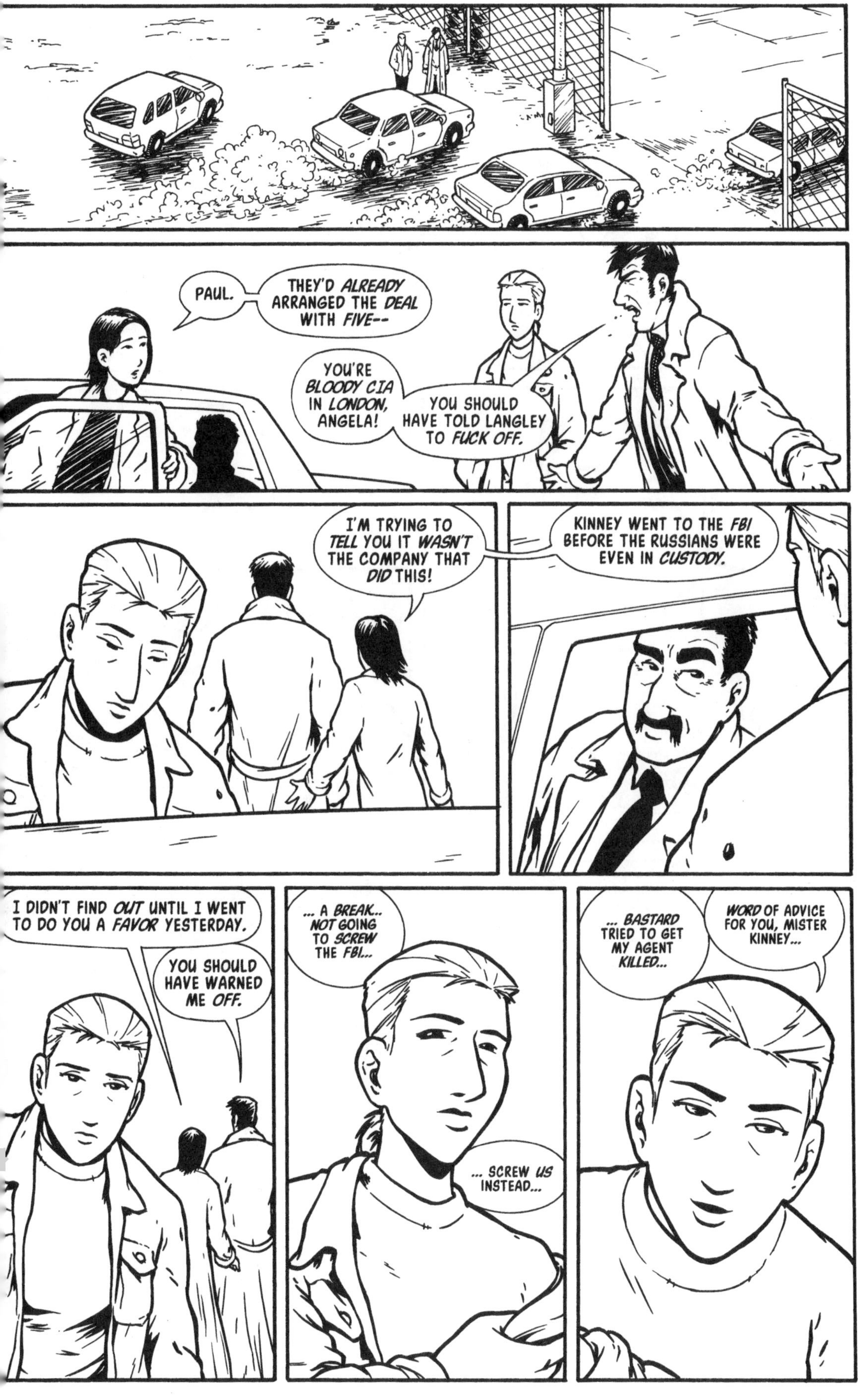
PAUL.
THEY'D *ALREADY* ARRANGED THE *DEAL* WITH *FIVE*--
YOU'RE *BLOODY CIA* IN *LONDON*, ANGELA!
YOU SHOULD HAVE TOLD LANGLEY TO *FUCK OFF.*
I'M TRYING TO *TELL* YOU IT *WASN'T* THE COMPANY THAT *DID* THIS!
KINNEY WENT TO THE *FBI* BEFORE THE RUSSIANS WERE EVEN IN *CUSTODY.*
I DIDN'T FIND *OUT* UNTIL I WENT TO DO YOU A *FAVOR* YESTERDAY.
YOU SHOULD HAVE WARNED ME *OFF.*
... A *BREAK*... *NOT* GOING TO *SCREW* THE *FBI*...
... SCREW *US* INSTEAD...
... *BASTARD* TRIED TO GET MY AGENT *KILLED*...
WORD OF ADVICE FOR YOU, MISTER KINNEY...

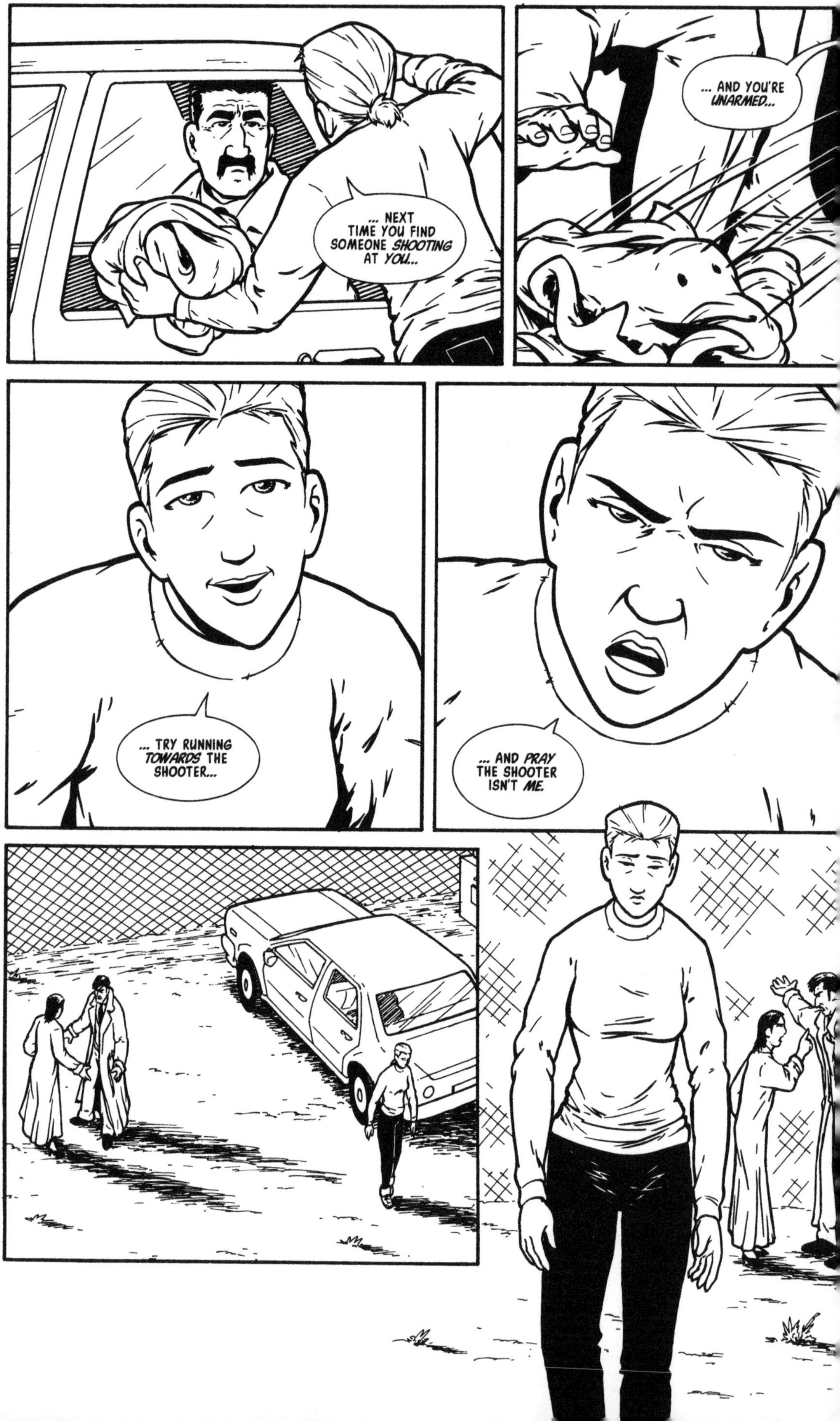
... NEXT TIME YOU FIND SOMEONE *SHOOTING* AT *YOU*...
... AND YOU'RE *UNARMED*...
... TRY RUNNING *TOWARDS* THE SHOOTER...
... AND *PRAY* THE SHOOTER ISN'T *ME*.

STAN SAKAI

The following short story is intended to take place between Chapters 1 and 2 of this story arc.

The story's artist, Stan Sakai, is the Eisner Award-winning creator of USAGI YOJIMBO, published by Dark Horse Comics.

STAN SAKAI

The following short story is intended to take place between Chapters 1 and 2 of this story arc.

The story's artist, Stan Sakai, is the Eisner Award-winning creator of USAGI YOJIMBO, published by Dark Horse Comics. Gray tones by Tom Luth.

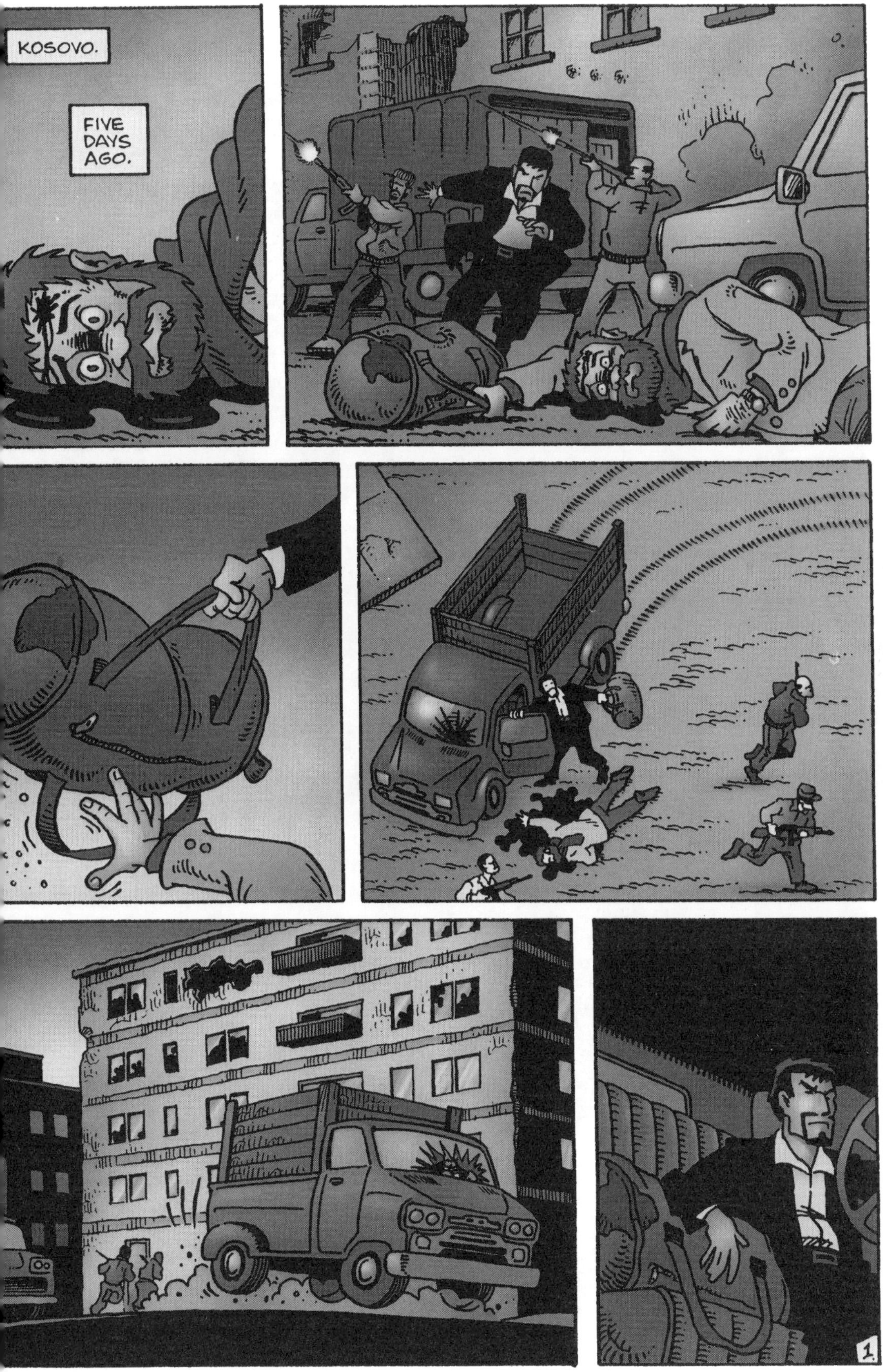
KOSOVO.
FIVE DAYS AGO.
1

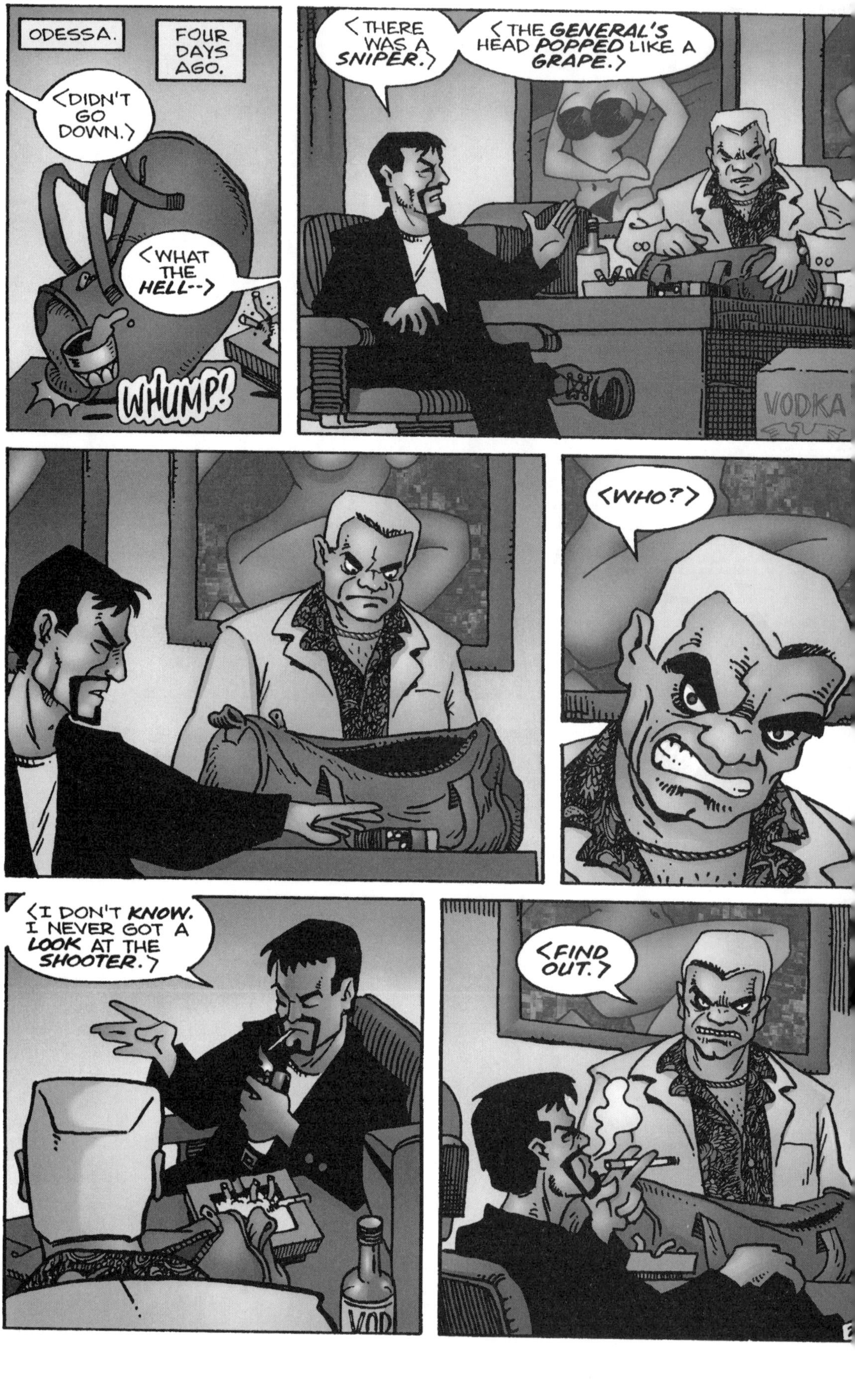
ODESSA.
FOUR DAYS AGO.
<DIDN'T GO DOWN.>
<WHAT THE HELL-->
WHUMP!
<THERE WAS A SNIPER.>
<THE GENERAL'S HEAD POPPED LIKE A GRAPE.>
VODKA
<WHO?>
<I DON'T KNOW. I NEVER GOT A LOOK AT THE SHOOTER.>
<FIND OUT.>

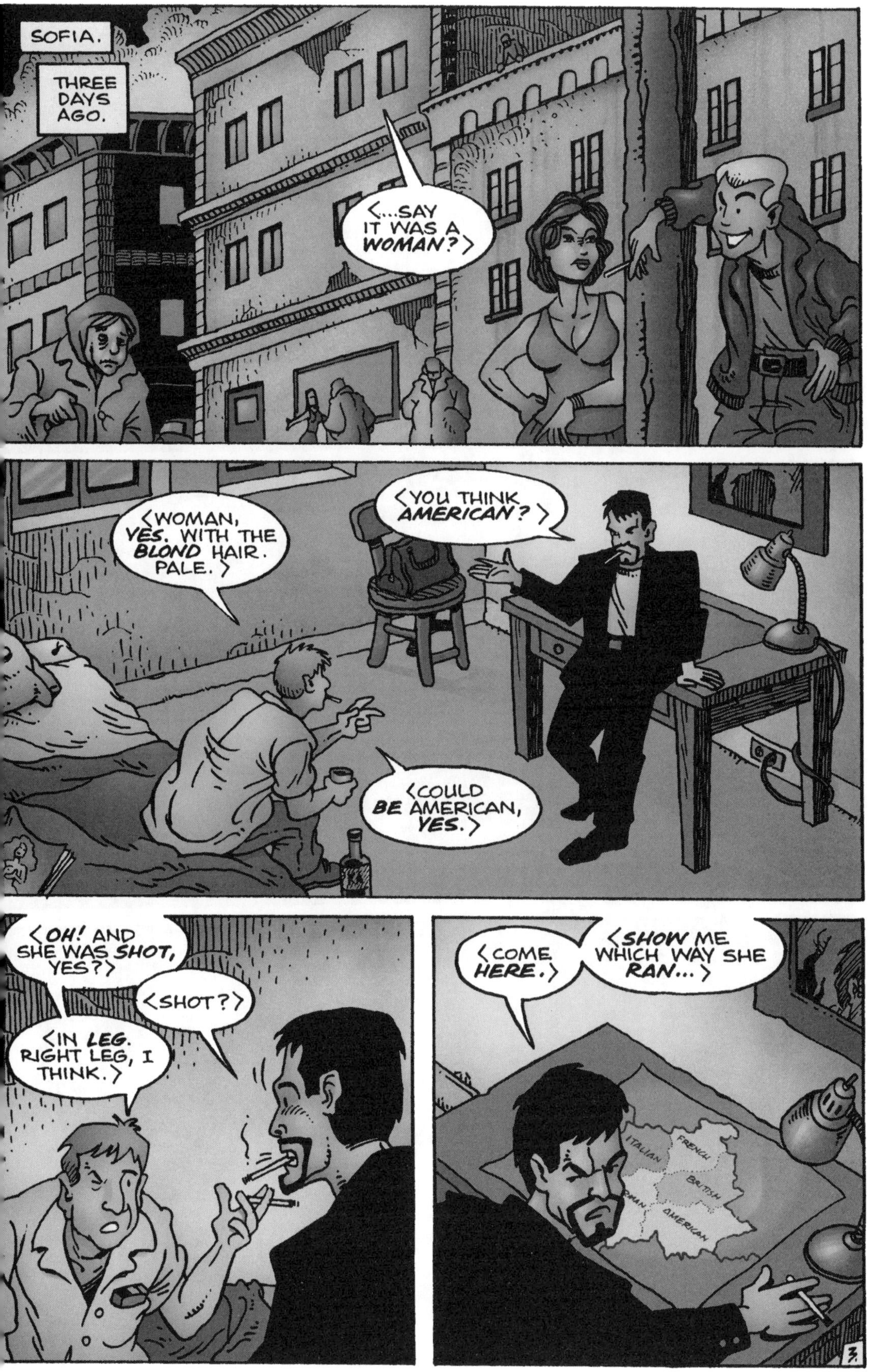
SOFIA.
THREE DAYS AGO.
<...SAY IT WAS A **WOMAN?**>
<WOMAN, **YES.** WITH THE **BLOND** HAIR. PALE.>
<YOU THINK **AMERICAN?**>
<COULD **BE** AMERICAN, **YES.**>
<**OH!** AND SHE WAS **SHOT,** YES?>
<SHOT?>
<IN **LEG.** RIGHT LEG, I THINK.>
<COME **HERE.**>
<**SHOW** ME WHICH WAY SHE **RAN...**>
ITALIAN
FRENCH
BRITISH
AMERICAN

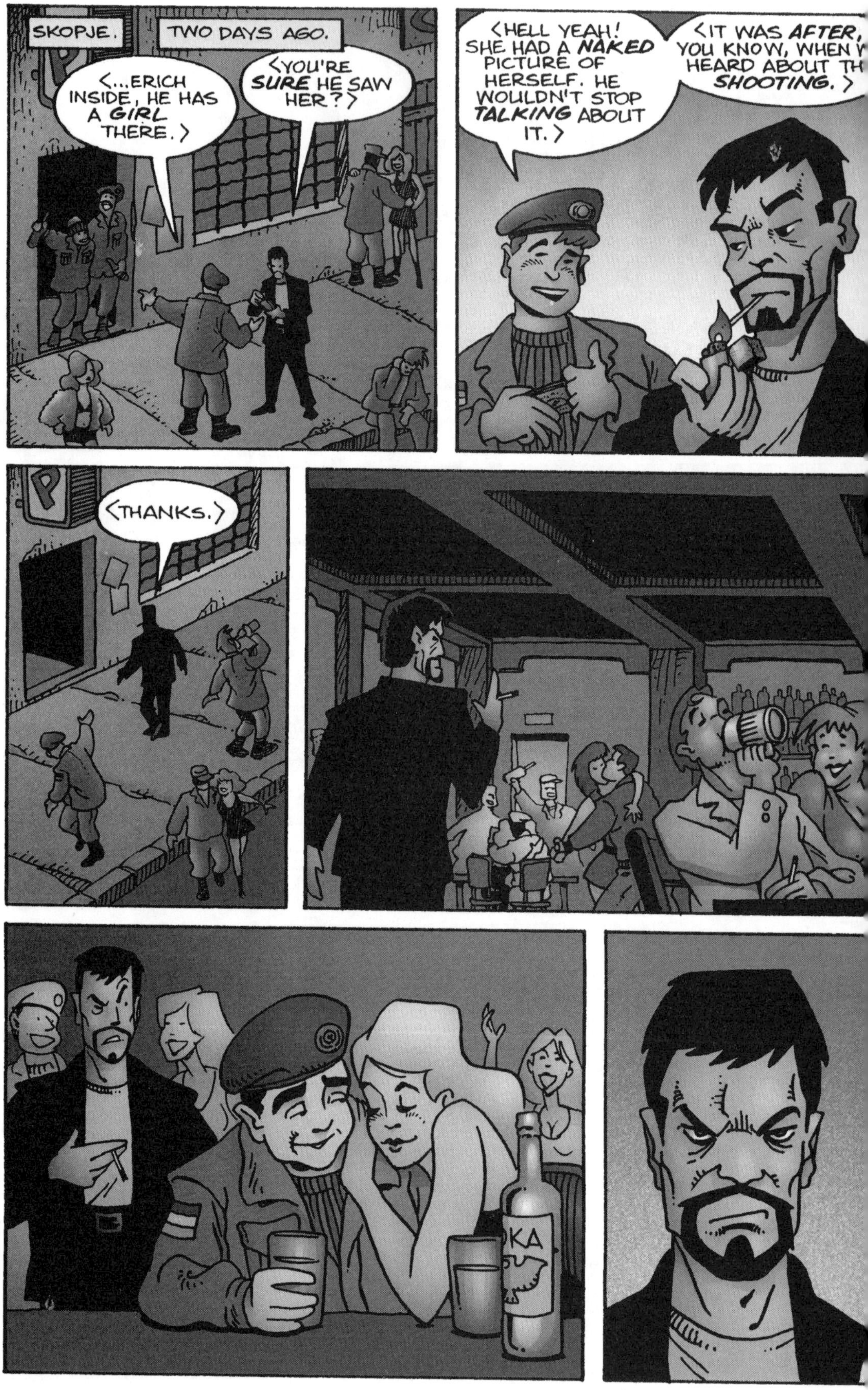
SKOPJE.
TWO DAYS AGO.
<...ERICH INSIDE, HE HAS A GIRL THERE.>
<YOU'RE SURE HE SAW HER?>
<HELL YEAH! SHE HAD A NAKED PICTURE OF HERSELF. HE WOULDN'T STOP TALKING ABOUT IT.>
<IT WAS AFTER, YOU KNOW, WHEN W HEARD ABOUT TH SHOOTING.>
<THANKS.>
KA

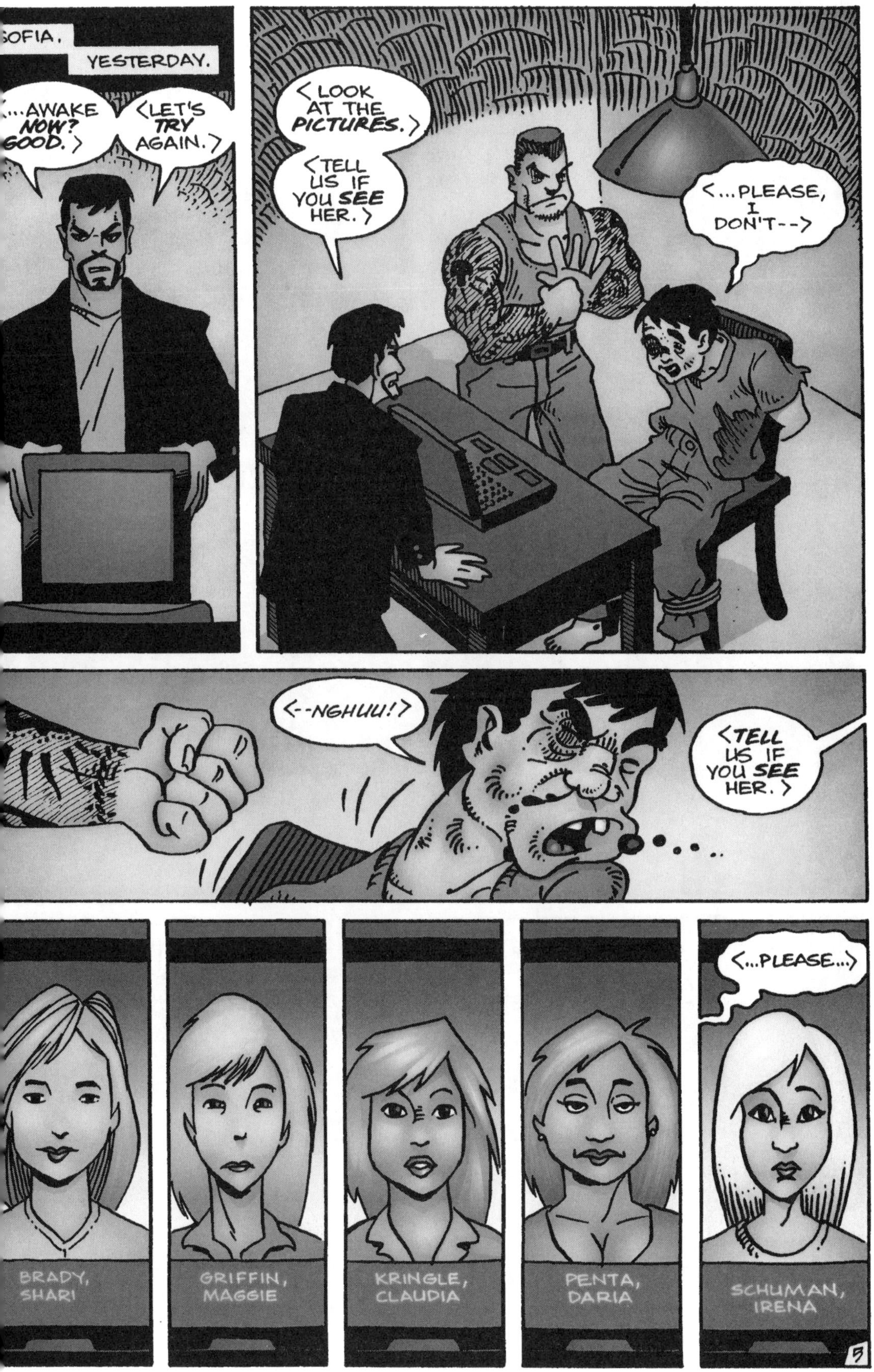
SOFIA.
YESTERDAY.
<...AWAKE NOW? GOOD.>
<LET'S TRY AGAIN.>
<LOOK AT THE PICTURES.>
<TELL US IF YOU SEE HER.>
<...PLEASE, I DON'T-->
<--NGHUU!>
<TELL US IF YOU SEE HER.>
<...PLEASE...>
BRADY, SHARI
GRIFFIN, MAGGIE
KRINGLE, CLAUDIA
PENTA, DARIA
SCHUMAN, IRENA

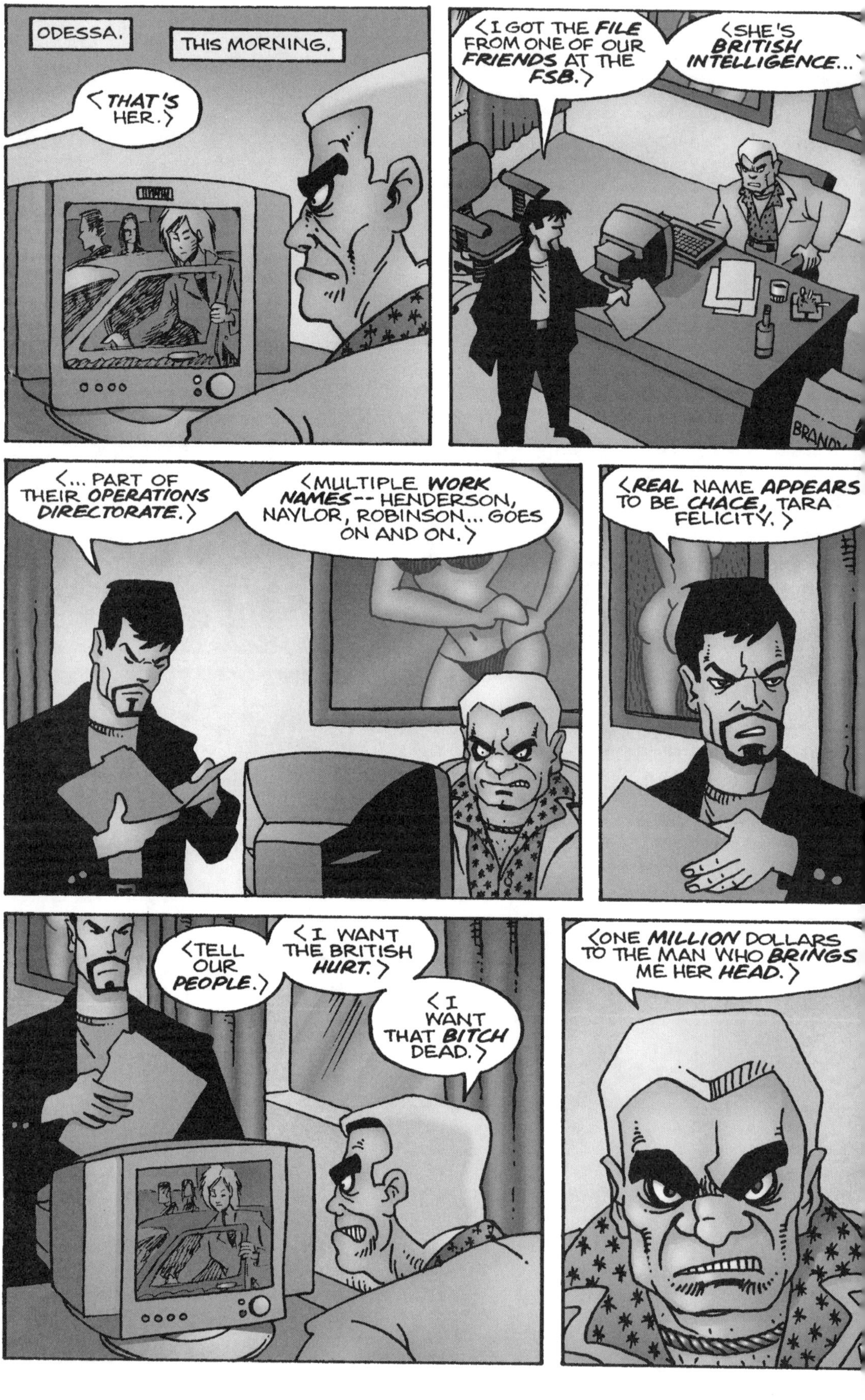
ODESSA.
THIS MORNING.
<THAT'S HER.>
<I GOT THE FILE FROM ONE OF OUR FRIENDS AT THE FSB.>
<SHE'S BRITISH INTELLIGENCE...>
<... PART OF THEIR OPERATIONS DIRECTORATE.>
<MULTIPLE WORK NAMES-- HENDERSON, NAYLOR, ROBINSON... GOES ON AND ON.>
<REAL NAME APPEARS TO BE CHACE, TARA FELICITY.>
<TELL OUR PEOPLE.>
<I WANT THE BRITISH HURT.>
<I WANT THAT BITCH DEAD.>
<ONE MILLION DOLLARS TO THE MAN WHO BRINGS ME HER HEAD.>

BASIC TRAINING

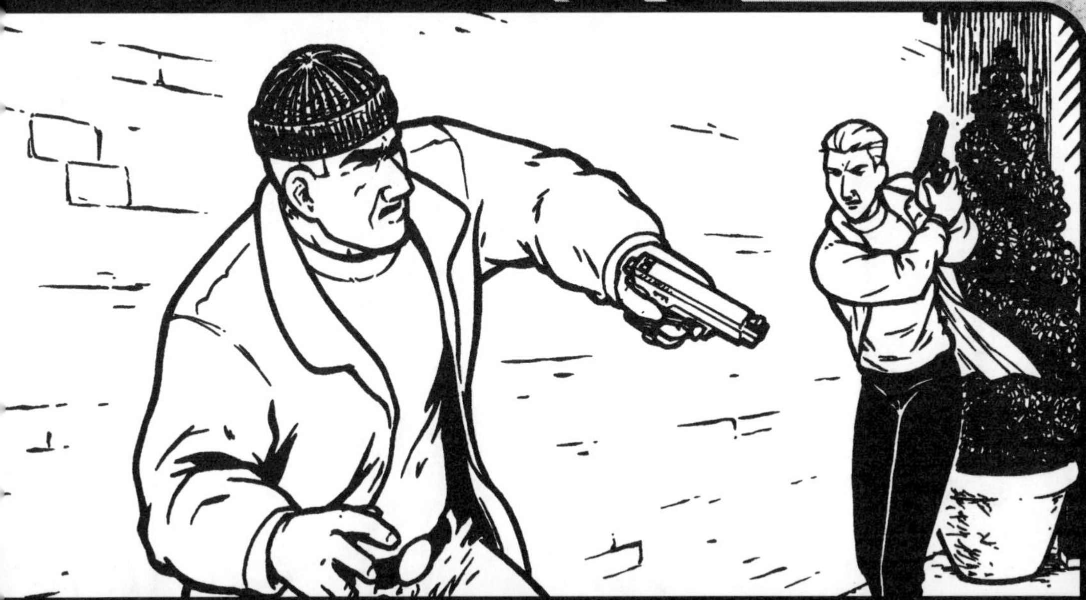

The following pages contain samples of some of Steve Rolston's development process, taking the characters from sketches to final designs, as well as looking at the layout/pencilling process.

Steve's first sketches...

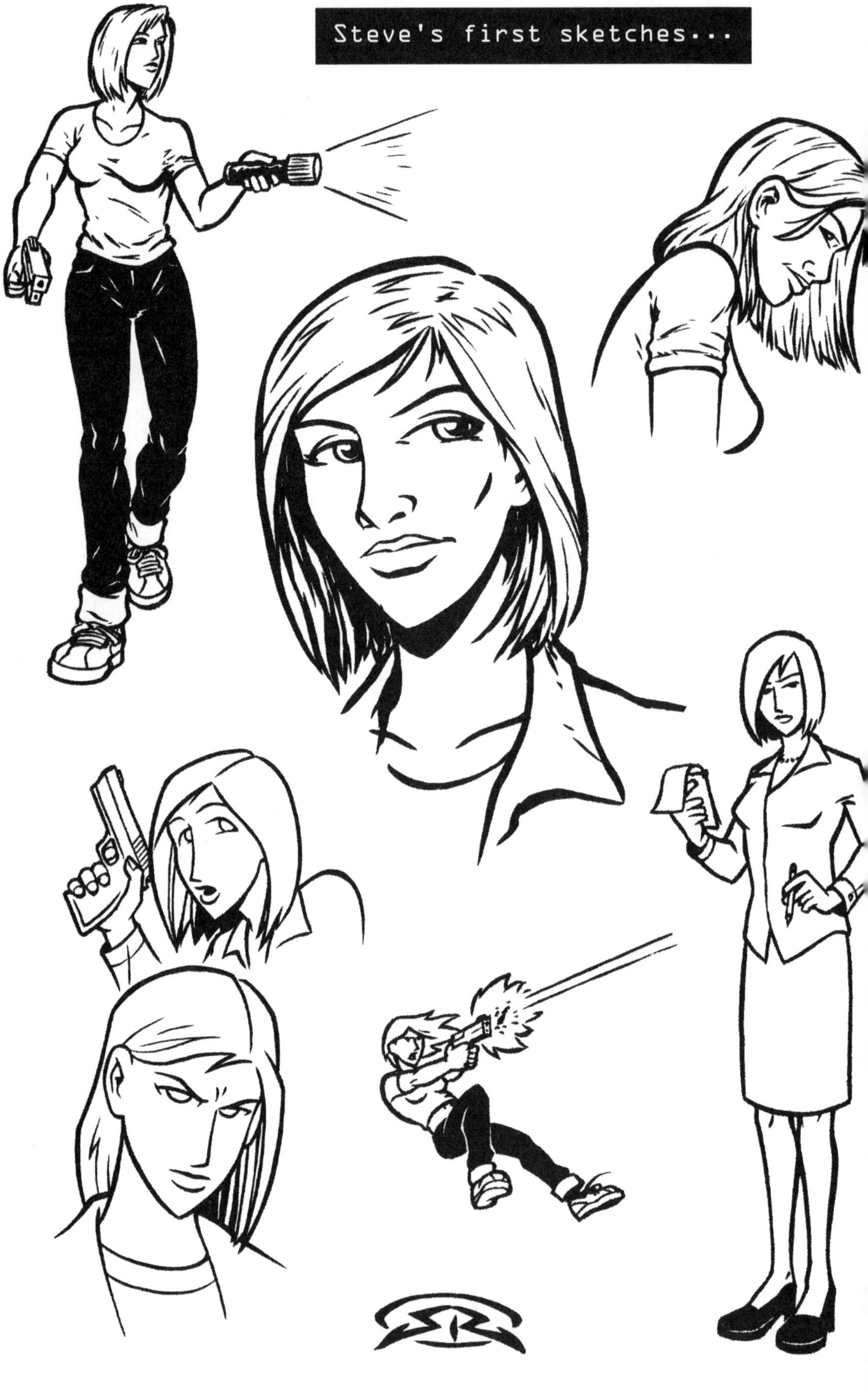

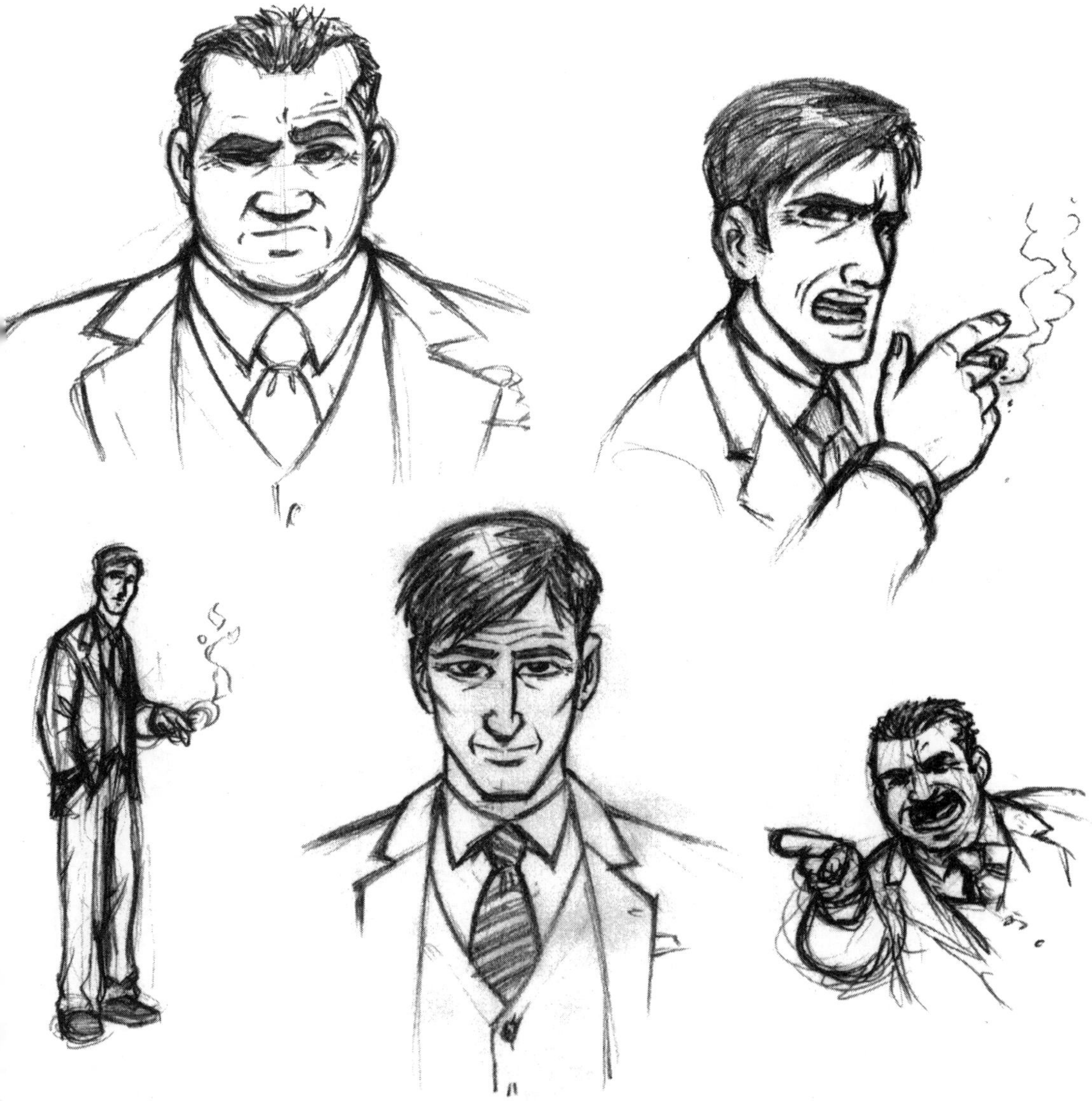

Original designs for Wallace, the Minder who most drastically changed by his final version

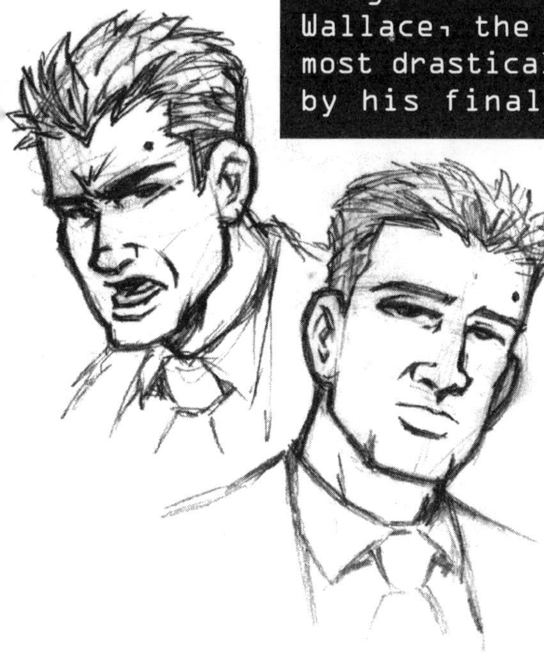

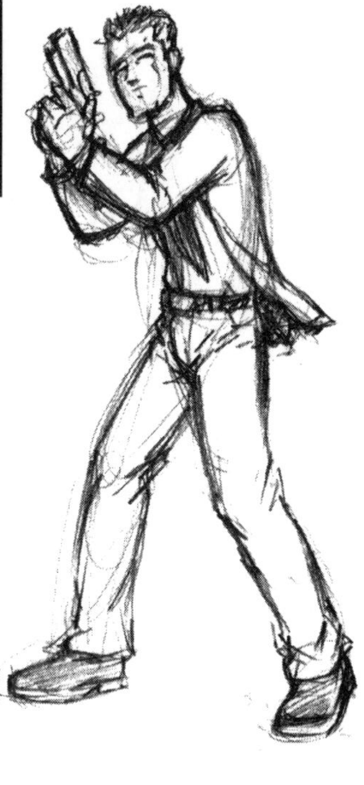

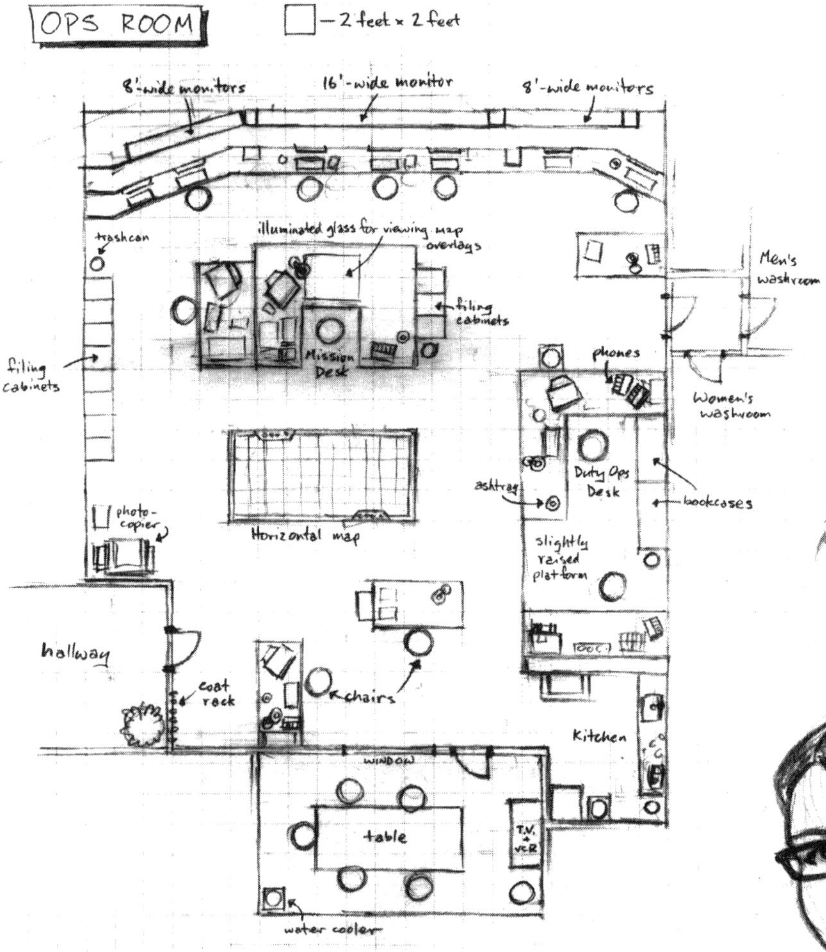
OPS ROOM
— 2 feet x 2 feet
8'-wide monitors
16'-wide monitor
8'-wide monitors
trashcan
illuminated glass for viewing map overlays
filing cabinets
filing cabinets
Mission Desk
Men's washroom
phones
Women's washroom
ashtray
Duty Ops Desk
bookcases
Horizontal map
photo-copier
slightly raised platform
hallway
coat rack
chairs
Kitchen
WINDOW
table
T.V. + VCR
water cooler

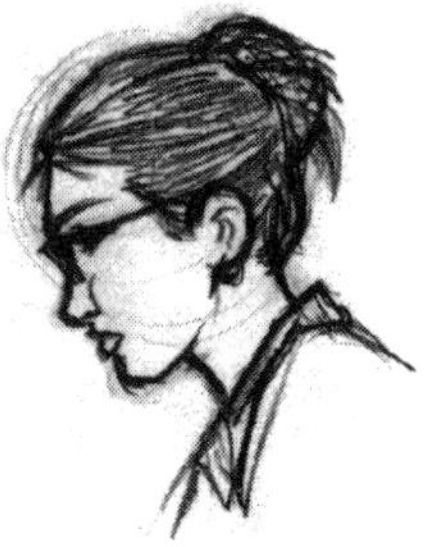

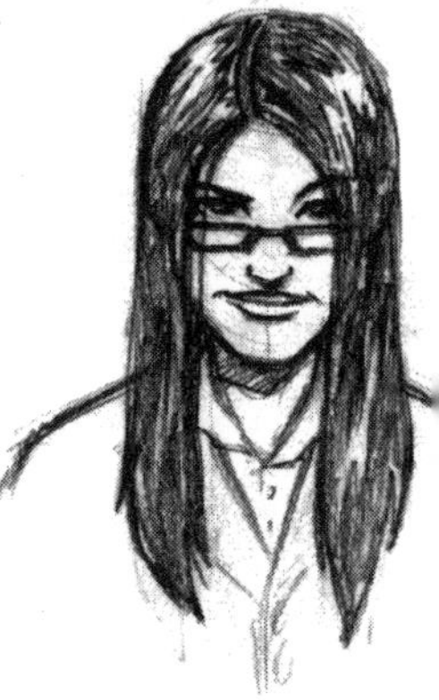

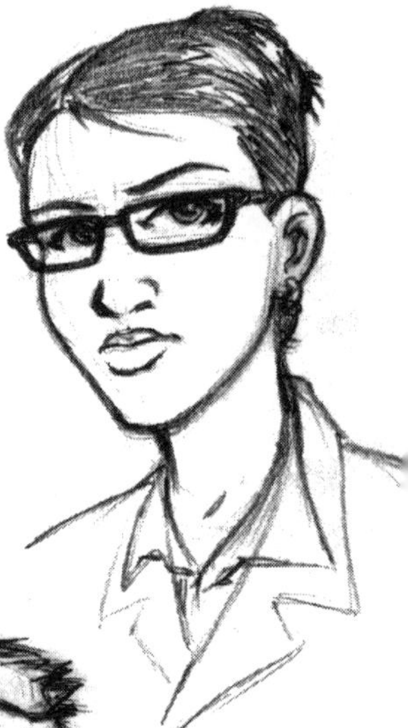

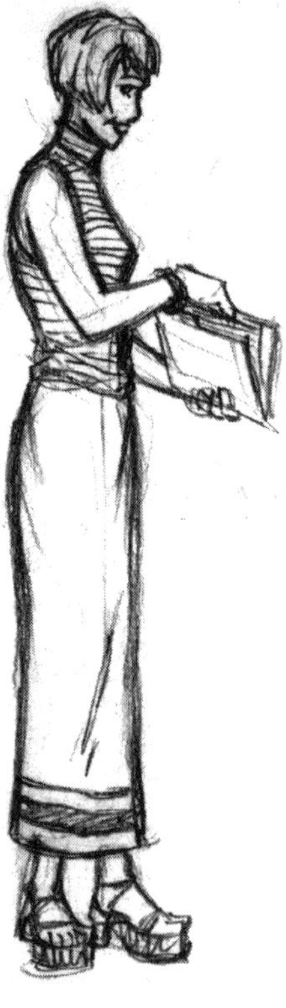

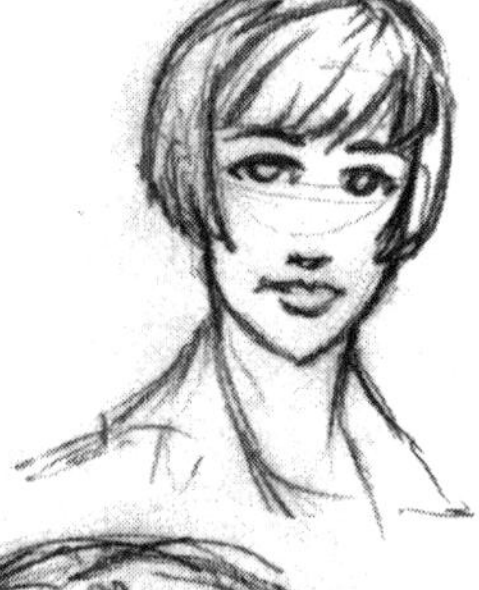

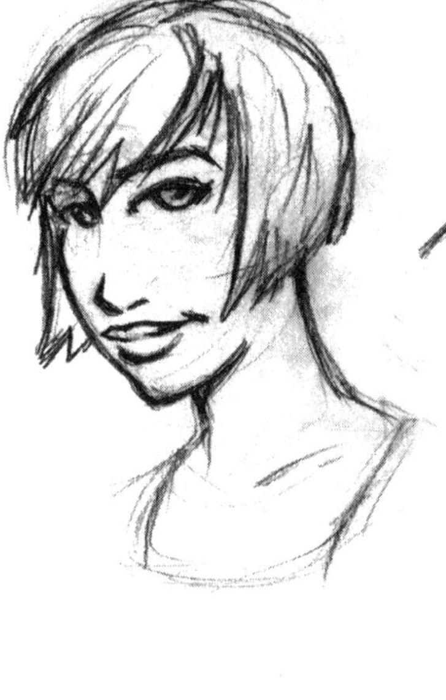

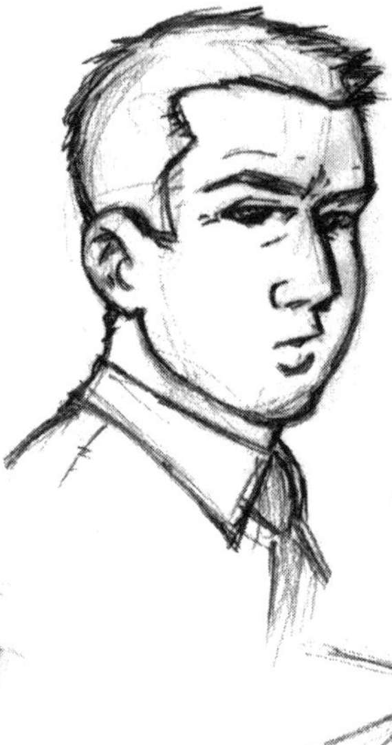

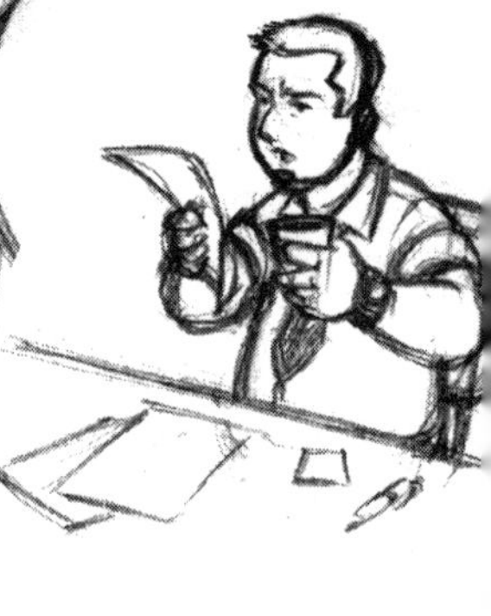

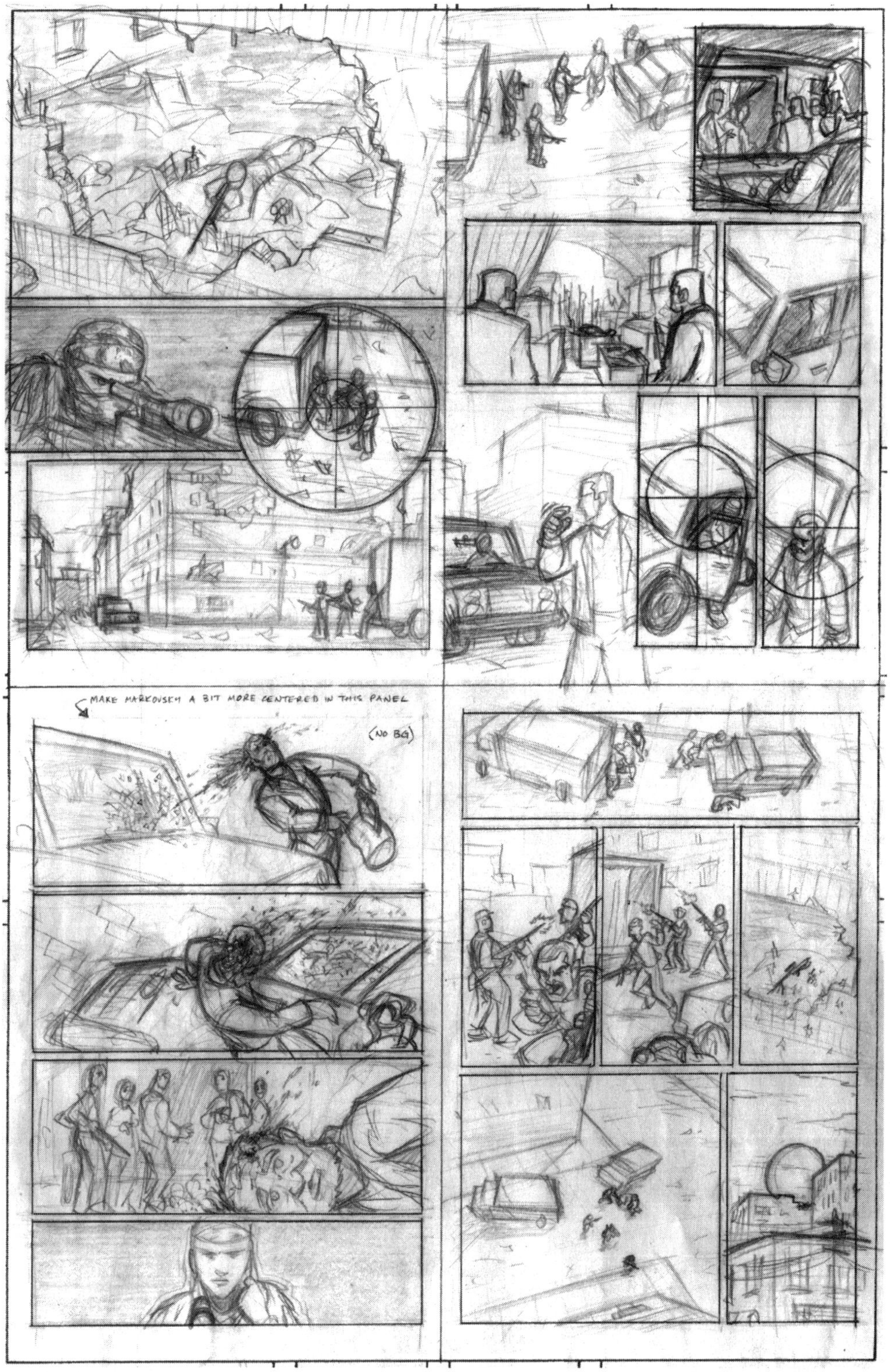
MAKE MARKOVSKY A BIT MORE CENTERED IN THIS PANEL
(NO BG)

This is an example of how Steve roughed out his pages at a smaller size before he started pencilling them. Figuring out the angles and positioning at this stage allowed him to make changes before starting the detailed work.

Cartoons done in response to stuffy critics demanding a more "realistic" style on QUEEN & COUNTRY.

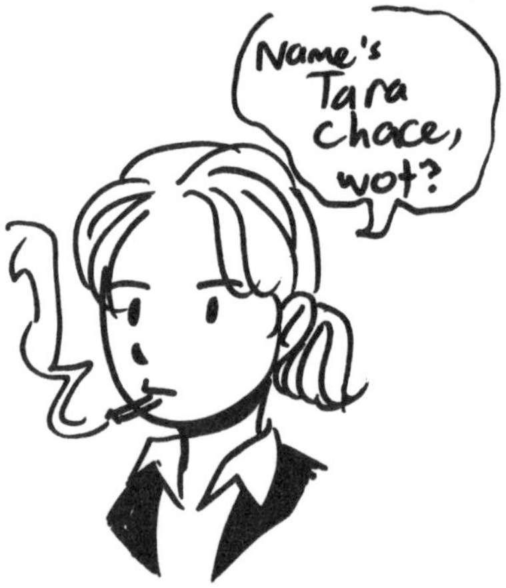
Name's Tara chace, wot?

Sketch by Bryan O'Malley

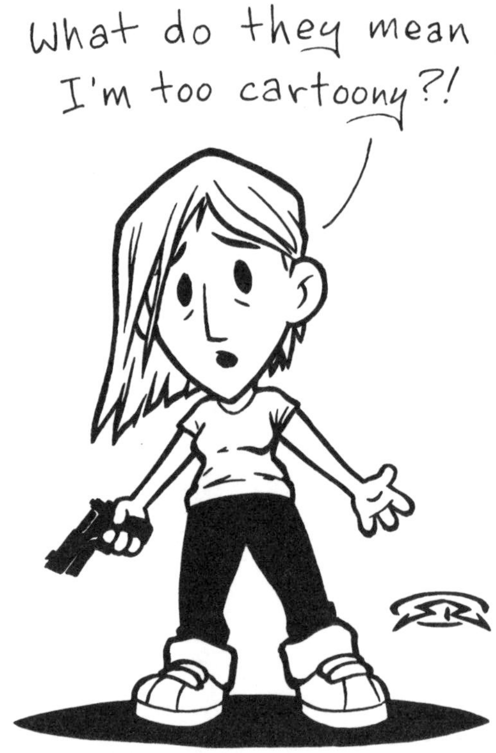
What do they mean I'm too cartoony?!

Cartoon by Steve Rolston

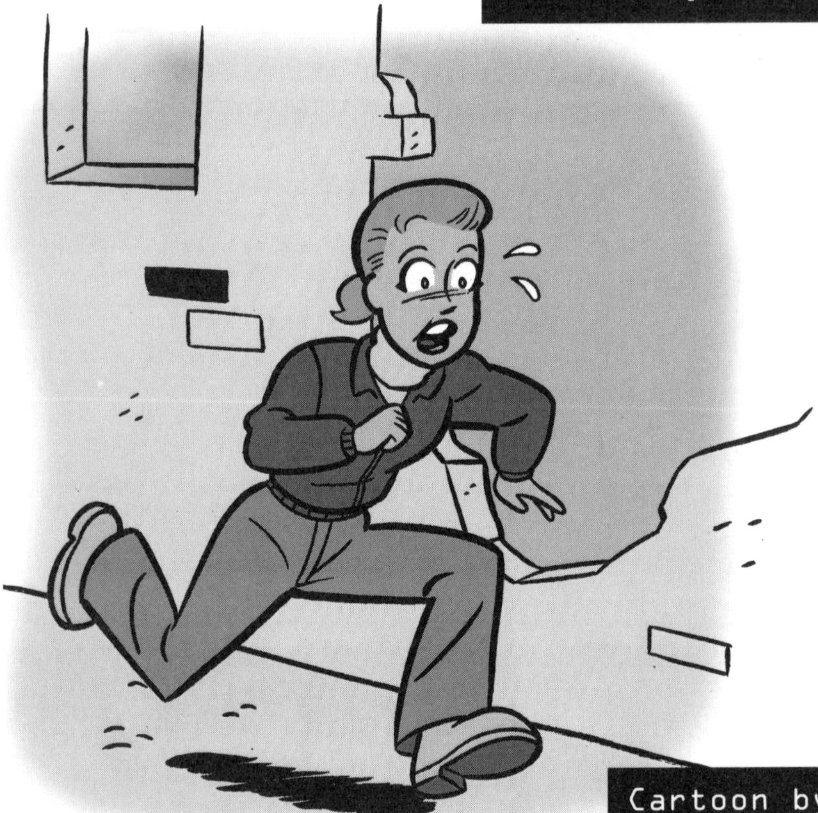

Cartoon by J. Bone

GREG RUCKA

Born in San Francisco, Greg Rucka was raised on the Monterey Peninsula. He is the author of several novels, including four about bodyguard *Atticus Kodiak*, and of numerous comic books, including the Eisner Award-winning *Whiteout: Melt*. He resides in Portland, Oregon, with his wife, Jennifer, and their son, Elliot.

www.gregrucka.com

STEVE ROLSTON

Born in Vancouver, BC, Canada, Steve was raised a little further north in a small town called Pender Harbour. After high school he moved to Vancouver to study classical animation at Capilano College. Upon graduating, he spent a couple years drawing storyboards for various cartoon shows. Seeking greater artistic satisfaction, Steve took a departure from animation work to pursue a career in the field of comic books. While honing his skills, he created two animated webcomics starring his own characters Jack Spade & Tony Two-Fist. In 2000, Steve landed his first professional comic gig—illustrating the first four issues of *Queen & Country*. His comic work since then includes a portion of Paul Dini's *Jingle Belle Jubilee* and all the artwork for *Pounded*, a miniseries written by Brian Wood. *Pounded* is a punk rock love story set in Vancouver, where Steve still lives.

www.steverolston.com

Other books by GREG RUCKA...

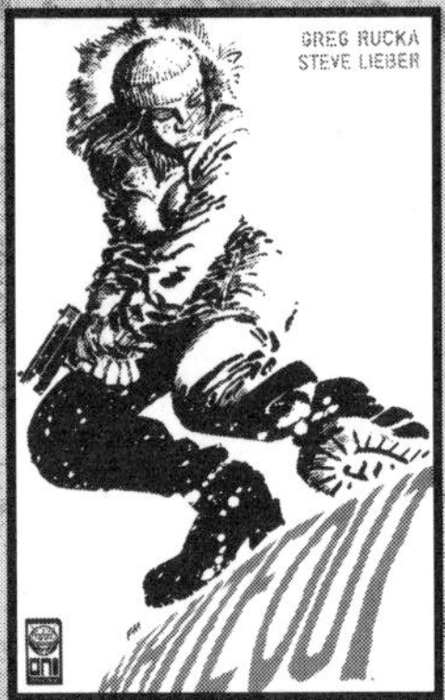
GREG RUCKA
STEVE LIEBER

Whiteout™
by Greg Rucka & Steve Lieber
128 pages, black-and-white interiors
$11.95 US, $16.95 CAN
ISBN 0-9667127-1-4

Whiteout: Melt™
by Greg Rucka & Steve Lieber
128 pages, black-and-white interiors
$11.95 US, $16.95 CAN
ISBN 1-929998-03-1

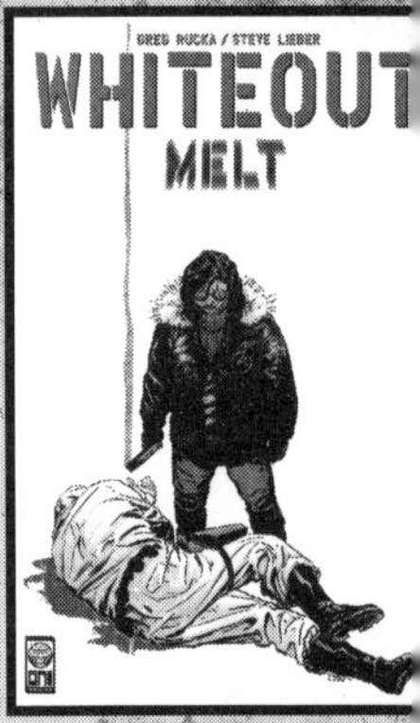
GREG RUCKA / STEVE LIEBER
WHITEOUT
MELT

"Whiteout's well researched, well written and expertly rendered. Don't buy it for those reasons, though. Buy it because Carrie Stetko's mouthy, freckled and cool..."
– Kelly Sue DeConnick, artbomb.net

THE ATTICUS KODIAK
Novels from Bantam Books...

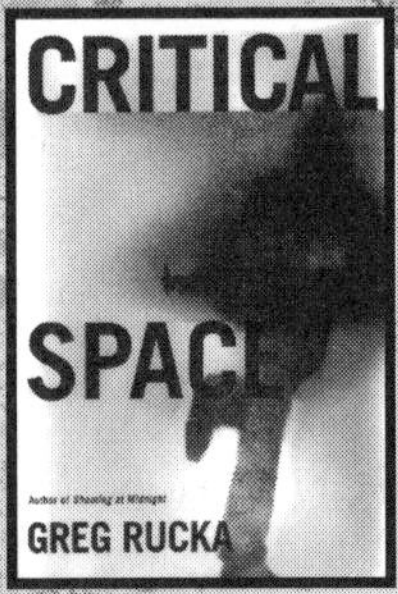
CRITICAL
SPACE
GREG RUCKA

Critical Space
hardcover edition
$23.95 US,
$34.95 CAN
ISBN 0-553-80132-5

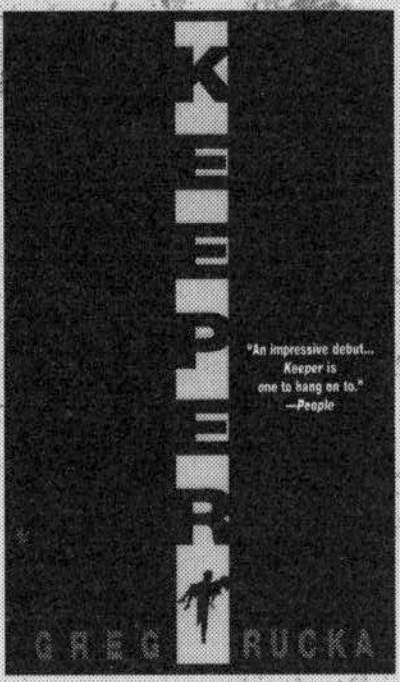
"An impressive debut... Keeper is one to hang on to." —People
GREG RUCKA

Keeper
$5.99 US,
$7.99 CAN
ISBN 0-553-57428-0

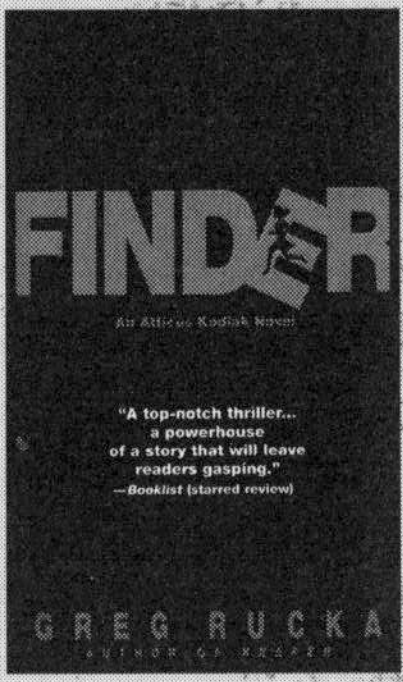
FINDER
"A top-notch thriller... a powerhouse of a story that will leave readers gasping." —Booklist (starred review)
GREG RUCKA

Finder
$5.99 US,
$7.99 CAN
ISBN 0-553-57429-9

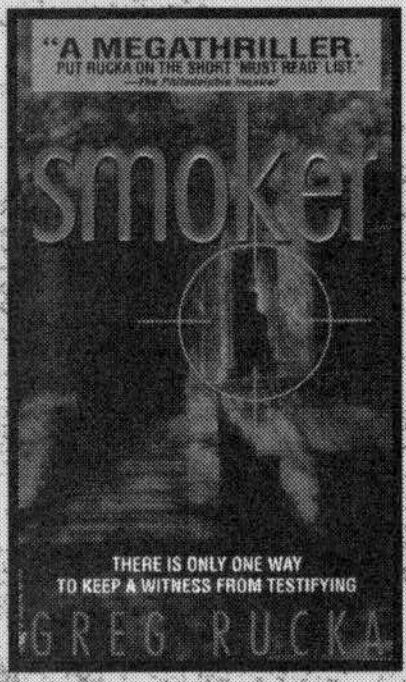
"A MEGATHRILLER.
smoker
THERE IS ONLY ONE WAY TO KEEP A WITNESS FROM TESTIFYING
GREG RUCKA

Smoker
$5.99 US,
$7.99 CAN
ISBN 0-553-57829-4

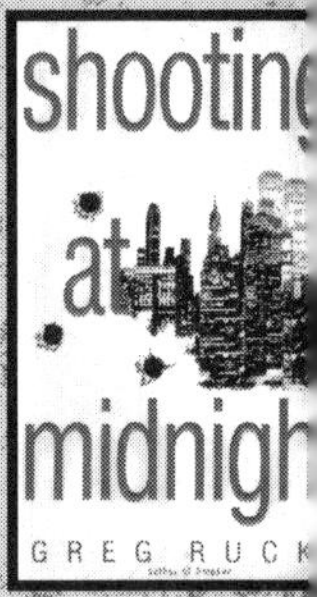

Shooting A
Midnight
$5.99 US,
$7.99 CAN
ISBN 0-553-578

"Rucka blends Spillaine's 'tough-guy' private eye with Chandler's noir insights and Hemingway's Spartan expression..."
– Statesman Journal, Salem, Oregon

AVAILABLE AT FINER BOOKSTORES EVERYWHERE

For a comics store near you, call **1-888-COMIC-BOOK**
or visit **www.the-master-list.com.**

For more information on more Oni Press books go to:
www.onipress.com

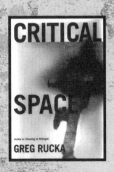